Reframing the Musical

METHUEN DRAMA
Bloomsbury Publishing Plc
50 Bedford Square, London, WC1B 3DP, UK
1385 Broadway, New York, NY 10018, USA
29 Earlsfort Terrace, Dublin 2, Ireland

BLOOMSBURY, METHUEN DRAMA and the Methuen Drama logo
are trademarks of Bloomsbury Publishing Plc

First published by Red Globe Press in 2019
This edition published by Bloomsbury, Methuen Drama in 2021

Copyright © Sarah Whitfield, and The Authors 2019

The Authors have asserted their right under the Copyright,
Designs and Patents Act, 1988, to be identified as Authors of this work.

All rights reserved. No part of this publication may be reproduced or
transmitted in any form or by any means, electronic or mechanical,
including photocopying, recording, or any information storage or retrieval
system, without prior permission in writing from the publishers.

Bloomsbury Publishing Plc does not have any control over, or responsibility for,
any third-party websites referred to or in this book. All internet addresses given
in this book were correct at the time of going to press. The author and publisher
regret any inconvenience caused if addresses have changed or sites have
ceased to exist, but can accept no responsibility for any such changes.

A catalogue record for this book is available from the British Library.

A catalog record for this book is available from the Library of Congress.

ISBN: HB: 978-1-352-00532-5
PB: 978-1-352-00439-7

Printed and bound in Great Britain

To find out more about our authors and books visit
www.bloomsbury.com and sign up for our newsletters.

Contents

Notes on Contributors

Rebecca Applin Warner is a composer and sound designer for musical theatre based in the UK

Sarah Browne is Head of the School of Performing Arts at the University of Wolverhampton, UK

Maya Cantu teaches on the Drama Faculty at Bennington College, US

Broderick Chow is Director of Teaching and Learning at Brunel University, London, UK

Wind Dell Woods is completing his PhD at University of California, Irvine, US

Donatella Galella is Assistant Professor at University of California, Riverside, US

Brian Granger is a composer/playwright and actor/director based in Nashville, Tennessee, US

Arianne Johnson Quinn is a PhD candidate at Princeton University, US

James Lovelock is Subject Leader in Musical Theatre at the University of Wolverhampton, UK

Sean Mayes is a New York-based music director, pianist and educator, US

Alejandro Postigo is Lecturer in Musical Theatre at London College of Music, UK

Phoebe Rumsey is a PhD Candidate at The Graduate Center, City University of New York, US

Sarah Whitfield is Senior Lecturer in Musical Theatre at the University of Wolverhampton, UK

Acknowledgements

My thanks go first of all to Nicola Cattini and Sonya Barker at Red Globe Press (formerly Palgrave) for their enthusiasm, dedication and continued support of this collection. The work would not have been completed without the particular support and encouragement of Nicholas Ridout, Donatella Galella, George Rodosthenous, Arianne Johnson Quinn, James Lovelock, Sarah Browne, Eric Glover, Sean Mayes, Brian Granger, Dwayne Keith Moon, Susannah Pearse, Bethany Doherty, and Janet Werther. The collection greatly benefited from the support of both the Music Theatre and Dance and Black Theatre Association at the Association for Theatre in Higher Education, and the opportunity to run a joint panel at the 2017 conference to further discussions around the research in its earlier stages. The discussions that came from this were vital to the project's subsequent development. The feedback of the anonymous peer reviewers has been enormously helpful in shaping the collection; thank you for your support and critical vision.

This book exists because of the difficult and important questions about musicals asked by my students, who in bringing their own lived experience to musical theatre studies made me aware of what work needed to take place. Their passion for the musical is as inspiring as it is contagious. I owe particular thanks to students who have asked the most difficult questions: Daniel Williams, Natasha Msanide, Joash Musundi, Martha Mondewa, Alexis Miller Warren, and the student LGBTQ+ Performing Arts research group at the University of Wolverhampton.

The support and encouragement of my husband, Jakob, as a critical friend and sounding board, has helped bring this project into existence, as has Ada and Emmy's patience.

The book is the work of the contributors, however, whose timely and diverse contributions are incisive, provocative and necessary in challenging the conversation around musical theatre, and it is dedicated to them and to those who use their work to make new things.

*

x   **Acknowledgements**

The editor and publisher would like to thank the following for the use of copyright text material in the book:

Sara Ahmed, for an extract from 'Making Feminist Points' (2013), taken from the online blog 'Feminist Killjoys' (available from: https://feministkilljoys.com/2013/09/11/making-feminist-points), used in the Introduction.

Joshua Lim So, for extracts from personal correspondence used in Chapter 2, 'Seeing as a Filipino: *Here Lies Love* (2014) at the National Theatre'.

Introduction

Sarah Whitfield

Framing and Reframing: Existing Ways of Looking

In an art gallery, a painting hangs on a wall. I stop, my eye called to it by the wooden rectangle that separates out the bit of the wall that is 'the art' from the rest. The frame does the work of telling me 'look *here*, not there, look at *this bit*. This is the bit that is art'. Even in paintings without frames, the blank wall around them becomes its own kind of frame: 'here is art and there is not-art'. Frames make a transition between two spaces, and shape the way we look at the art in the middle. The musical, while plainly another kind of art, has been framed in various ways that shape how it is 'seen' and understood. These frames may be what we bring with us, our personal histories of encounters with musicals, perhaps what we might have performed in or listened to before. Popular histories may shape how we put musicals in order, or categorize them: glossy coffee table books and TV histories illustrated with beautiful pictures of the so-called Golden Age era of musicals. We may share cultural references to the musicals 'that were always on the telly when we were growing up'. But, just as significantly, critical theories and academic approaches to the musical do this work too. They shape the way the musical is taught in colleges and universities, and ripple out of academia more broadly, impacting on how the form is seen and understood in public discourse.

This collection is called *Reframing the Musical: Race, Culture and Identity*, because it sets out to reconsider the musical through new critical frames and approaches, or approaches which have been drawn from outside musical theatre studies. It begs the question – what is the problem with existing frames, with existing ways of looking? Each chapter of this book responds to limitations in how the musical has been understood;

whether in the way in which existing approaches have framed issues of race, culture and identity, or in the way in which the history of the musical has been shaped (the musical's historiography). The problem with the existing 'frame', then, is that some people, places and events have been privileged as more important, more worth remembering and paying attention to than others: public discourse around the musical has minimized, ignored and erased the contributions and presence of many marginalized people. And as musical theatre studies as a discipline has developed, the repeating of this historiography repeats what Sara Ahmed has called '*these techniques of selection*, ways of making certain bodies and thematics core to the discipline and others not even part' (emphasis in original, Ahmed, 2013). What we think happened in the past (and what we think *did not*) shapes how we understand the present, and what we can imagine as possible in the future.

The historiography of the musical (the writing of the musical's history) is my focus here. Histories that revolve around Thomas Carlyle's much-criticized argument that 'the history of the world is but the biography of great men' (1840) seem products of another age, but stories of the musical's development tend to reinforce this generation-to-generation way of understanding the form. The story of the musical tends to rely on individuals and the contribution of certain kinds of practitioners being prioritized over others, primarily composers, librettists and lyricists, and perhaps directors and choreographers; occasionally 'star' performers may be recorded. The contribution of some figures to the musical is seen as so artistically significant that they are not paid only a wage but also royalties for their artistic and creative copyright. The work of these figures shapes the 'history' of the musical, romanticized through popular histories of the musical's development before and after the so-called Golden Age. One of its earliest iterations is in Leonard Bernstein's 1956 TV documentary on the American musical, where he notes the connection between the musical and proper European art forms, reassuring any viewers that the musical was 'steadily moving in the direction of opera' (in Bernstein, 1969, p. 183). In this narrative the serious musical can be seen in a proto form in *Show Boat* (1927) and then evolves fully with *Oklahoma!* (1943) – the Golden Age of musical theatre begins. One major popular historian of the musical,

David Ewen, writes that *Oklahoma!* saw lyricist Oscar Hammerstein II 'transcend[ing] the techniques and skills of his trade to arrive at the higher purposes [...] of a true poet' (1968, p. 162).

The Golden Age brings about dramatic integration, unity, and artistry to a form previously dedicated to entertainment – and instigates a period in which the musical can be considered a proper art form. The problematic performance practices of vaudeville and of other earlier precursors to the musical, like minstrel shows, were *fixed* by the arrival of high(er) art and the dramaturgically integrated musical. The emphasis on dramaturgical integration as part of a strategy to value the musical as a serious art form places specific emphasis and value on Broadway and West End theatre, and on the Hollywood musical. As a result, the complex variety of kinds of musical theatre production become overlooked in making a better, more dramaturgically pleasing, story. Todd Decker notes that Bernstein's TV documentary omits 'black-cast musicals and black performers entirely' in framing a historiography of the Broadway musical (2009, p. 12). The historiography of the musical has crafted a version of a history where the achievements of one generation of musical theatre writers gets 'developed' and progressed by the next. The bid to make the musical culturally serious has had serious consequences on what kinds of musicals and what kinds of people the story has included.

This story of the musical has clearly lasted, since 60 years after Leonard Bernstein it still dominates the reception of the musical as a form. One example can be seen in the widespread news interest about *Hamilton* (2015): here, one British newspaper critic writes that Lin-Manuel Miranda's Pulitzer Prize-winning musical is part of the 'ancestral' revolutionary thinking of the musical as a form:

> Jerome Kern and Oscar Hammerstein's *Show Boat* (1927), George and Ira Gershwin's *Porgy and Bess* (1935), and *South Pacific* (1949) – by Hammerstein and Richard Rodgers – all explored racial prejudice – and gave opportunities to non-white performers – at a level that American spoken theatre took decades to match.

(Lawson, 2017)

The (white) men in this story are giving the opportunity to be seen to non-white performers that they would otherwise supposedly not have had access to (the more complex issues of Jewish American identities, particularly during the 1920s and 1930s, are usually ignored). This is echoed in contemporary histories of the musical, which still place people of colour as the recipient of white generosity. In reference to the first African American performer to appear in a traditionally 'all-white' revue, historian Ethan Mordden writes that 'it was [Florenz] Ziegfeld who integrated Broadway, when he hired Bert Williams for *Follies of 1910*' (2013, p. 101). Bert Williams is reduced from a highly skilled performer and practitioner who could command audiences to a mute beneficiary of Ziegfeld's business acumen and progressive politics. Not only does this undermine Williams, but Monica White Ndounou's work suggests it is entirely factually inaccurate, since she establishes that he had already appeared in Victor Herbert's *The Gold Bug* (1896) with his performing partner George Walker (2012, p. 60).

Michel-Rolph Trouillot, in his work on power and the production of history, destabilizes what gets to be history (to use the vocabulary I have been using so far, what is framed as history) by examining power structures which shape the writing of that history. He argues:

> [...] history reveals itself only through the production of specific narratives. What matters most are the process and conditions of production of such narratives. [...] Only through that overlap can we discover the differential exercise of power that makes some narratives possible and silences others.

> (Trouillot, 1995, p. 25)

As a whole this collection reframes what narratives are possible within the story of the musical as a form, and crucially, within its future. In this introduction I want to respond to Trouillot by considering one of the most lasting narratives in musical theatre historiography, perhaps slightly less Great Man than what might usefully be called the Cool White Guy narrative. This is a story of the musical where benevolent white men get to extend their spaces and be heroes for doing so, where it is white men who get to do almost all the cool, important, revolutionary stuff.

The 'Cool White Guy' Narrative in the History of Musical Theatre

In order to explore the relationship between legitimizing the musical and the way in which it has instilled racialized hierarchies in whose story gets told, I need to first declare my own position and record my own naivety in seeing the consequences of this story of the musical. For many years I tried to work out how and why musical theatre studies, and those professionally involved with the form, had spent so long trying to culturally legitimize the musical. During my PhD I paid attention to how the cultural value of the musical as 'less than' opera required a kind of cultural 'acting up' – of suggesting that some musicals were as good as operas, perhaps because of a genius composer, a visionary lyricist or an epic scale. I spent considerable time unpicking how this value-based history had worked in sorting out *better* or *worse* musicals as a primary approach (so Andrew Lloyd Webber is less like opera than Stephen Sondheim, so his musicals are 'worse' than Sondheim's). Yet for me to spend so long pursuing this narrative without seeing how tangled up musical theatre studies is in race and identity reveals my own white privilege: I failed to see that as a consequence of its bid to be culturally serious, unintended or not, the 'possible narrative' of the musical requires 'a differential exercise of power' in what it is prepared to allow non-white people to do, and what it is prepared to acknowledge they have done in its history.

To call back to Trouillot, this 'possible narrative' of the history of the musical relies on white supremacist thinking, because it excludes a more complex reality: the musical as a form exists because of Black performance practice and the work of African American performers, creatives, and collaborators racialized as Black. This may seem shocking to white people since white supremacism tends to conjure up images of neo-Nazis or the Ku Klux Klan, but critical race theory positions this as the way society is structured to benefit white people. White supremacism is not only what Frances Ansley calls the 'self-conscious racism of white supremacist hate groups', but also what she lays out as a structural reality:

> [...] a political, economic and cultural system in which whites overwhelmingly control power and material resources, conscious and unconscious

ideas of white superiority and entitlement are widespread, and relations of white dominance and non-white subordination are daily reenacted across a broad array of institutions. White supremacy produces material and psychological benefits for whites, while extracting a heavy material and psychological price from blacks.

(Ansley, 1997, p. 592)

This understanding of white supremacy is perhaps uncomfortable for white people, who may be prepared to acknowledge that white privilege exists – but less so the specific costs and consequences of this privilege. Donatella Galella notes that white people's fear of being called out as racist betrays 'a liberal understanding of white supremacy rooted in individuals rather than in racial capitalism in which we are all complicit' (2016). As a white person it is more comfortable to think about racism as an individual choice rather than a system embedded into daily life which explicitly benefits white people at the cost of people who are racialized as non-white. Kimberlé Crenshaw recounts that at the beginning of Black Studies as a discipline, 'interrogating racial power from the inside out – was to some a discordant, uncomfortable and even shocking experience' (2011, p. 1290). Unpicking the way in which a dominant culture maintains its power is uncomfortable, but interrogating the ways in which 'racial capitalism' has shaped our understanding of one of the most popular forms of Western popular culture is vital. In his work interrogating whiteness in Hollywood movies, Daniel Bernardi writes that representations of race in films have a 'real impact in real people's lives'; and that 'to question cinema [...] is to resist ideology' (2007, p. xvi). The musical has a very real impact on real people's lives; it continues to shape national and personal ideologies, so too the arguments and ideas that frame it as a form.

Understanding the way in which default whiteness, and other kinds of normativity, have been at the heart of the musical and its historiography is a key part of assessing what and who has been missed. Who gets represented in glossy histories and contemporary TV documentaries on the history of the musical has real consequences on the people reading or watching those accounts. Seeing Bert Williams as the recipient of Ziegfeld's good intentions misses the far more complex reality of understanding Williams' negotiation of racist structures and expectations in the late nineteenth and early twentieth centuries. It overlooks the considerable work of theorists such as Camille Forbes who have addressed Williams' performance practice, arguing that he refused expected 'representations of the black man as primitive, and dared the audience to look at their biases, to recognize their prejudicial notions regarding the black man' (2004, p. 623). In order to successfully operate, the Golden Age historiography of musical theatre studies (which is essentially the same thing as the Cool White Guy Narrative) requires a number of uncritical assumptions to work. Perhaps the most crucial of these is that Broadway and the West End must be the main destination for musical theatre shows and practitioners: what happens there counts, what happens elsewhere is only important if it is a precursor to the 'main event'. As a result, musicals that explicitly challenge white dominant voices are an exceptional event, because the boundaries for success have been so tightly framed. Vaudeville that leads to Broadway is important, but the TOBA circuit (Theatre Owners Booking Association), historically known as the 'Chitlin circuit', is not.

Much of this is highlighted in the way Noble Sissle and Eubie Blake's *Shuffle Along* (1921) has been historicized as a one-off blip in the narrative of the musical. In his overview of American musical theatre, John Kenrick writes that after *Shuffle Along* closed, 'the renaissance of Black musical theatre quickly subsided and the genre would not appear with any frequency until another half a century had past' (2010, p. 191). This immediately reveals problems in what counts as 'Black musical theatre' on Broadway; Kenrick's categorization occludes the popularity of all-Black casts on Broadway during the 1930s. If Kenrick is referring to a lack of Black composers and theatre creatives, then there are numerous examples which would disprove this, not least composer/performers Eddie Hunter and Fats Waller in the late 1920s and 1930s, lyricist Andy Razaf also during this period, poet Langston Hughes' work in the 1930s and Duke Ellington's work in the 1940s. Many Black practitioners and performers moved beyond Broadway to networks of touring circuits (TOBA) and regional centres of performance such as Chicago, and into the film industry (for a detailed history of this period see Robinson, 2007, pp. 167–179).

Traditional histories of the musical have struggled to reconcile outwardly racist performance practices with readings which see them as sites of resistance. In describing *Shuffle Along*, Kenrick writes that '[it] was still burdened by hateful conventions. Most of the black skinned cast still felt it necessary to black their faces' (2010, p. 190). While blackface was used by white performers to reproduce racist tropes through exaggerated caricatures in minstrel shows, Cedric J. Robinson argues that in contrast to white performers putting on blackface, 'Black minstrels represented the anguish, the privations, and the pain of plantation life and the singular achievement of Black religion in providing an escape' (2007, p. 147). Considering blackface as solely a 'hateful' tradition allows a narrative where visible moments of racism can be seen in the context of imagined (and false) racial progress: it is reassuring for white people to think 'well, things were bad *then* but we would not accept that *now*'. But crucially, it also diminishes the agency of performers, who were operating from inside racist and racialized performance practice, as Stephanie Batiste, in her work uncovering Black performance practice in Depression-era musical theatre, notes:

> To assume that African Americans are unable to imagine and enact them-selves as empowered subjects promotes a naive view of power. It denies African Americans a full spectrum of social and cultural agency. It is also quite simply historically inaccurate.

(2011, p. 3)

Much of David Savran's work has considered the juxtaposition of cultural values around music, theatre, and race, unpicking the stratification of cultural values and musical theatre in the 1920s. This decade, he notes, saw 'theater professionals intent on the elevation of the legitimate theater [...] made distinctly anxious by the ubiquity of a low-class music that emerged from African Americans, eastern European Jews, and other immigrant groups' (2009, pp. 4–5). He addresses the way in which *Shuffle Along* 'modernized musical comedy' by making jazz and tap dancing 'obligatory on Broadway' (Savran, 2009, p. 76) in a wider survey which considers the intersection of racial and class identity. More recent approaches to writing histories of American musical theatre have covered *Shuffle Along* in serious depth, but still in terms of its relation-ship to the Golden Age/integration narrative: '[it] was hardly a giant step in the direction toward the integrated musical' (Wollman, 2017, p. 67). Wollman argues that ultimately the success of this musical, which she notes led to all-Black revues, frequently produced by Lew Leslie (who was white), 'denied performers their agency and thus tamped the possi-bility of a black theatre truly by, about, and for, black spectators' (2017, p. 69). Yet in his essay on the Chitlin circuit and the kinds of Black theatre it produced during the 1920s and 1930s, Henry Louis Gates, Jr. (2001) suggests that it produced theatre 'for, by, and about' Black people. Musical theatre's tight focus on the geographical real estate of Broadway is problematic.

The significant historical and performance analysis that has taken place of musical theatre practitioners within African American and Black diaspora studies has not always been reflected or responded to in musical theatre scholarship. There is a need to include the work of scholars from other disciplines, particularly from critical race theory and critical whiteness studies. Indeed, race and identity studies in musical theatre have tended to be relegated to sections of whole col-lections rather than placed as the centre of the discussion. Such sepa-ration has been repeated in other kinds of identity studies – especially in terms of LGBTQ+ identities – and unsurprisingly has limited work around intersectional identities. In the context of exploring contem-porary musical theatre as an industry, composer Michael R. Jackson argues: 'Casting should be part of a larger project that aims to decenter whiteness as the primary reference point in the stories non-white bodies populate'; he goes on to call for new musicals which will 'upend our expectations of default whiteness in musical theatre' (2015). Without a complex unpicking of the minimizing of Black performance prac-tice, whiteness continues to be the primary reference point of both the musical theatre industry and the field of scholarship around it. To borrow this term from Jackson, challenging expectations of default whiteness (and the correlated other dominant settings which assume straightness, able-bodiedness, binary-genderedness and so on), mean that established stories about the history of the musical start to fall apart.

Recognizing Jewish and LGBTQ+ Identities within this Narrative

One result of attempting to emphasize the quality of musical theatre in comparison to opera has been the focus on text-based archival traces as a way of asserting the artistic integrity of the musical. One benefit of this is the inclusion of the important work of Jewish composers and lyricists in the development of the form. The remarkable work of scholars, and in particular Andrea Most (2004), becomes central in understanding the complex ways in which the musical can be considered as a site of the construction of Jewish American identities. As these stories testify, the musical does have a complex heritage: clearly, alongside episodes of hateful anti-Semitism and homophobia, the industry has been used by people who identify as part of marginalized groups in order to gain representation and to construct complex identities (for example the Jewish American transition). People who identify within the LGBTQ+ community have found ways to work within the heteronormative musical, subverting it with songs of unrequited yearning (as in Noël Coward's work) or radically re-envisioning what the musical can do (in the case of Stephen Sondheim). The contribution that many marginalized groups have made to the musical has been the recipient of what Eric Lott (1993) calls 'love and theft' by the dominant culture of white heteronormativity; that is to say, their work has been interpolated, misappropriated, fetishized, or ignored. This is not a one-way process, and performance practices have passed backwards and forwards between cultures – albeit with likely monetary discrepancies in who got paid more for them. But the extent to which Black performance practice has been minimized and erased from the musical's historiography is astonishing; and it has largely been done through an overt emphasis on written text (words and music) and a minimizing of performance as a practice which allows for any personal agency and creativity.

Challenging Established Ways of Knowing

Performance theorist Susan Melrose raises the question: 'what might be the implications [...] of the premise that *established ways of knowing condemn us to inadequate ideas?*' (emphasis in original, 2007). I would argue that established ways of knowing and retelling the history of the musical are inadequate to deal with its complex reality in all its guises, beyond Broadway as a location, beyond the contributions of the Cool White Guys. This is what this collection, then, is aiming to do in its reframing. The transnational depth and breadth of the scholarly work contained in it, and of its contributors with their variety of lived experience and approaches, testifies to the urgency behind this collection. There are many more stories to be told, and there are other ways of looking which can help uncover and address these missing stories. How does musical theatre studies negotiate and respond to interventions from other related areas of research such as popular culture studies, film studies, disability studies, critical race theory and critical whiteness theory, and LGBTQ+ studies?

Existing Approaches to Reframing the Musical

This collection joins a growing number of texts that address how Black and other marginalized and suppressed groups have appeared, and how their identities have been represented and constructed through popular performance and the musical. While this is not a comprehensive list, it sets out the current moves towards reframing and recovering performance practice. Daphne Brooks' vital positioning of Black performers as enacting resistance often considers the relationship between white composer and Black performance as an occupation (see Brooks, 2006 and 2014). This kind of repositioning is a key part of the wider field of Black studies, which, as Darlene Clark Hine notes, explicitly sets out to recover resistance which appears 'veiled or dissembled'; the field works to 'unravel and reveal the myriad rituals and cultural creations that nurture and sustain oppositional consciousness while appearing to signal acquiescence, accommodation, and adaptation' (Hine, 2014, p. 14). Some approaches have been in specific historical case studies: James Wilson offers an extensive unpicking of the work of performers such as Florence Mills and Ethel Waters, noting how these two women in particular managed to play expected racist stereotypes while often subverting them (Wilson, 2011, p. 153). David Krasner's work on Aida Overton Walker (1996) is similar, while he also gives a clear overview of Black performance practice during the Harlem Renaissance (2002). Stephanie Batiste's (2011) work on Depression-era performance and practices of resistance and agency is extremely important in reconceptualizing musical theatre from this period.

This is continued in work which approaches race with a focus on contemporary performance practice, such as E. Patrick Johnson's significant work on Black and Queer bodies (2003), and his collaborative work with Ramon Rivera-Servera (2016). Other work which makes important interventions into performance and racial identity includes: Angela Chia-yi Pao's work on race and ethnicity in American theatre (2010); Anna Cheng's work on *Racial Melancholia* (2002); Brian Herrera's work about constructions of Latin(x) identity in performance (2015); Carol Oja's work on *West Side Story* and Bernstein, which explores these issues at length (2014, 2009); Josephine Lee's work on the imagined Japan of *The Mikado* (2010), which does the same; and Elizabeth Craft's important work on *In the Heights* (2011), which is particularly useful in framing *Hamilton*'s subsequent relationship with an audience who mostly have not seen the actual show. Work on the film musical has considered the implications of how the musical has been adapted to the stage: on *The Jungle Book* see Clark et al., 2017. Warren Hoffman considers the performance and construction of race, as well as drawing on critical whiteness studies in considering the assumption of white identities within Broadway musicals (2014). Within hip hop studies, Nicole Hodges Persley's work provides a vital historiography of musicals in both the UK and the US that draw on rap and hip hop (2015). Many of the chapters in this collection respond to and build on this work, and these sources may well be important for you as a reader when you set about your own responses to other musicals.

This Book and its Structure

In order to reframe the musical and to challenge existing power structures, the stories we as academics and students need to tell must shift, just as we demand better representation from the musicals we go and see on stage. Part of this shift in reframing is a call to do better by being deliberatively inclusive in edited collections such as these, and actively redistributing resources and attention both in who and what we work on, and how we work. In editing this book, I deliberately invited scholars and practitioners with minoritized identities to approach this task of reframing the musical, and also junior scholars whose work tended towards interdisciplinary approaches. As a result, the book brings together an exciting collection of academics, with a diverse range of critical approaches and methodologies. It is by no means a complete approach, and there are necessarily gaps – particularly around representations of disability and mental health and well-being in the musical. As these conversations continue there is also a need to think further about intersectional identities, to address aspects of other identities that are not written about here. This book is the next step in a series of conversations about the musical. Queer feminist critical theorist Sara Ahmed has called for radical shifts in the way we approach our scholarship:

> We need feminist and anti-racist critique because we need to understand how it is that the world takes shape by restricting the forms in which we gather. We need this now; the time for this is now. We need this critique now, if we are to learn how not to reproduce what we inherit.
>
> (Ahmed, 2013)

In order to establish such a critique in reframing the musical, then, this book is split into three sections, not according to a purely chronological approach but rather to make connections between methodologies and critical approaches.

In the first section, **Reframing Identity/Identities**, Donatella Galella, Broderick Chow and Brian Granger's chapters explore and reposition how musicals build and perform identities, and how audiences receive and interpret what is offered to them. In Chapter 1, Galella offers an urgent unpicking of the complex relationship between white storytellers and Black lives by focusing on the musical *The Fortress of Solitude* (2014), written by the late composer-lyricist Michael Friedman. Galella argues that the musical, which originated at the Public Theatre in New York, 'offers glimpses of interracial possibility'. She makes the powerful argument that the musical demonstrates 'alternate ways of listening, telling stories, and flying above structural racism' in its willingness to stage white privilege. She draws out of the musical a potential model for how scholars might achieve similar work: 'To tell the stories of the United States and of musical theatre history, scholars must also tell the stories of black Americans.'

In Chapter 2, Broderick Chow responds to the production of *Here Lies Love* that he saw in 2014 at the National Theatre, London. The musical, based around the life of Imelda Marcos, written by David Byrne and Fatboy Slim, also emerged out of New York's Public Theatre. Chow draws on his own identity 'as a "Pinoy", albeit a half-Chinese Pinoy who grew up in Canada and now lives in London, England' to establish the critical position of '*seeing as a Filipino*', a term he defines as articulating 'a specific position that I, as a diasporic subject, find myself compelled to take up when confronted with a history that has haunted my life since the beginning'. Chow notes that scholarly and critical approaches to this musical reveal the 'colonial gaze'; not least in the musical's historiography, something he argues has not been 'expansive enough to admit non-Western or hybridized forms'. The chapter offers a powerful reading of *Here Lies Love* and its use of theatricality, which Chow argues 'troubled and tore apart a neocolonial narrative of third-world dictatorship and first-world democracy that so often characterizes representations of Asia'.

Finally in this section, Brian Granger's urgent discussion of *The Lion King* (1997) in Chapter 3 begins with his sharing of his own powerful experience of being an African American audience member in the theatre of the Broadway musical. He contrasts existing responses to the musical which focus on the problematic representations of Africa in the animated film by drawing our focus to 'the complex pleasures and powers of live theatre'. He considers how the pleasure of the live theatrical encounter is mediated through the 'sensory – and in some aspects consumable – pleasure of the black body'. Drawing on Stephanie Batiste's critical methodology and conceptualizing of the 'real and unreal' Black body, Granger sets out to be 'both celebratory and critical' of the musical as a whole. He asks: 'What is meaningful about this peculiar performance, appearing near the end of the twentieth century and yet remaining, more than two decades later, so entwined in contemporary discourses of race, culture, and identity?' Ultimately, Granger argues that 'Disney's *The Lion King* on Broadway is a vital sign for understanding civic and racialized presence in the early twenty-first century'.

In the second section, **Challenging Historiographies**, Maya Cantu, Arianne Johnson Quinn, Sean Mayes, Alejandro Postigo, and Phoebe Rumsey address and restore missing histories of musical theatre: each author takes a different approach to case study missing stories or perhaps different ways of looking at known material. In Chapter 4, Cantu recovers the work of Ada 'Bricktop' Smith (1894–1984), the little-known performer and practitioner, by challenging problematic and limiting concepts of her most important contribution as that of Cole Porter's muse. She argues that Bricktop's career was 'defined by acts of racial, cultural, and national border-crossing', yet Bricktop 'remains an overlooked presence in histories of musical theatre, to which she made significant contributions as a maker, mentor, and agent of artistic inspiration'. By carefully establishing an accurate historiography for the kinds of labour Bricktop carried out, Cantu powerfully reinstates her into the narrative of musical theatre development in the 1920s. Ultimately Cantu reasserts the need to incorporate performance practice within the history of musical theatre, and to reconsider the role of locations outside of Broadway and the West End as places where musical theatre is further developed.

In Chapter 5, Arianne Johnson Quinn reframes readings of perhaps *the* most well-known creative practitioner in existing histories of the musical, Oscar Hammerstein II. She focuses on his work and reception in the UK as a way to consider his global influence, challenging 'his ability to craft the image of ambassador of American progress and equality and white liberal saviour who rescues the stories of racial minorities ... reflected in the pervasive narratives surrounding his work'. She considers both the original British premiere of his collaboration with Richard Rodgers, *South Pacific*, in 1951, and the much later British premiere of *Carmen Jones* in 1991, directed by Simon Callow. Johnson Quinn suggests that 'the very issues of race and equality that Hammerstein attempted to tackle in both of these librettos unintentionally reified attitudes of race and difference through the mythos of progressive theatre'. The chapter is particularly useful in the context of the wider collection, since in turning back to a key figure within the established historiography of the musical, Johnson Quinn considers how well-established parts of the musical's narrative must be attended to, alongside the lesser known stories which are recovered elsewhere.

Professional music director Sean Mayes carries out an urgent and complex restoration of this role in Broadway theatre, asking: 'Why has the contribution and the significance of the music director gone unrecognized?' Mayes writes from his own experience, noting that he wants to 'as a Black practitioner, shed distinct light on how this has particularly afflicted practitioners of colour whilst also acknowledging the problems that all minority practitioners experience'. He explores the way in which, in what he calls the music director's *lost labours*, 'the evidence of their creation and maintenance has been predominantly all but lost'. Mayes draws on critical race theory to explore the 'duality of facing discrimination both via role and via race'. He points to the huge number of practitioners whose contributions are yet to be explored, while urgently calling for better documentation of the work contemporary music directors carry out.

In his chapter, Alejandro Postigo carries out a rigorous historical positioning of the intercultural development of musical theatre in Spain in the twentieth and twenty-first centuries. Postigo's work models potential responses to Chow's call for more 'expansive historiographies' of the musical, and as a result, his chapter works as a case study for the way other kinds of musical theatre histories and locations are a necessary part of reframing the musical. Postigo considers the *zarzuela* and its relationship with global touring Broadway productions; the *zarzuela*, originally a 'popular response to the monarchic impositions of foreign genres', is 'a lyric-dramatic genre that has married music and theatre in Spain for over 365 years'. Postigo notes that while American musicals did appear in Spain, the form remained connected to folk and local traditions, with European influences from Italy and France. It was only after the collapse of the Franco regime and the rise of pop music that musical theatre shifted in Spain, when Spanish producers turned to the American musical: 'Spain's youth demanded new styles of music and theatre coming from abroad, effectively wanting to forget about anything related to the long years of the dictatorship'. In the twenty-first century, Postigo notes that 'the international influence of Anglophone culture facilitates the exportation of musicals everywhere by somehow collapsing and replacing other cultural systems'.

Finally, in this section, Phoebe Rumsey focuses on Savion Glover's choreography for *Shuffle Along – Or The Making Of The Musical Sensation of 1921 And All That Followed* (2016) in Chapter 8. Rumsey explores how the production, a short-lived Broadway musical, stages and disrupts the historiography of the American musical by emphasizing how the work of Black performers and creatives has been minimized in official accounts. She notes that the performers on stage 'culturally and politically present the archive of the show', as orchestrated by Glover and director George C. Wolfe. She argues that 'Glover's choreography has both an embodied sense of the past and a boldness to it that directly re-declares the African American ownership of tap in musical theatre'. This chapter fits into one of the key themes of the collection in considering how recognizing embodied performance reframes the whole, and ultimately reveals the limitation of existing historiographies. Just as in Mayes' chapter, it points to the range of work which is waiting to be done to transform the stories we tell about the musical.

In **Musical Structures: Identity and Social Change**, chapters bring a range of critical methodologies to exploring constructions of identity in key musicals. Two of the chapters in this section respond to Lisa Kron and Jeanine Tesori's *Fun Home* (2015) but with different methodologies and focuses; this allows the reader to see how different critical frames highlight different aspects of the same musical – in effect confirming the value of reframing as a flexible and repeatable concept rather than a finished product. Composer Jeanine Tesori's 'significant output' has, as Rebecca Applin Warner notes in Chapter 9, 'received little in the way of serious critical musicological responses'. In her chapter, Applin Warner argues that 'the richness of musical language that is found in Tesori's work demonstrates the sophistication of craft which places a dramaturgical approach at the heart of the compositional process'. To explore this Applin Warner carries out close readings of musical motifs, to establish how Tesori creates 'a musical relationship between Alison and her family that supports Alison's quest for an understanding of her own identity, and her lived experience as a lesbian within her family unit'.

In Chapter 10, Sarah Browne positions *Hair* (1967) as a musical which has been often overlooked in the way 'history, culture and power collide to produce powerful commentaries on racial and gender inequality in the US'. Her work unpicks the complex representations of identity of African American masculinity in the musical; Browne suggests that this

is an overlooked area in existing scholarship on *Hair*, which has tended
to focus on the white male roles. She uses musicological and cultural
studies to read 'Colored Spade' as a protest song, arguing that it encapsulates the civil rights movement of the 1960s: the 'shift from integration to
highlighting and reinforcing difference'. She argues that these representations of African American masculinity in *Hair* present its audience with 'a
complex set of signs that perhaps speak loudly of the potential dangers the
civil rights movement posed to the dominant, white mainstream culture'.
Browne makes several calls to action, one of which is to invite 'scholars of
musical theatre to develop and adopt analytical approaches which stem
from other disciplines'; ultimately her work highlights the value of investigating 'the social and artistic structures which have dictated the ways in
which we understand identity and its associated performance'.

The musical is often (as part of celebrations over its 'diversity') assumed
to be some kind of gay art form: to pick one of potentially thousands of
examples of this, an interview with Hugh Jackman in *The Times* in 2017
explained to the reader that Jackman's 'considerable experience of musical
theatre on Broadway has won him Tonys, and inspired some of the more
persistent "secretly gay" rumours any straight actor ever endured' (Vernon,
2017). In Chapter 11, in response to these kinds of deeply problematic
assumptions about the musical, James Lovelock invites us to ask whether
'the supposed "queerness" of the musical theatre genre has been utilized as
an excuse to maintain an impoverished queer heritage within a genre that
is uniquely positioned to externalize the idiosyncrasies of what it means to
be queer'. He considers productions which have brought the lived experience of LGBTQ+ people to the foreground: *The Color Purple* (2005), *Yank!*
(2017), *Fun Home* (2015), and *Everybody's Talking About Jamie* (2017). He
uses these musicals to make a powerful call for musical theatre studies to
move away from limited binaries in discussing sexuality and gender 'and to
begin to consider bisexual, asexual, transgender and genderfluid identities'.

In Chapter 12, Wind Dell Woods' important consideration of *Hamilton*
(2015) explicitly addresses racial identity in considering how the musical
avoids staging Black revolt and doing the kind of anti-racist work Galella
calls for at the beginning of this book. Since the public discourse around
Hamilton wants to make it as revolutionary as *Oklahoma!*, Johnson
Quinn's earlier unpicking of Hammerstein is particularly illuminating in

providing a context for the work that Woods carries out. While there are an ever-growing number of critical responses to this hugely popular number, this chapter makes for particularly challenging reading for fans of the musical, since in it Woods argues that the musical conflates 'immigrant(-ness)' with 'slave(ness)'. He draws our attention to the unlovely features of this musical, by fearlessly laying out its revolutionary limitations. Woods calls for 'a deeper interrogation, not merely of what the play does *with* the past, but what it does *for* the present'. Ultimately, he argues that 'Miranda's dramaturgical forgetting' offers 'a romanticized notion of American (neo) liberal multicultural progress centred on the figure of the non-black immigrant'. Woods notes that 'the erasure of the black captive and indigenous population is the condition of possibility for the American immigrant narrative to emerge'.

Woods powerful unpicking of how *Hamilton* constructs identity while forgetting African American identity connects with one of the key themes of this collection: how some stories are remembered and retold, and others are not. Writing new musicals and reframing existing ones is not finished, and this one collection is not enough; clearly no single text can cohesively address the losses of individuals and marginalized or suppressed groups. There are many more gaps in scholarship that need to be urgently addressed and many more musicals that need to be unpicked. Each chapter in the book equips you with potential models and case studies that you can use in your own recoveries and reframing work – inviting *you* to tell the other stories of the musical.

References

Ahmed, S. (2013) Making Feminist Points, *feministkilljoys* [online]. Available at: https://feministkilljoys.com/2013/09/11/making-feminist-points. Accessed 19 June 2018.

Ansley, F.L. (1997) White Supremacy (And What We Should Do about It). In Delgado, R. and Stefancic, J. (eds.), *Critical White Studies: Looking Behind the Mirror* (pp. 592–595). Philadelphia, PA: Temple University Press.

Batiste, S.L. (2011) *Darkening Mirrors: Imperial Representation in Depression-era African American performance*. Durham, NC: Duke University Press.

Bernardi, D. (2007) Introduction: Race and Contemporary Hollywood Cinema. In Bernardi, D. (ed.), *The Persistence of Whiteness: Race and Contemporary Hollywood Cinema* (pp. xv–xxvi). London: Routledge.

Bernstein, L. (1969) American Musical Comedy: Broadcast on 7 October 1956. In *The Joy of Music* (pp. 157–184). London: Panther Books.

Brooks, D. (2006) *Bodies in Dissent: Spectacular Performances of Race and Freedom, 1850–1910.* Durham, NC: Duke University Press.

Brooks, D.A. (2014) Open Channels: Some Thoughts on Blackness, the Body, and Sound(ing) Women in the (Summer) Time of Trayvon. *Performance Research*, 19(3), 62–68. Available at: http://dx.doi.org/10.1080/13528165.2014.935171. Accessed 17 January 2017.

Carlyle, T. (1840) On Heroes, Hero-worship, and the Heroic in History, by Thomas Carlyle. Available at: www.gutenberg.org/files/1091/1091-h/1091-h.htm. Accessed 20 June 2018.

Cheng, A.A. (2002) *The Melancholy of Race: Psychoanalysis, Assimilation, and Hidden Grief, Race and American Culture.* Oxford and New York: Oxford University Press.

Clark, E., Galella, D., Jones, S.A. and Young, C. (2017) 'I Wanna Be Like You': Negotiating Race, Racism and Orientalism in The Jungle Book on Stage. In *The Disney Musical on Stage and Screen: Critical Approaches from 'Snow White' to 'Frozen'* (pp. 185–204). London: Bloomsbury Publishing.

Craft, E.T. (2011) 'Is this What it Takes Just to Make it to Broadway?!': Marketing *In the Heights* in the Twenty-First Century. *Studies in Musical Theatre*, 5(1), 49–69.

Crenshaw, K.W. (2011) Twenty Years of Critical Race Theory: Looking back to Move Forward. *Connecticut Law Review*, 43(5), 1253–1354.

Decker, T. (2009) 'Do You Want to Hear a Mammy Song?': A Historiography of Show Boat. *Contemporary Theatre Review*, 19(1), 8–21.

Ewen, D. (1968) *The Story of America's Musical Theater* [Rev. ed.], Philadelphia, PA: Chilton Book Co.

Forbes, C.F. (2004) Dancing with 'Racial Feet': Bert Williams and the Performance of Blackness. *Theatre Journal*, 56(4), 603–625. Available at: https://muse.jhu.edu/article/175883. Accessed 25 June 2018.

Galella, D. (2016) Why Diversity? Plenary – All-Conference Plenary 1: Diversity in Theatre and Higher Education, given at Association for Theatre in Higher Education Conference 2016, Chicago, IL.

Gates, H. L., Jr. (2001) The Chitlin Circuit. In Elam, H.J. and Krasner, D. (eds.), *African-American Performance and Theater History: A Critical Reader* (pp. 132–148). Oxford and New York: Oxford University Press.

Herrera, B.E. (2015) *Latin Numbers: Playing Latino in Twentieth-Century U.S. Popular Performance*. Ann Arbor, MI: University of Michigan Press.

Hine, D.C. (2014) A Black Studies Manifesto. *The Black Scholar*, 44(2), 11–15.

Hoffman, W. (2017) *The Great White Way: Race and the Broadway Musical*. New Brunswick: Rutgers University Press.

Jackson, M.R. (2015) Unpacking 'Diversity' In Musical Theatre, *HowlRound*. Available at: http://howlround.com/unpacking-diversity-in-musical-theatre. Accessed 25 January 2018.

Johnson, E.P. (2003) *Appropriating Blackness: Performance and the Politics of Authenticity*. Durham, NC: Duke University Press.

Johnson, E.P. and Rivera-Servera, R.H. (eds.) (2016) *Blacktino Queer Performance*. Durham, NC: Duke University Press Books.

Kenrick, J. (2010) *Musical Theatre: A History*. London: Continuum.

Krasner, D. (1996) Rewriting the Body: Aida Overton Walker and the Social Formation of Cakewalking. *Theatre Survey*, 37(2), 67–92.

Krasner, D. (2002) *A Beautiful Pageant: African American Theatre, Drama, and Performance in the Harlem Renaissance, 1910–1927*. New York: Palgrave Macmillan.

Lawson, M. (2017) Hamilton is Creative and Radical in the Proud Tradition of Musical Theatre. *The Guardian*. Available at: www.theguardian.com/commentisfree/2017/dec/26/hamilton-radical-musical-theatre-groundbreaking. Accessed 26 January 2018.

Lee, J. (2010) *The Japan of Pure Invention: Gilbert and Sullivan's The Mikado*. Minneapolis: University of Minnesota Press.

Lott, E. (1993) *Love and Theft: Blackface Minstrelsy and the American Working Class*. New York: Oxford University Press.

Melrose, S. (2007) The (Written) Confessions of an Uneasy Expert Spectator, *Professor S F Melrose*. Available at: www.sfmelrose.org.uk. Accessed 24 February 2016.

Mordden, E. (2013) *Anything Goes: A History of American Musical Theatre*. New York: Oxford University Press.

Most, A. (2004) *Making Americans: Jews and the Broadway Musical*. Cambridge, MA: Harvard University Press.

Ndounou, M.W. (2012) Early Black Americans on Broadway. In Young, H. (ed.), *The Cambridge Companion to African American Theatre, Cambridge Companions to Literature* (pp. 59–84). Cambridge: Cambridge University Press.

Oja, C.J. (2009) West Side Story and The Music Man: Whiteness, Immigration, and Race in the US during the Late 1950s. *Studies in Musical Theatre*, 3(1), 13–30.

Oja, C.J. (2014) *Bernstein Meets Broadway: Collaborative Art in a Time of War, Broadway Legacies*. New York: Oxford University Press.

Pao, A.C. (2010) *No Safe Spaces: Re-casting Race, Ethnicity, and Nationality in American Theater*. Ann Arbor, MA: University of Michigan Press.

Persley, N.H. (2015) Hip-hop Theater and Performance, In Williams, J.A. (ed.), *The Cambridge Companion to Hip-Hop* (pp. 85–98). Cambridge: Cambridge University Press.

Robinson, C.J. (2007) *Forgeries of Memory and Meaning: Blacks and the Regimes of Race in American Theater and Film before World War II*. Chapel Hill, NC: University of North Carolina Press.

Savran, D. (2009) *Highbrow/Lowdown: Theater, Jazz, and the Making of the New Middle Class*. Ann Arbor, MI: University of Michigan Press.

Trouillot, M.-R. (1995) *Silencing the Past: Power and the Production of History*. Boston: Beacon Press.

Vernon, P. (2017) Hugh Jackman: The Greatest Showman, Being Bullied on Set and his Take on the Weinstein Scandal. *The Times*, 30 December. Available at: www.thetimes.co.uk/article/hugh-jackman-the-greatest-showman-being-bullied-on-set-and-his-take-on-the-weinstein-scandal-3ckp2s3vs. Accessed 8 February 2018.

Wilson, J.F. (2011) *Bulldaggers, Pansies, and Chocolate Babies: Performance, Race and Sexuality in the Harlem Renaissance*. Ann Arbor, MI: University of Michigan Press.

Wollman, E.L. (2017) *A Critical Companion to the American Stage Musical* (Critical edition). New York: Bloomsbury Methuen Drama.

Note on Terms Used

This collection brings together the work of academics from a variety of disciplines with a range of voices and different lived experiences: the practitioners and researchers reflect methodological approaches across many different practices. While the book uses consistent spellings and conventions across each of the chapters for the sake of the reader, individual terms or descriptors that describe racial and cultural identities have remained (as have individual preferences about capitalization of experience and identity). This can sometimes cause confusion, for example for British students the term 'people of colour' is unusual, as BAME (Black and Asian Minority Ethnic) has become the preferred term in the UK. The contributor's terms have been used in each chapter: they often draw on individual choice, expertise, and cultural lived experience and preferences about individual identities.

Part I

Reframing Identity/Identities

1

'Superman/Sidekick': White Storytellers and Black Lives in *The Fortress of Solitude* (2014)

Donatella Galella

At the top of the musical *The Fortress of Solitude*, the audience hears a black soul singer croon on a shaky record. The record skips. Mingus Rude later plays the record in full for his best friend Dylan Ebdus, as the number 'Superman/Sidekick' comes to life on stage. The musical follows Dylan in 1970s Brooklyn, an outer-borough of New York City, where his white family is one of the few living on Dean Street and where he befriends Mingus. Abandoned by their mothers, the white boy and black boy bond over the soulful music of Mingus' father and over their magic ring that enables them to fly. But racial difference and inequality separate them. While Dylan gains entrance to an elite high school and becomes a music critic dedicated to African American artists, Mingus ends up in prison with his dreams of becoming a famous visual artist shattered.

But in 'Superman/Sidekick', Dylan and Mingus share a moment of interracial harmony. Mingus' father Barrett Rude, Jr., the lead of the musical group The Subtle Distinctions, intones on the record, 'I could be Superman ... If only I could fly' (Friedman, 2015).[1] He dons a red and blue robe evoking Superman's cape, echoed in Mingus and Dylan's red and blue striped clothes. By the end of the song, the tempo quickens as he becomes empowered, dropping the modal of 'could' and preparing to learn to fly. His voice soars in the long-held, triumphant note as if he were flying. Mingus uses this song as a jumping-off point, to imagine what if he, too, could fly and write his graffiti art on otherwise impossibly high walls. In an inversion of the trope of the white boy playing the protagonist to the black best friend, Mingus says that Dylan could be his sidekick. By replaying this Motown-inspired song, changing the lyrics to embrace superpowers, and layering it with Mingus and Dylan singing of flying, 'Superman/Sidekick' in *The Fortress of Solitude* models how songs and superheroes can enable alternate ways of listening, telling stories, and flying above structural racism. But the dramatization of black–white intimacies comes at a price. In the actual framing of the musical, Dylan plays the narrator, while Mingus plays the sidekick.

In order to critique racism and to imagine spaces without racism, *The Fortress of Solitude* relies upon white authorization. The main character, Dylan, is white, and so are almost all of the artistic creators behind the musical: director Daniel Aukin, librettist Itamar Moses, composer-lyricist Michael Friedman, and the original novelist Jonathan Lethem. And yet, what remains of the musical is an original cast recording from Ghostlight Records that privileges blackness. This chapter traces the power dynamics of storytelling when white artists and characters recount black lives and music. After laying out the background of the musical adaptation and key terms from critical race theory, the chapter uses close readings of songs, literary scholarship, interviews with Friedman, and historical context to conduct its analysis. By starting with a black singer's voice, *The Fortress of Solitude* and this very introduction suggest how to shift the centre to blackness. The musical does more than merely include black Americans. It reveals blackness as the necessary core. *The Fortress of Solitude* importantly pinpoints mixed race spaces, amplifies black characters, and stages the differing impacts of structural white supremacy on Dylan versus Mingus. By making Dylan the narrator, Aukin, Moses, and Friedman illuminate how the white protagonist fashions histories, appropriates blackness, and disavows complicity in racial hierarchy. The book centres on Dylan, yet the score centres on black voices and interracial spaces. Friedman incorporates black musical genres, including Motown, disco, gospel, soul, funk, R&B, and hip hop. Even so, white artists crafted these songs, and the storyline draws meta-theatrical attention to the creation of not only Dylan's story, but also of this musical. Deliberately underscoring racial and aesthetic tensions, *The Fortress of Solitude* highlights the unequal socio-political life chances for white and black Americans and imagines interracial friendship through music and a magic ring.

But for that to be possible, the musical must rest upon whiteness. By pointing out the white frame itself, or reframing the frame, this musical shows clearly how white is also a race and how whiteness mediates story-telling. *The Fortress of Solitude* ultimately insists upon the responsibility of those with racial privilege to do anti-racist work, from the art they make to the scholarship they write.

Origin Stories: Making the Musical and Making Race

The origin story of *The Fortress of Solitude* musical begins with author Jonathan Lethem. In 2003, this award-winning white Jewish American popular fiction writer published a novel of the same title (a reference to the Superman comics universe). A semi-autobiographical coming-of-age story with fantastic elements, *The Fortress of Solitude* defies easy categorization. Drawn to Lethem's novel, director Daniel Aukin reached out to composer-lyricist Michael Friedman on whether adapting the novel into a musical seemed viable. Given the significance of music to the story, they imagined that *The Fortress of Solitude* could sing. Aukin had off-Broadway directing experience, while Friedman is perhaps best known for his work with The Civilians, a New York-based group that makes theatre out of its creative investigations into subjects like climate change, as well as his scores to *Bloody Bloody Andrew Jackson* (2006) and *Love's Labour's Lost* (2013). For the book, they recruited Itamar Moses, a playwright and screenwriter whose most recent musical work has been another adaptation, *The Band's Visit* (2017).

In the transition from page to stage, the theatre artists wielded the possibilities and dealt with the limitations of live musicals. They materialized the songs of The Subtle Distinctions, sampled existing songs like 'Play that Funky Music', and lifted lines from Lethem's novel. But they also had to condense this 500-page work into a couple of hours on stage. The musical streamlined black–white dynamics, whereas the novel also includes old Puerto Rican men and Chinese students in the community. In addition, the novel could let the characters literally fly, whereas the stage, as feminist theatre theorist Jill Dolan has noted, 'elides this flight of hopeful fantasy because the actors' bodies are inevitably visible and earth-bound' (Dolan, 2015, p. 300). In 2014, *The Fortress of Solitude* premiered at the Dallas Theatre Center in Texas and then transferred to the Public Theater in New York City, an institution that has a history of supporting Friedman's works, as well as progressive musicals from *Fun Home* (2014) to *Hair* (1967), another text that examines blackness, as Sarah Browne discusses in Chapter 10 of this volume.

To understand how race and power operate in *The Fortress of Solitude*, it is crucial to understand these concepts as explained by critical race theorists. In *Racial Formation in the United States* (1994), a foundational text for the sociology of race, Michael Omi and Howard Winant locate how race has changed since the civil rights movement, from the 1960s onwards, seeing it as historically based rather than natural and stagnant. They conceive race as a social construct with no basis in biology, yet with measured, patterned effects in how different racialized groups are valued. Racialization names the process of making race. Race becomes racism when people sort others into hierarchical categories, not only on an individual basis but on a systemic one. In other words, racism is not just when someone yells a racial epithet; it is also when people with resources and influence keep that power for people like themselves. In the context of the twenty-first century United States, the system remains white supremacy. People with white skin have white privilege; they receive benefits such as better education, cleaner environments, and more jobs with fewer qualifications. Civil rights attorney and scholar Michelle Alexander has documented in *The New Jim Crow* how black Americans experience discrimination at every level of the justice system, from being disproportionately arrested and charged with more serious crimes all the way through jury convictions and job applications that ask if you have ever committed a felony (Alexander, 2012). Academics across disciplines from critical whiteness studies to black feminism have illuminated how race and racism continue to shape lives and institutions, even as most white Americans deny the existence of racial inequalities (Pew Research Center, 2016). These scholars bring to light how whiteness forms a race often thought of as invisible or neutral, and how race must be considered as intersecting with other axes of identity, such as gender. Musical theatre becomes a potent place for investigating racial dynamics because of the interactions of different racialized bodies and the stories that they express through song and movement in front of an audience processing racialized meanings (Galella, 2015).

For this chapter, three ideas from critical race theory and performance studies are particularly helpful in grasping racial dynamics in *The Fortress of Solitude*. First, American Studies scholar George Lipsitz has dubbed the ways that whites, as a group, shore up their privileges the 'possessive investment in whiteness', as if privileges were property with increasing value distributed to whites and denied to people of colour (1998, p. viii). To comprehend how white people commodify people of colour – that is, make them safe and consumable – radical black feminist bell hooks suggests the term 'eating the other' (1992). Dominant white culture treats marginalized cultures like spices added to an existing dish. White people retain their privilege as arbiters of taste, enjoying the thrill of interacting with others, while avoiding the negative consequences of racism on actual people of colour. Finally, black performance studies scholar Daphne Brooks invented the term 'Afro-alienation acts', which '[call] attention to the hypervisibility and cultural constructions of blackness' instead of taking blackness as an inevitable, generalized given (2006, p. 5). Putting these notions together, this chapter looks to how Dylan invests in whiteness and eats the other, but also how *The Fortress of Solitude* highlights and criticizes white dominance through its performances of Afro-alienation acts. Even though racism structures life and art, this chapter shows how *The Fortress of Solitude* offers glimpses of interracial possibility.

Racialized Spaces and Sounds

In addition to the interracial intimacies staged in the number 'Superman/ Sidekick', *The Fortress of Solitude* imagines the block, the physical space of Dean Street, as a place for mixed race community. In the 1970s, the predominantly working-class of colour neighbourhood of Gowanus in northwest Brooklyn included Latinx people, black people, and white people. To set the stage for this memory musical and his friendship with Mingus, in the opening number Dylan recalls his mother, her vision, and their neighbours. She celebrates the block where everyone sings a different song, 'But if they all sing together then it can't be wrong.' As Dylan introduces each character, they introduce new music. They sing of who they will be when they grow up, who they will remember, and of not forgetting who they are and where they belong. Although the themes of time and memory link the songs, they do not specify character and circumstance. Through these snippets of songs, Friedman conjures how people listen to and sing along to songs. Pop songs become associated with moments in people's personal lives, so that when they are replayed they bring up those memories, though the lyrical content may not be directly related to the situation at hand. The songs layer, coming in and out, and they do not harmonize exactly; to do so would suggest a sameness of experiences across racial gaps. Friedman adds, 'I think the democracy of the opening number is extremely important to me, which is that the opening number has no protagonist and Dylan maybe is our guide to it, but he doesn't sing […] it's not counterpoint, like they don't all fit together. They actually just collide' (Friedman, 2017). The composer-lyricist proffers the street as a utopian space where each person sings side by side and holds onto their differences. But, by the end of the number, Dylan's mother abandons the family. Perhaps her conception of interracial togetherness is not so easily realizable.

In her valorization of music as the key to togetherness, Dylan's mom specifically champions records by black American artists. When Mingus shares his father's music with Dylan, beginning with The Subtle Distinctions' 'Superman', the boys develop an intense adolescent friendship. In turn, Dylan shares with Mingus a ring from his mother. Named for legends Bob Dylan and Charles Mingus, they have a special musical connection. Just like their namesakes, Dylan draws inspiration from black artists, and Mingus sings within black musical traditions. Their interracial intimacy over music, superhero comic books, and the ring endow them with superpowers, or at least what feels to them like flying, as the ensemble repeats 'sing a song of two boys flying' in the number 'Take Me to the Bridge'. In these magical moments, the boys soar above the institutional racism that tries to separate them and ground them. On stage, silhouettes show them flying, while the physical actors stand on stage and lean forward with their arms extended. Choreographed by African American dancer-choreographer Camille A. Brown, the stage picture demonstrates the impossibility of really taking flight and the difficulty of dismantling systemic white supremacy, yet stirs an anti-racist imagination.

In the score to *Fortress of Solitude*, black voices are the heart of the musical. Friedman composed the songs for The Subtle Distinctions, citing his work as a 'jukebox musical with a jukebox that never existed' (quoted in Churnin, 2014). Specific popular black American musical styles, which change over time as Dylan and Mingus grow up, inspired this score. In 'Bothered Blue', for example, Friedman echoes the social justice songs of 1970s Motown like Marvin Gaye's 'What's Going On'. Although the lyrics begin by lamenting the loss of a lover, the colours take on racial dimensions. Barrett Rude, Jr. riffs that white is the colour 'Of a world that seems to have no place for me'. His song names how whiteness shapes the world and appears to provide no room for people of colour, and no means for them to obtain racial justice.

Unlike the novel, which uses only third-person omniscient narration and Dylan's first-person narration, the musical lends voices to black characters to speak for themselves. In 'Gentrification, Authenticity and White Middle-Class Identity in Jonathan Lethem's *The Fortress of Solitude*', Matt Godbey argues: 'Told from Dylan's perspective, though, the novel can only allude to the black perspective and perhaps its strongest statement about race is Mingus's relegation to the periphery of narrative about the gentrification' (2008, p. 147). Meanwhile, in the 11 o'clock number of the musical, the climax that showcases a forceful (often solo) performance, Mingus claims ownership of his own narrative: 'This is the story of what really happened to Mingus Rude'. With each iteration, he emphasizes that he will speak his truth on the operations of the prison-industrial complex, the racial and economic mechanisms for keeping disproportionately black and Latino people in cages. He employs the passive voice, 'what really happened to', indicating the forces foisted upon black people. Using hip hop, Friedman gives Mingus a new musical idiom to express himself that is different from the rest of the score, as the narrative moves into the 1980s. After Mingus shoots his grandfather in self-defence, he becomes an inmate and returns to prison repeatedly for minor offences. Mingus describes the violence within prisons and his survival techniques: lifting weights, selling his artistic skills, and learning to appear invisible. In the refrain, he sings of running, though he cannot escape, and of flying, though he cannot see the sky. Mingus follows his father in aspiring to soar like Superman. Cultural studies scholar Devika Sharma points out that 'the motif of flying is a magic countermove to the long history of material and symbolic incarceration shared by the black characters' (2014, p. 671). In 'Black Movements: Flying Africans in Spaceships', Soyica Diggs Colbert (2014) traces this oral-literary tradition to stories of enslaved black people flying back to Africa and representing struggles over life and death. The superhero fantasies of Mingus's and Dylan's youth cannot protect the black boy in the real world, where black Americans face greater obstacles than whites. His class privilege from his father's success as a popular soul singer cannot save him either. When Mingus is released, he encounters the gentrification of Brooklyn, where whites and wealth have been pushing out poor residents of colour. Under strict parole terms, he encounters police eager to catch him with marijuana or spray paint to send him back to prison. Black men are not presumed innocent but already guilty. Under the three strikes rule in states like New York, people convicted of three felonies were automatically sentenced to extremely harsh sentences, even a lifetime in prison. Mingus has no space for freedom. The musical illuminates the differing life outcomes for people with differently coloured skin. Although Mingus sold and consumed drugs with Dylan, white characters receive second chances whereas black ones do not. Mingus ends up in prison with another young black man from Brooklyn, Robert, while their drug-dealing white friend Arthur ends up buying real estate on the block.

White Privilege

For stories and critiques of racist systems to take centre stage, a white protagonist has to be the narrator making that possible. While black music plays, from start to finish, Dylan frames the musical. He turns out to the audience, breaking the fourth wall as he directly tells his story through other people's stories. Dylan does not condemn racial inequality outright but views his inheritance as deserved. His possessive investment in whiteness leads him to believe that he 'earned [his] place' to attend a top high school by passing the entrance exam, in contrast to Mingus.

He fails to consider how black students might not be encouraged to take the test in the first place. Their friendship never recovers from their separation in high school. Having internalized his mother's liberal lessons and love of black music, Dylan becomes a journalist who repackages old records on compact discs. He persuades a producer to reissue The Subtle Distinctions' music, and he pens the liner notes, literally telling his version of this black musical group's history. A kind of white saviour, he provides the opportunity for a new generation to hear The Subtle Distinctions. Eating the other (to use bell hooks's term), Dylan consumes and sells difference as he retains his white privilege. But his actions are not intentionally oppressive; indeed, he seeks to recuperate Mingus's washed-up father and to give the black music that has shaped his life its due. Then again, his well-meaning actions indicate that the terms for including blackness rest upon foundational whiteness. To put it another way: Dylan must guide the narrative in order for black stories and sounds to be heard.

This racial dynamic mirrors the production of *The Fortress of Solitude* itself. Based in part on Jonathan Lethem's experiences growing up in Brooklyn, Dylan serves as a surrogate for the white author, and for the white musical creative team of Aukin, Moses, and Friedman. It is not Barrett Rude, Jr. who wrote the songs for The Subtle Distinctions but Michael Friedman. Traditionally white institutions with predominantly white audiences, the Dallas Theatre Center and the Public Theater allocated resources to these white artists and not to others. Speaking in 2017, an age of Donald Trump's overtly racist and popular policies from the Muslim ban to the Mexican wall (Coates, 2017), Friedman reflected on the musical, 'It's a project where it will always be by white men writing about a perspective of white men, and it's very possible that the world does not need that perspective much right now' (2017). But at the very least, *The Fortress of Solitude* does the work of showing that perspective to be subjective. For another artistic venture, during the 2016 US presidential election, Friedman travelled across the nation to interview Americans and put their words verbatim to song. When asked about his white privilege in providing a platform for other voices, he said, 'I have chosen to use the power I have in that way and that can be that I have not voluntarily relinquished my power. Which is another option. And one I'm not brave enough to do' (2017). Rather than lashing out or becoming defensive about his position and actions, Friedman acknowledged honestly the decisions that he has made in how to use his white privilege. He, Aukin, and Moses could have invited more black artists to the creative team or given up their opportunity to others. Nonetheless, as individual acts, neither option necessarily dismantles structural racism. They are part of a larger system in which resources tend to go towards whites, so systemic change requires whites as a group to make racial equality a reality.

The musical importantly provides a critique of Dylan's white privilege and, taking a step back, that of the white co-creators. Like the novel, it 'points to its own representational restraints' (Sharma, 2014, p. 674). In Chapter 2, Broderick Chow analyses *Here Lies Love* (2014), another musical by white men at the Public Theater, and similarly suggests that the Imelda Marcos disco musical prompts critical awareness of personal positionality and constructed performance. As for *The Fortress of Solitude*, young adult Dylan has a girlfriend named Abby, who, though narratively underdeveloped, offers sharp insight into Dylan's character. Her song 'Something' serves as a crucial Afro-alienation act in drawing attention to the politics of blackness and whiteness. She shows self-awareness in noticing his collection of records and comic books, wondering if she too is part of the collection as the black girlfriend, just like his 'black best friend on Dean Street'. Instead of talking about his life and how he knows Mingus and Barrett Rude, Jr., Dylan changes the subject and puts on black records. Abby calls him out for how he decontextualizes and romanticizes history: 'You said those people's lives don't matter/Only the songs'. These lyrics take on greater resonance in light of the Black Lives Matter movement, which arose in 2012 in response to the acquittal of George Zimmerman, who had killed Trayvon Martin, a young, unarmed black man in Florida. To create distance, Dylan glosses black people as 'those people' and asserts that their lives do not matter. At the same time, he believes that the songs wield profound truth 'Because they sing their pain'. In his contradictory reasoning, he views music as separate (and separable) from people and politics, even as he locates authenticity in black people's personal and political racial struggles. In discussing the influence of black music on white artists, Lipsitz '[warns] against a kind of romanticism that looks so hard for individuality, emotion, and an aesthetic rendering of social pain that we overlook the collective, material, and political dimensions of our lives' (1998, p. 129). When Abby asks Dylan, 'Will you ever learn to sing anything but other people's pain?', he answers by singing lyrics originated by Barrett Rude, Jr. Although he sings the pain of black struggle, Dylan is simultaneously using the vehicle of black music to convey his own pain from his mother abandoning him and him abandoning Mingus. His life is the soundtrack of racial politics, no matter how hard he tries to remove himself from the obligation to raze racial hierarchy. By including this number, Aukin, Moses, and Friedman implicitly critique themselves as white artists mobilizing black sounds, stories, and struggles to compose *The Fortress of Solitude*. Rather than appearing to side with Dylan and his apparently objective white frame, the musical artists call out the privileges of who gets to tell whose story. It is at this point that Mingus breaks out into 'The Ballad of Mingus Rude' to tell his tale and criticize the racist prison-industrial complex.

In the end, Dylan confronts his past. When he visits Mingus in prison, he offers the magic ring in an attempt to repair the rift between them. But restoring interracial intimacy is not that simple. As hooks argues, 'Whether or not desire for contact with the Other, for connection rooted in the longing for pleasure, can act as a critical intervention challenging and subverting racist domination, inviting and enabling critical resistance, is an unrealized political possibility' (1992, p. 22). Dylan's desire for Mingus's friendship and for black musical culture does not equate to anti-racist action. Mingus rejects Dylan, who instead gifts the ring to Robert. Another black kid from the block, Robert had bullied Dylan when they were growing up, but Robert had nothing and no one to support him. While in the novel he accepts the ring and jumps off the prison tower to his death, the musical implies that he successfully flies away, leaving room for the fantasy of escape from the systemic confinement of unequal racial conditions. In a light but earnest a cappella voice, Mingus is able to finish singing the 'Superman' lyric from his father's record that kept skipping at the start of the musical. *The Fortress of Solitude* names what holds back black Americans but, premiering in 2014 in an age of Barack Obama's presidency, the musical also imagines hope, change, and flight if only people of colour were granted greater opportunities.

'Middle Spaces'

In the finale, 'Middle Spaces', Dylan recognizes the racial politics of his narration and the utopian messiness of racial equity yet continues to insist on the potential of music to bring people together. Friedman explains, 'he has been seduced and fooled by pop music' as an easy way to solve the fundamental racial problems of the United States (Friedman, 2012). Dylan reflects that he created the song list, speaking literally to the music compilations that he produces and figuratively to the stories that he tells to comprehend his life and relationships. An unreliable narrator, he sings of his friendship with Mingus and how they could fly, or at least that is how he sees it, highlighting the ambiguity between perception and reality. Did the ring actually grant Dylan and Mingus superpowers? Yes, according to Dylan, though he also shares that truth is grounded in his perspective; it is not objective. Through this self-consciousness, he and the musical's creators model responsible storytelling for people with white privilege. Although they become aware of the difficulties to making interracial harmony, they insist repeatedly in the refrain: 'the song makes a space'. Dylan sings with his voice straining on 'refrain', 'And the refrain/Circles and circles…'. Instead of presuming that he knows the answers and can pose a clear-cut, step-by-step solution to abolishing white supremacy, he has humility in recognizing the limits of the song. Anti-racist work can be messy, awkward, and circular. The song breaks apart and repeats fragments from the first number. Friedman has written a song that critiques songs. Dylan persists because the song makes a space for whites and people of colour to imagine a world without racism. The space is not merely a white one that includes a few people of colour but one made in the middle, in a magical place where black Americans can sing and fly. In the entire score, there is not a single number with only white voices, demonstrating that blackness and interracial relationships provide a necessary, fuller sound.

With its refreshing honesty in addressing racial dynamics while holding onto new ways of forming mixed race community, *The Fortress of Solitude* proffers a model for place making and for historiography, the ways that people come together and recount narratives. To tell his story, Dylan must also tell the story of Mingus. To tell the stories of the United States and of musical theatre history, scholars must also tell the stories of black Americans.

In 2017, three years after the premiere of the off-Broadway production, Aukin, Moses, and Friedman continued to revise this musical as they planned for future productions. But that September, Friedman passed away from HIV/AIDS complications, and the musical theatre community lost a brilliant, leftist artist. The work of *The Fortress of Solitude* remains unfinished, and so is the work of students, educators, researchers, and activists to make a space where white people are willing to be sidekicks to black superheroes.

Note

1. All lyrics from *The Fortress of Solitude* musical come from the original cast recording.

References

Alexander, M. (2012) *The New Jim Crow: Mass Incarceration in the Age of Color-blindness*. New York: New Press.

Brooks, D. (2006) *Bodies in Dissent: Spectacular Performances of Race and Freedom, 1850–1910*. Durham: Duke University Press.

Churnin, N. (2014) Theater: 'Fortress of Solitude' Composer Talks About the Theatrical Challenge he Couldn't Refuse. *Dallas News*. Available at: www.dallasnews.com/arts/arts/2014/03/19/theater-fortress-of-solitude-composer-talks-about-the-theatrical-challenge-he-couldnt-refuse. Accessed 10 August 2017.

Coates, T. (2017) The First White President. *Atlantic*. Available at: www.theatlantic.com/magazine/archive/2017/10/the-first-white-president-ta-nehisi-coates/537909. Accessed 27 November 2017.

Colbert, S.D. (2014) Black Movements: Flying Africans in Spaceships. In DeFrantz, T.F. & Gonzalez, A. (eds.), *Black Performance Theory* (pp. 129–148). Durham: Duke University Press.

Dolan, J. (2015) Seeing Broadly: A Cultural Omnivore's Menu. *Theatre Journal*, 67(2), 295–309.

Friedman, M. (2012) 'The Song Makes A Space: Michael Friedman at TEDx-East', TEDx Talks. Available at: www.youtube.com/watch?v=LQ3KdEoPts0. Accessed 27 November 2017.

Friedman, M. (2015) *The Fortress of Solitude. Original Cast Recording.* CD. New York: Ghostlight Records.

Friedman, M. (2017) Interview with the author. 24 April 2017.

Galella, D. (2015) Redefining America, Arena Stage, and Territory Folks in a Multiracial *Oklahoma!. Theatre Journal*, 67(2), 213–233.

Godbey, M. (2008) Gentrification, Authenticity and White Middle-Class Identity in Jonathan Lethem's *The Fortress of Solitude. Arizona Quarterly*, 64(1), 131–151.

hooks, b. (1992) *Eating the Other. Black Looks: Race and Representation* (pp. 21–39) Boston, MA: South End Press.

Lethem, J. (2003) *The Fortress of Solitude.* New York: Doubleday.

Lipsitz, G. (1998) *The Possessive Investment in Whiteness: How White People Profit from Identity Politics.* Philadelphia, PA: Temple University Press.

Omi, M. & Winant, H. (1994) *Racial Formation in the United States from the 1960s to the 1990s.* 2nd ed. New York: Routledge.

Pew Research Center. (2016) On Views of Race and Inequality, Blacks and Whites Are Worlds Apart. Available at: www.pewsocialtrends.org/2016/06/27/on-views-of-race-and-inequality-blacks-and-whites-are-worlds-apart. Accessed 10 August 2017.

Sharma, D. (2014) The Color of Prison: Shared Legacies in Walter Mosley's *The Man in My Basement* and Jonathan Lethem's *The Fortress of Solitude. Callaloo*, 37(3), 662–675.

2

Seeing as a Filipino: *Here Lies Love* (2014) at the National Theatre

Broderick D.V. Chow

Before my mother was born, my grandfather, Vincente Veloso Yap, bought a piece of land in Makati, a city to the south of Manila. According to my mother, the youngest of seven children in a middle-class Chinese *mestizo* family, Makati was nothing when the family moved there. 'Just empty lots', she says, 'everyone said why are you buying in Makati, but your *ah-kong* ['grandfather' in Hokkien] knew.' After being devastated in the Second World War, Makati was rebuilt. Real estate values soared, and Makati became a hub for commerce and finance.

In 1975, Makati was amalgamated into the National Capital Region, or 'Metro Manila', by Governor Imelda Marcos, First Lady of the Philippines. The Yap family, fearing the political climate, had already emigrated to Canada, keeping ownership of the compound but little else. My mother met my Chinese father in Vancouver, British Columbia, and in June 1982, I was born. On 21 August 1983, a little over a year later, Senator Benigno (Ninoy) Aquino, Jr., an outspoken opponent of President Ferdinand Marcos, stepped off his plane at the Manila International Airport in Parañaque, after three years of self-imposed exile. He was immediately shot in the head by an unknown assailant. The assassination, which many maintain was ordered by Marcos, was a touch-paper for the People Power or EDSA Revolution, against martial law and the Marcos kleptocracy. In 1986, Ferdinand and Imelda Marcos fled the country, airlifted by United States Air Force rescue helicopters from the roof of Malacañang

Palace, carrying millions of dollars in jewellery and cash. In February 1986, Ninoy Aquino's widow, Corazon, assumed the presidency.

I wonder what the conversations among my mother, her sisters and brothers were like during this time. I overheard snatches about the Marcoses, the Aquinos, Philippine politics during my childhood, but this would be beyond my four-year-old comprehension. Also, I was Canadian, and the Philippines might as well have been imaginary considering the paradisiacal images I saw of the country in the travel agent brochures we kept longingly under the coffee table: blue lagoons and impossibly green hills, rice terraces, a boat swaying gently off a white sand beach in Boracay. In 1987, President Aquino appeared on the cover of *Time* magazine as their Woman of the Year; I sensed that this Chinese *mestiza* woman who looked like my auntie was important. In 1990, I went to the Philippines for the first time. I was in Grade Two and I hated it. It was too hot. The house was dusty and smelled of coconut oil. I didn't understand why my cousin had a Super Nintendo but we still had to take a shower with a *tabo* and a bucket. Everyone spoke perfect English with me, but Tagalog or Hokkien with each other, which felt like cheating. Since that first trip, I've been to the Philippines many more times. I've watched Makati transform as high-rises and shopping malls take over the landscape. You can walk for hours in air-conditioned splendour. I've learned more about Philippine culture, language, and history, as well as its theatre, music, and song-and-dance. I have developed an identity for myself as a 'Pinoy', albeit a half-Chinese Pinoy who grew up in Canada and now lives in London, England.[1]

This embodied history accompanied me to my viewings of *Here Lies Love*, which opened the refurbished Dorfman Theatre at London's Royal National Theatre (NT) in October 2014.[2] First produced at New York City's Public Theater in 2013, *Here Lies Love* was conceived as a concept album by David Byrne and Fatboy Slim before being staged by director Alex Timbers, known for his experimental musical works (including *Rocky* on Broadway and the emo rock musical *Bloody Bloody Andrew Jackson*). The show's concept is broadly 'immersive', although not in the wandering, exploratory sense popularized by companies like Punchdrunk. The audience is placed on a dance floor, with the Dorfman's flexible architecture transformed into a nightclub. The action largely takes place on a long gangway and several raised platforms, slightly higher than the audience. The story covers the life of Imelda Romuáldez Marcos, including her youth as a beauty queen in the poor province of Leyte, Visayas, her glory days as a politician, and the People Power Revolution that brought down the Marcos regime. It depicts the brutality of martial law, though throughout, the constant, throbbing music with a strong 4/4 beat compels the audience to dance.

When the 'Imelda Marcos Musical' was announced at the National, I was prepared for the worst. The idea of white British audiences happily dancing along to such a recent story of corruption, violence, and brutality was an unbearable prospect. After all, what did they know about Philippine history? Or Filipinos? I often heard 'Filipino' used as a quick signifier for 'Third World Poverty' by TV comedians; jokes about Filipino/a maids, houseboys, and sex workers were common. Despite the 2007 census recording over 200,000 people of Philippine descent in the United Kingdom, Filipino/as are largely invisible in the British media, and even British-Filipino/a celebrities such as Myleene Klass are often not known to be Filipino/a at all. Furthermore, despite significant progress made since the Royal Shakespeare Company's (RSC's) *The Orphan of Zhao* controversy in 2012 (Chow, 2014), British theatre has a significant problem with yellowface casting and erasure of East Asian actors in general. If Denise Van Outen were cast as Imelda, I promised myself, I would shut down the production myself. However, once the cast was announced, the first all-East Asian cast I had ever seen outside of Asia, my trepidation turned to excitement. On the day of the performance I felt overwhelmed by the significance of it all: *I am going to the Royal National Theatre in London, to see a show about the Philippines.* 'Please don't mess this up!' I tweeted.

They didn't mess it up. *Here Lies Love* played to tremendous critical praise and full houses of enthusiastic audiences. Yet, in the aftermath of the production, reading reviews and having discussions with others, I had a nagging feeling that perhaps I was reading the production in a different way. While I was full of personal intense praise for *Here Lies Love*, and agreed with the general positive reception of the show, at the same time I felt my praise was of a different order, a kind of *dissensus* in consensus that demonstrates how disagreement is rarely binary. Critical praise around the production seemed to focus on the novelty of the concept, its juxtaposition of form and narrative that were implicitly indexed to 'West' and 'East', which was the corollary of criticism that its theatrical innovations were insufficiently complex to present this historical moment. But I didn't see this production as a juxtaposition. It felt, for me, like an exceedingly Filipino show. This disagreement in the reception of form marked a positionality where I was, in essence, *seeing as a Filipino*. I do not mean that owing to my Filipino heritage I hold a privileged interpretative position in relation to others. Nor should the analysis that follows be taken as representative of the community. Rather, I use the phrase *seeing as a Filipino* to articulate a specific position that I, as a diasporic subject, find myself compelled to take up when confronted with a history that has haunted my life since the beginning. This position of seeing is also bound up with the position of *being seen*, that is, being legible as Filipino/a. Therefore, it is a position one is 'hailed' into. In his 1952 essay 'The Fact of Blackness', Frantz Fanon unpacks a moment of being *seen* as black by a child: 'Look, a Negro!' (1952, p. 258). The child's hail forces Fanon to discover his Otherness, as a black man, for a white gaze, 'an object in the midst of other objects' (1952, p. 257). The white gaze undoes Fanon's 'corporeal schema', his dialectical understanding of his body in the world, replacing it with a 'racial epidermal schema' (1952, p. 258). Fanon (1952, p. 259) writes of being suddenly burdened by a 'triple person': 'I was responsible at the same time for my body, for my race, for my ancestors' (1952, pp. 258–259). Something similar, I contend, takes place when one watches a Filipino show *as* a Filipino: I became aware of my presence in the audience at the National Theatre as guarantor for the authenticity of the spectacle taking place, the white gaze curtailing my interpretative abilities. Seeing as a Pinoy is thus about accepting the position to which I am hailed to parse and interrogate other layers of colonial and decolonial 'seeing'.

I am most interested to challenge a neocolonial reading by which the representation of Third World politics must function as a history lesson for Western audiences, and in doing so adopt a realist or documentary aesthetic. The politics of *Here Lies Love*, from my position of seeing, are embedded in its affective and excessive theatricality, which should be understood in relation to the performance culture of the Philippines. In other words, my analysis of the musical reframes the work as an embodied and affective intervention into Philippine culture, history, and identity. In this chapter I connect the production's concept and staging to forms of what I would call, after Nicanor Tiongson (quoted in Diamond, 1996, p. 146), 'Filipinized' performance, that is, forms that were brought to the Philippines during its colonial history but are an essential part of its hybrid culture. Thus, the production's central conceit is not a clever form of Brechtian distancing, a Western container for a Southeast Asian story, but rather a means of conveying, via a fundamentally participatory performance tradition (see Fernández, 1996), precisely how the Marcos regime survived for so long: through a combination of state violence and the manipulation of appearance. It conveys the affective nature of populist politics, something that neither the realist book musical nor naturalistic representation can properly capture. Seeing *Here Lies Love* as a Filipino, I argue, interrupts and complicates established narratives around representation and reception that might lead us to wring our hands over or dismiss a musical by two white British men, staged in America and the UK, about one of the darkest moments in Asian history.

Benevolent Assimilation: The Philippines and the Colonial Imaginary

To contextualize my reading of *Here Lies Love* we must firstly examine its position in what I call the 'colonial imaginary'. The archipelago was first 'claimed' for Spain in 1521 by Portuguese colonizer Ferdinand Magellan, and the first Spanish settlers arrived with Miguel López de Legazpi in 1565. After 300 years of colonial rule, a successful revolution took place in 1898, ignited in part by the satirical writings of Chinese *mestizo* polymath José Rizal. However, in that same year, as part of the concessions for the Spanish-American war, the islands were given to the United States, who suppressed further rebellions. The Philippines thus became a colony of the United States, who described its role as a

form of 'benevolent assimilation' (McKinley, 1898). President William
McKinley stated:

> there was nothing left for us to do but to take them [...] and to educate the
> Filipinos, and uplift and civilize and Christianize them, and by God's grace
> do the very best we could do by them, as our fellow men for whom Christ
> also died. And then I went to bed and went to sleep and slept soundly.
>
> (McKinley in Chuh, 2003, p. 44)

McKinley's statement shows the American colonizing mission to be especially paternalistic, placing the Philippines in the structural position of
the child who requires 'saving'. The US aimed to establish an American-
style democracy in Asia, which also served a strategic purpose since the
Philippines would act as an important military base in the Pacific during
World War II. During the war, the islands were captured and occupied
by Japan, only to be recaptured by the Americans in 1945. Finally, after
nearly 400 years of colonization, on 4 July 1946 the Philippines became
an independent republic under President Manuel Roxas.

As Lucy Mae San Pablo Burns points out, American colonization did
not operate only through a repressive state apparatus (colonial government), but also through 'ideological state apparatuses [of] education,
culture, and health care' (Burns, 2013, p. 63). These ideological state
apparatuses enacted, to draw from Catherine Ceniza Choy's concept,
a form of 'corporeal colonization' (2003). The most persistent of these
apparatuses is American popular culture, including dance, music, and
fashion, which continues to exert a strong influence. Filipinos in the
homeland and the diaspora routinely speak of 'colonial mentality', an
internalized oppression that expresses itself in a distinct preference for
American (or non-Filipino) food, culture, and language, and a talent for
gaya, or imitation (David and Okazaki, 2006).

This history underlines the first number of *Here Lies Love*, the
strangely titled 'American Troglodyte'. Accompanied by choreography
(by Annie-B Parson) in the dance vocabulary of commercial pop and
music video, 'American Troglodyte' is an energetic way to bring the
audience into the world of the piece. There is, too, an additional 'jolt'
of seeing an all-East Asian cast costumed for a nightclub in black jeans,

t-shirts, leather jackets, and little black dresses, rather than the traditional worn signifiers of Asianness on the musical theatre stage: rags,
rice-paddy hats, *kimono*, and *qi-pao*. Crucially, though, this number is
not a *juxtaposition* of Western cultural form and Asian bodies. Rather,
from my position, it reads as a presentation of a historically determined
post-colonial subjectivity. Through the 'list' song format, we see that
what might be straightforward satire of excessive traits of American
culture ('gigantic cars') are counterbalanced by banalities ('income tax')
and other aspects that have been fully adopted as part of Philippine
culture ('basketball'). Furthermore, the staging and choreography
would not be out of place in any of the music television shows popular
in the Philippines such as *Eat Bulaga* or *ASAP*.[3] The sheer pleasure
taken in the performance of 'American Troglodyte', and indeed the rest
of *Here Lies Love*, complicates the notion that it is simply a number
about what Renato Constantino calls 'cultural Westernization' (in Tadiar,
2009, p. 27). Anthropologist Fenella Cannell's study of Bicolano pageantry (including the performance of *baklas*, an indigenous 'third-gender'
identity) is helpful in understanding this distinction: 'imitation in the
Philippines [...] has a particular meaning and the fact that it incorporates
"Western" models should not lead us to confuse it with mere derivative-
ness; in Bicol, imitation of content can constitute a self-transformative
process' (1995, p. 224). In other words, 'American Troglodyte' embodies the process by which the Filipino/a subject negotiates identity *through*
American signifiers and forms, mirroring the same process on a national
level of a people forming a *positive* identity after only emerging as a people
through the anti-colonial struggle (Tadiar, 2009, p. 266).

As I danced along to Byrne and Fatboy Slim's music and seductive
beats, I thought about this idea of the Pinoy subject, divided from itself.
It resonated with my own negotiations of Filipino identity, further complicated by my being half-Chinese, and Canadian by nationality. *Here
Lies Love*'s use of 'disco', both in music and staging, for me, was a perfect
representation of a fundamental aspect of a culture defined through
the struggle against (neo)coloniality. Yet critical response to the show
tended to focus on the novelty and innovation of the 'concept', attributed to its British and American creative team. Victoria Sadler, in the
Huffington Post, for example, first poses the question of the juxtaposition

of narrative and form ('why has the life of Imelda Marcos been set to a club soundtrack?') before attributing the innovation to Byrne's fascination with Imelda Marcos's 'love of the New York club scene' (Sadler, 2014). Indeed, it is true that Marcos was fascinated with American nightlife and music but, as I have explained, this is by no means exceptional. Other critics in London, New York, and the most recent production in Seattle have pointed to the novelty of the concept, or 'big idea' (Brantley, 2013; Billington, 2014; Letts, 2014; Berson, 2017), though perhaps such critical gestures can be justified by the economies of theatre marketing. More indicative of a certain Anglo-American critical position is musical theatre academics Millie Taylor and Dominic Symonds's reading of the piece, where they state: 'This show's significance then – what allows it to get away with the bold *incongruities* of this theatrical conceit – is in the make-up of its concept' (2014, p. 72, emphasis added). They go on to state that 'to frame the biographical story of a political matriarch within the milieu of the contemporary club scene may seem rather anachronistic' (p. 70). The use of *anachronistic* is perhaps a slip, but a significant one nonetheless. The use of a historically specific sound (disco) to accompany a story of the 1970s is, obviously, perfectly *synchronous*. Taylor and Symonds' appraisal of the concept as anachronistic therefore points to a colonial gaze by which the colonized subject is fixed in an 'essentialized past' (see Hall, 1990, p. 225).

The familiar historiography in which the concept musical (usually associated with white male innovators such as Stephen Sondheim or Bob Fosse) is the postmodern zenith of a modern form that began with the 'integrated musical' is not expansive enough to admit non-Western or hybridized forms, such as the Philippine *sarsuwela*. An indigenized form of the Spanish *zarzuela*, *sarsuwela* is romantic comedy-drama, interspersed with songs and dance, typically set against a backdrop of important local and community social, political, and economic issues. According to Philippine theatre scholars Sir Anril Pineda Tiatco and Amihan Bonifacio-Ramolete (2010, p. 307), it 'served as a venue to release unexpressed emotions against the colonial masters, Spanish or American'. Seen in relation to Asian theatre history, then, *Here Lies Love* is less a conceptual innovation than a piece informed by a traditional cultural form, an extension of a political theatre that during colonization and martial law learned to communicate through 'indirection' (Fernández, 1996, p. 129).

I argue that the production's politics operate indirectly through its 'excessive theatricality'. Timber's staging should be seen less in relation to recent developments in 'immersive theatre', more to Fernández's conceptualization of *palabas* (performance) as a particular orientation in Philippine theatre. It is an invitation for the audience to play witness to the theatricality of politics. By providing discrete and shifting roles for the audience, the piece goes further than simply dramatizing the Marcoses' predilection for glamour, exhibition, and spectacle. It instead embodies the way Imelda sought to manage the *mise-en-scène* of her political spectacle, literally scripting a role for each social actor in Philippine politics.

Theatricality and the 'Fantasy-Production' of the Marcoses

In a recent article for Seattle's *The Stranger*, Asian American performance artist Sara Porkalob takes issue with the production's 'spectacle': *Here Lies Love* 'musically remakes and recirculates Filipina femininities to commercialize and reconstruct US and Philippine history for marketable, danceable consumption' (Porkalob, 2017). Porkalob argues that the onstage glamour and theatricality obscures the fact that Marcos was a complex, intelligent figure in her own right. Largely, this is a problem of form, as the concept does not allow for a demonstration of interiority ('true character'). The audience is thus seduced by the glamour of the production without reflecting on 'the Philippines' national trauma and America's role in it' (Porkalob, 2017). Porkalob's critique reflects similar handwringing over the seductive nature of the production in other cities; for example, Michael Billington in *The Guardian* writes, 'the lack of a libretto means we never fully understand how the Marcos regime survived as long as it did'.[4] Taylor and Symonds (2014, p. 73) declare 'audience members are blind to the fact that moments before they have willingly and enthusiastically – but mindlessly – danced to [Marcos's] tune'. Porkalob's critique gives me pause: where is the possibility for a rupture in the glossy veneer of the Imelda fairy tale?[5] However, while the images and music of *Here Lies Love* are certainly seductive, I suggest that the politics of the production lie in its disclosure of the work of theatricality in producing complicity.

Imelda, portrayed at the NT by Australian actress Natalie Mendoza, kneeling still in a blue dress, in front of Peter Nigrini's projection of Leyte, an island in the Visayas region, in monsoon season. She sings the first verse of the title song in this *tableaux vivant*, the costumes and sepia-toned video creating a nostalgic image. Byrne's choice to begin the narrative at this point (rather than with, for example, Imelda's childhood, or her later arrival in Manila) creates an intertextual allusion to Andrew Lloyd Webber and Tim Rice's *Evita*, which similarly begins with a teenage Eva in her provincial hometown. However, while Eva's longing for Buenos Aires is played authentically, Byrne's lyrics are more ambiguous. Though the song in style and position in the show is a traditional 'I wish' song, the lyrics are strangely declamatory and self-aggrandizing. Their simplistic statement of the given circumstances ('I'm just a young girl from Leyte') serves the same function as the subtitles in the projection. They are also direct quotations of Imelda Marcos (indeed, many of the show's lyrics are verbatim texts). Already in Imelda's first appearance, we bear witness to the obvious presentation of self, and the management of the theatrical image. This is not without a touch of irony; as the song reaches its chorus Mendoza pulls out a microphone as the female ensemble appears behind her, dressed identically in white, dancing with useless paper parasols – we've established it is monsoon season.

The disarticulation of the *mise-en-scène* and the disintegration of music and narrative from this first appearance of Imelda foreground the fact that spectacle is also a form of labour. *Here Lies Love* is theatre that does not hide its seams. Timbers and company use devices drawn from popular, rather than prestige, theatrical forms, including the fashion show (the platforms of David Korin's set at several points form runways); the pantomime (the two-dimensional cardboard sets of 'The Rose of Tacloban'); and the magic show (during the number 'Sugartime Baby', Imelda and Ferdinand's traditional wedding *terno* and *barong tagalog* are ripped off to reveal matching polka-dot swimming costumes). The reference to stage magic and 'quick-change' performance is significant, as stage magic is not about an audience being 'fooled' into believing magic really exists, but rather about being moved by the magician's skill at creating, via material things, a fantasy. The recognition of a trick, in other words, is what is astonishing.

The production does not attempt to present Imelda's interior life. The number 'Solano Avenue', for example, uses techniques drawn from music videos or pop concerts in order to subvert what in other musicals might be an emotional duet. In it, Imelda confronts her old friend and maid Estrella Cumpas (played at the NT by Gia Macuja Atchinson), who raised her as a child, after Estrella has given an interview on Philippine TV that skewers much of Imelda's self-mythologization. The maudlin lyrics reflect the depth of Imelda's betrayal, yet they are staged in the style that recalls R&B duets such as Brandy and Monica's 'The Boy Is Mine', including choreography that is played strictly towards the audience. We never forget that this production is being played *for* us. As I watched the production on the dance floor of the Dorfman Theatre, I was never seduced into empathizing with Imelda Marcos, but I had complex feelings of being impressed, astonished, and *moved* by this Filipina icon, and Mendoza's deeply embodied performance. This is a crucial distinction.[6] By refusing to psychologize a historical figure, in contrast to *Evita* or indeed, *Hamilton*, *Here Lies Love* embodies the theatrical-political process by which consent and complicity were manufactured.

Famously, Imelda Marcos loved to perform, specifically, to sing, and her favourite genre was/is *kundiman*, Tagalog love song. She has a fine soprano and excellent breath control well suited to *kundiman*, which generally expresses devotion or longing for an absent lover. Her signature tune is 'Dahil Sa'yo' ('Because of You'), composed by Miguel Velarde, Jr. in 1938, which she sang at political rallies, for heads of state, and for US President Lyndon Johnson at the start of the Vietnam War (Balance, 2010, p. 130). Christine Bacareza Balance connects this preference to perform musical lamentations to Imelda's tendency to openly weep on television, suggesting that 'Imelda's power to charm and deceive [is] a gendered corollary to her husband's legislative and military power by force' (Balance, 2010, p. 121). By performing 'Dahil Sa'yo', whose first lyrics are 'Dahil sa iyo, nais kong mabuhay' ['Because of you, I yearn to live'], for US Heads of State, for example, 'the ballad [...] performed the Philippines' dependence upon the United States when, in reality, the Cold War political relationship between the two nations was more aptly codependent' (Balance, 2010, p. 130). This performative diplomacy, which gendered or 'feminized' (Tadiar, 2009) the Philippines' international role, was an enormously important part of the Marcoses' politics.[7] I want to extend Balance's reading of Imelda's theatrical politics here; Imelda's politics were not only theatrical in the sense of a personal performance, but also in the sense of managing the wider *mise-en-scène*. Imelda Marcos was also Governor of Manila, and as Governor reshaped the city into a global metropolis. Consolidating 16 municipalities into one suddenly made Manila into an Asian mega-city similar to Hong Kong or Singapore, and projected a modern face to the Philippines in order to attract flows of capital (Tadiar, 1993, p. 154). Imelda launched numerous cultural projects including 'film festivals, historically themed parks, [and] international conferences' (Rafael, 2000, pp. 122–161), and above all, the construction of the Cultural Center of the Philippines (CCP), a massive complex not unlike the NT. The CCP was built in a prestigious location on Manila Bay; its construction ran 35 million pesos over budget and was finished with the assistance of US loans of around 7 million USD. It is well known today for having inadequate parking, as Marcos assumed audiences would be drawn exclusively from the middle and upper classes, who in Manila typically have private chauffeurs. The Manila Film Centre, on the south-west of the complex, is said to be the most haunted building in the Philippines due to an accident during its construction when 12 low-paid workers fell and were buried in quick-drying cement, their bodies remaining in its foundations to this day (Lace, 2012).[8] The CCP is an apparatus that enables Filipino/as to 'appear' in a certain way (cosmopolitan, educated, cultured), at the same time as it conceals, or to use a more pointed political term, 'disappears', vast inequalities in the nation. In a similar oscillation of appearance/disappearance, Imelda's reinvention of Metro Manila required the construction of a large number of flyovers, which created, according to Tadiar, an archipelago of urban islands connected by flyover bridges (Tadiar, 1993). These flyovers allow traffic to pass directly over the slums of Tondo and San Andres, but also illustrate the new way residents of Manila were to imagine themselves and to perform: as discrete selves, in flows of traffic within a free flow of commerce.

The fact that, as anyone who has been to Manila knows, these flyovers and new highways immediately became choked and blocked with traffic is perhaps an ideal illustration of the contradictions of neoliberalism.

The Marcoses theatricalized political performance on an individual level as a glamorous political couple, as well as on the level of a kind of national *theatrum mundi* which enabled the people to perform a certain role. Their 'conversion of politics into spectacle' is what enabled them, according to Vicente L. Rafael, to marry neoliberal capitalist economics with a more traditional Philippine practice of 'patronage', so that the Marcoses were positioned as the origin of capitalist circulation (Rafael, 2000, p. 142). I argue that the staging of *Here Lies Love* is analogous to this process, as it works to affectively and literally 'move' the audience around Imelda Marcos as the symbolic centre of gravity. It embodies, and shows the labour of, what Neferti Tadiar calls 'fantasy-production', which is her concept for the state manipulation of the codes of the national and international socio-symbolic practices that 'organise what we take to be "reality"' (Tadiar, 2004, p. 29). The gimmick of *Here Lies Love* is to tell this history as disco. The coup is to show that it really was disco.

Palabas; Outro

After my second viewing of *Here Lies Love*, I wrote up my initial responses to the piece in a rough essay and sent it to an acquaintance of mine in the Philippines, a playwright. He wrote back, intrigued yet wondering,

> how do these audiences let themselves be immersed by the entire almost hallucinatory experience of excess and disco, and when does the 'distancing' take effect, where one's mind is suddenly pricked by the notion that there had been so much squalor and death and disgust behind everything?
>
> (So, 2014)

It is a fair question, and one I cannot answer in terms of a general audience response. In terms of narrative, Byrne's vision is more critical of the Marcoses than not. Throughout the theatrical manipulations, a counter-narrative

emerges, as Ninoy Aquino (played in London by Dean John-Wilson) trans-
forms into a convincing socialist voice. When he is murdered, the audience
is moved, in the show's most drastic scenographic change, into a traditional
end-on configuration, forming the people at Aquino's funeral, and the
'People' in the abstract sense. The style of music drastically changes for 'Just
Ask the Flowers', sung by Aquino's mother (Li-Tong Hsu), a soft ballad
that turns into a stirring protest song, including the slogan of the People
Power Revolution, 'Tama Na! Sobra Na!' ['Enough already!']. Finally, the
Dorfman's disco transformation is stripped away, the work lights go up,
and the DJ (Martin Sarreal) sings 'God Draws Straight (but with crooked
lines)', accompanied only by a guitar. This final number is made up of
quotations from participants in the People Power Revolution. The audience is positioned *as* the People, watching the helicopters fly away from
Malacañang. If there is a distancing, it is in these final, calculated moments.

However, for me there is a secondary, but equally important politics
to *Here Lies Love*. What struck me, 'pricked' me, most of all in the setting
of the Royal National Theatre, a concrete cultural complex not unlike
the CCP but built 10 years later, was a cast of East Asian actors from
Britain, Europe, and the Philippines, staging Asian history. *Here Lies
Love*'s excessive theatricality and its continuous hailing of the audience,
I suggest, reveals the agency of the performers, within a text composed
by a white British man and directed by a white American man. It stages
palabas. In Tagalog, the word *palabas* simply means 'performance', but
it also means 'outward' (*pa* – towards; *labas* – exterior). In her lexicon
of Philippine theatre, Doreen Fernández (1996, p. viii) uses this dual
meaning to highlight the social dimension of performance for Filipino/
as ('a people to whom performing is part of living'): *palabas* is 'peo-
ple-based and community oriented, whether it be school play or fiesta
spectacle or protest theatre'. Patrick Flores (2005) takes this further; for
him, *palabas* is a mode of being that is aware of one's self-presentation
and tries to manage the effects such presentation has on others. For
Flores, 'there is a deliberate agency at work in a gesture of performance
or the process of making something appear and making it appear in a
particular way' (Flores, 2005, n.p.). *Palabas* is revealed in the gestures
of *Here Lies Love* that disarticulate its theatrical components; which
refuse sympathy; and which constantly remind the audience that all this

is being performed for them, to have an intended effect. In a British theatrical context where East Asian performers so rarely appear at all, watching a cast of East Asian actors stage *palabas* in this way was truly powerful.

Bearing witness to the agency and pleasure of staging history, for me, began to strip away layers of colonial gaze in which the Filipino/a is the object, and not the subject of history. It troubled and tore apart a neocolonial narrative of third-world dictatorship and first-world democracy that so often characterizes representations of Asia. It forced me to consider the complexity of the embodied history that leads me to see and be seen as a Filipino, my position in relation to both the diaspora and the homeland. But most of all it made me consider the affective nature of populism, which remains dangerous as recent events have shown. As I write this essay, President Rodrigo Duterte is waging his violent war on drug dealers and gangs, while enjoying an approval rating in some areas of upwards of 90 per cent. In the face of such repression and populist fervour, *Here Lies Love* perhaps appears quaint, ineffective. But perhaps its all-consuming focus on surface and appearance serves to remind us of what has been disappeared.

Notes

1. Filipino/as have a love of nicknaming and abbreviation, and Pinoy is a colloquialism for Filipino. Technically, being half-Chinese, I am a 'Chinoy'.
2. This chapter is my analysis of two viewings of the piece in two very different audience positions. I first saw the piece in October 2014 on the 'dance floor', and again in December 2014 from the gallery level.
3. For an example of this kind of 'party' television, see www.youtube.com/watch?v=-LsHoKBgXaU (Geronimo 2017).
4. It is interesting to note that Porkalob is Filipina American, which attests to my earlier point that 'seeing as a Filipino' should not represent a community response.
5. It is interesting to note that online comments on Porkalob's piece suggest she underestimates the Seattle audience; at least three comments note that while they were ignorant of the subject matter before seeing the production, the production provoked them into researching the history of the Marcoses.

6. I might compare this response to my response watching Tony Kushner's *Angels in America*, which similarly portrays a historical 'monster', in this case, Roy Cohn. Unlike in *Here Lies Love*, Kushner's psychological realism in the midst of cosmic magic does elicit a sympathetic response to Cohn's illness and death from me (as well as many audience members).
7. This is staged in *Here Lies Love* in the number 'Please Don't'.
8. It was rumoured at the time that 169 lives were lost in this accident, but in 2005 it was found that 12 had died, which demonstrates the depth of mistrust for the Marcoses (Lace, 2012).

References

Balance, C.B. (2010) *Dahil Sa Iyo:* The Performative Power of Imelda's Song. *Women and Performance*, 20(2), 119–140.

Berson, M. (2017) Review: Seattle Rep's bold 'Here Lies Love' is an interactive spectacle. *Seattle Times*, 21 April. Available at: https://www.seattletimes.com/entertainment/theater/review-here-lies-love-is-a-swirling-dynamic-first-ladys-biography-to-a-disco-beat/. Accessed 17 August 2017.

Billington, M. (2014) *Here Lies Love* Review: David Byrne and Fatboy Slim Show Lacks Substance. *The Guardian*. 14 October. Available at: www.theguardian.com/stage/2014/oct/14/here-lies-love-byrne-marcos-review. Accessed 17 August 2017.

Brantley, B. (2013) A Rise to Power, Disco Round Included. *New York Times*, 28 July. Available at: www.nytimes.com/2013/04/24/theater/reviews/david-byrnes-here-lies-love-at-the-public-theater.html. Accessed 17 August 2017.

Burns, L.M.S.P. (2013) *Puro Arte: Filipinos on the Stages of Empire*. New York: New York University Press.

Cannell, F. (1995) The Power of Appearances: Beauty, Mimicry, and Transformation in Bicol. In Rafael, V. L. (ed). *Discrepant Histories: Translocal Essays on Filipino Cultures* (pp. 223-258). Philadelphia: Temple University Press.

Chow, B.D.V. (2014) Here Is a Story for Me: Representation and Visibility in *Miss Saigon* and *the Orphan of Zhao*. *Contemporary Theatre Review*, 24(4), 507–516.

Choy, C.C. (2003) *Empire of Care: Nursing and Migration in Filipino American History*. Durham and London: Duke University Press.

Chuh, K. (2003) *Imagine Otherwise: On Asian Americanist Critique*. Durham and London: Duke University Press.

David, E.J.R. & Okazaki, S. (2006) Colonial Mentality: A Review and Recommendation for Filipino-American Psychology. *Cultural Diversity and Ethnic Minority Psychology*, 12(1), 1–16.

Diamond, C. (1996) Quest for the Elusive Self: The Role of Contemporary Philippine Theatre in the Formation of Cultural Identity. *TDR: The Drama Review*, 40(1), 141–169.

Fanon, F. (1952)[2000] The Fact of Blackness. In Back, L. & John, S. *Theories of Race and Racism: A Reader* (pp. 257–266). London and New York: Routledge.

Fernández, D.G. (1996) *Palabas: Essays on Philippine Theatre*. Manila: Ateneo de Manila University Press.

Flores, P. (2005) *Palabas (Curatorial Note for Danas: Palabas Exhibition)*. Manila: Cultural Center of the Philippines.

Hall, S. (1990) Cultural Identity and Diaspora. In Rutherford, J. (ed.), *Identity, Community, Culture, Difference* (pp. 222–237). London: Lawrence and Wishart.

Lace, K. (2012) The Ghost in Manila Film Center. *Philippine Urban Legends*. 17 February. Available at: http://philurbanlegends.blogspot.co.uk/2012/02/ghost-of-manila-film-center-this-is-not.html. Accessed 17 August 2017.

Letts, Q. (2014) *Here Lies Love* Review: I Can't say I Was Emotionally Involved but Novelty is the Intention. *Daily Mail*, 14 October. Available at: www.dailymail.co.uk/tvshowbiz/article-2791847/here-lies-love-review-t-say-emotionally-involved-novelty-intention.html. Accessed 17 August 2017.

McKinley, W. (1898) McKinley's Benevolent Assimilation Proclamation. *Filipino.biz.ph - Philippine Culture*. Available at: www.msc.edu.ph/centennial/benevolent.html. Accessed 17 August 2017.

Porkalob, S. (2017) The Problem of Spectacle in David Byrne's *Here Lies Love*. *The Stranger*, 24 May. Available at: www.thestranger.com/slog/2017/05/24/25166370/the-problem-of-spectacle-in-david-byrnes-here-lies-love. Accessed 17 August 2017.

Rafael, V.L. (2000) *White Love and Other Events in Filipino History*. Manila: Ateneo de Manila University Press.

Sadler, V. (2014) Theatre Review: David Byrne and Fatboy Slim Team Up for *Here Lies Love*. *Huffington Post*, 13 December. Available at: www.huffingtonpost.co.uk/victoria-sadler/here-lies-love-review_b_5978968.html. Accessed 17 August 2017.

So, J.L. (2014) Email, 30 November [personal communication].

Tadiar, N.X.M. (1993) Manila's New Metropolitan Form. *Differences: A Journal of Feminist Cultural Studies*, 5(3), 154–178.

Tadiar, N.X.M. (2004) *Fantasy-Production: Sexual Economies and Other Philippine Consequences for the New World Order*. Hong Kong: Hong Kong University Press.

Tadiar, N.X.M. (2009) *Things Fall Away: Philippine Historical Experience and the Makings of Globalization*. Durham and London: Duke University Press.

Taylor, M. & Symonds, D. (2014) *Studying Musical Theatre: Theory and Practice*. London: Palgrave.

Tiatco, S.A.P.T. & Bonifacio-Ramolete, A. (2010) Performing the Nation Onstage: An Afterthought on the University of the Philippines Sarsuwela Festival 2009. *Asian Theatre Journal*, 27(2), 307–332.

3

Disney's *The Lion King* on Broadway (1997) as a Vital Sign for Understanding Civic and Racialized Presence in the Early Twenty-First Century

Brian Granger

Introduction

My first experience as an audience member for *The Lion King* on Broadway is at a 2pm matinee performance at its Minskoff Theatre location on Broadway, in New York City on 13 April 2011. The show begins, importantly, with a sound that is identifiably black African, as the African actor playing Rafiki, whom I recognized from her character's similar colours in the film, enters and belts out an accappella musical phrase in Zulu using the Isicathamiya vocal style. This style, originating with Zulu mine workers, is characterized by strong vocals that begin alone and then are joined by a rhythmic call-and-response choral support. It is a sound that resonates with other black expressive practices across many transnational and transoceanic networks (an aesthetic solidarity I will henceforth refer to as 'black'). She is standing slightly bent-kneed, holding a staff in one hand and thrusting her other hand out into space as if commanding or signalling to the world she sees before her. As the unseen chorus joins in, also singing in Zulu and echoing her musical line, I can hear this gorgeous 'black' sound above and behind me at the same time. As these additional voices enter the sonic space, a variety of costumed and puppet-carrying actors also enter, each one of the actors representing various African animals and signalling the start of the 'Circle of Life' opening number. This 'Noah's Ark'-style procession is widely recognizable from the earlier, animated film version, as well as from the television commercials and movie trailers that have aired for both the film and the Broadway musical. Emotionally, the opening scene is disarming. I see several audience members of various ages in tears. How beautiful it is to see so many brown-skinned bodies on a Broadway stage, to see such a creative representation of the film's animal life – embodying such a palpable love of nature that it almost feels spiritual – and to hear so many full-throated black voices! Oh! To hear them, wrapping around me like a hug.

*****

Disney's 1994 animated film *The Lion King* and its musical theatre stage adaptation in 1997 continue to be widely beloved, but the initial popularity of the musical was due to its faithfulness to the film plot. Fans of the 90-minute film were pleased to see that most of what they remembered and expected to see on stage was preserved in the longer and more detailed stage adaptation, running at two hours and 40 minutes with an intermission. The original film only had a handful of songs, and some of these were part of the background score. *The Lion King's* creative team on Broadway retained the basic plot of the film and its handful of songs, which had all been quite popular, and then added more music to transform the lucrative, award-winning film property into a fully fledged musical, one that became equally lucrative and award-winning.

The plot parallels between the Broadway stage musical and the animated film have understandably led to the stage musical not being fully appreciated as a distinct work by most of the commentators who were (rightly) critical of the film. Kirk A. Hoppe (2005) sees *The Lion King* film as 'a parable of patriarchy, heterosexual monogamy, and racial hierarchy', which, in its circulation on video and DVD throughout American homes, reinforces the meanings of the imaginary African space throughout the country. This imagined, Disney Africa depends on audience recognition of Africa as a beautiful, austere monolith – symbolized in the figure of the lion king, and more concretely, in Pride Rock, which looks over its film and stage musical worlds. Africa here is a place of unity and an endless source of unproblematic inspiration – an entire continent that is beautifully abundant in nature and untapped, consumable resources, but strangely unpopulated by humans who would understand exactly how abundant and how consumable it all is. The capitalist, touristic desire of Disney's representations of Africa casts the experience with the continent in *The Lion King* story as a wholly family-friendly and aesthetic experience. In both the film and stage plots, Disney's Africa is an Eden-like, utopian space. However, this notion of a raw paradise, ready to be tamed and ruled by a strong male figure, embodies problematic socio-political ideologies that Hoppe argues have been central to the way the United States and the larger West have looked at Africa. Africa-as-Eden ideologies have fostered almost all of the negative cultural representations of the continent that we have ever seen in our national and popular imaginations.

Because the *Lion King* animated film story can easily be read as a parable of these problematic socio-political ideologies, critics of *The Lion King* film who bristle at the spectacle of African animal pageantry and its distance from African realities often use a similar line of argument for the Broadway show and assert that the stage musical accomplishes the same problematic work as the original animated film. For example, Maurya Wickstrom's much-cited 1999 essay from *Theatre Journal*, 'Commodities, Mimesis, and *The Lion King*: Retail Theatre for the 1990s', argues that the stage version is merely a clever incarnation of the film, and that both film and stage version are commodities masked as art (Wickstrom, 1999). Wickstrom's criticisms are insightful and important. Yet in her largely Marxist reading of the film and stage versions, her unexamined binary between commodity on the one hand and pure art on the other obscures the complex pleasures and powers of live theatre.

It should be remembered that most Broadway musicals, as commercial entertainments, do not make a critique of consumption, and the lack of this particular critique within most musicals should not be the basis of aesthetic judgements made about them. Furthermore, when we consider the theatre as a code system, we need to understand that this type of consideration disassembles the sensory impact that theatre has on us as members of the audience, as argued effectively by Bert O. States in his important discussion of semiotics (States, 1987, p. 7). *The Lion King*, as an artistic work, produces code systems, and scholars have rightly identified some of these codes as being sexist, racist, and classist. But joining these codes are those produced in the phenomenological, sensory experience one has sitting in the theatre. This phenomenological experience works against the totalizing reading of the show as wholly problematic and oppression-supporting that some of *its* critics have levelled against it, and yet this experience is provided to the audience primarily by the sensory – and in some aspects consumable – pleasure of the performing black body.

In thinking through theories of the performing black body here, I am indebted to Stephanie Leigh Batiste's important book *Darkening Mirrors: Imperial Representations in Depression-Era African American Performance* (2011). Although the scope of Batiste's case studies in the book are limited to the early twentieth century, I work from her understanding, which she shares with many other scholars of black performance, that black performance itself is a working out, as well as a new creation, of theory within and through the symbolic and actual black body – a body that according to Batiste is 'material and metaphorical, real and unreal' (Batiste, 2011, p. 14). Batiste's understanding of the 'real and unreal' black body is particularly relevant to understanding *The Lion King* on Broadway and its larger symbolic function as a reflection of our twenty-first century historical moment, since director Julie Taymor's innovations give us black cast members who present themselves as simultaneously real (the actor we can see) and unreal (the anthropomorphized animal character we are meant to follow through the musical's story). The exoticism and primitivism that developed through, and was so frequently evident in, performances during the 1930s additionally makes Batiste's study helpful in encounters with the neo-exoticism of Disney's *The Lion King* story. Batiste's operating metaphor of the 'darkening mirrors', encountered at an amusement park's House of Mirrors, resonates with my similarly specular focus here on Taymor's double event, encountered within an internationally successful Broadway musical set in an imagined 'Africa' (that we are encouraged not to really see/read as 'Africa').

Significantly, *The Lion King* on Broadway is already over 20 years old (the animated film even older) and will reach its 25th anniversary in 2022. The stage musical reached its first threshold of canonical maturity in 2017, when the 20th anniversary of its continuous run on Broadway was publicly marked by a handful of celebratory and critical publications. It is, at the time of this writing (2018), the highest-grossing musical in Broadway history. When considered together under the single label 'Disney's *The Lion King*', it is easy to see how the source film, the plethora of branded *Lion King* merchandise, state-sanctioned educational materials and cross-marketed artefacts, as well as the domestic touring and international *Lion King* musical stage productions themselves, all represent an awe-inspiring beast of cultural expression. These distinctions make the film and stage musical worth continued critical examination for years to come.

This chapter seeks to be both celebratory and critical, and asks readers: 'What is meaningful about this peculiar performance, appearing near the end of the twentieth century and yet remaining, more than two decades later, so entwined in contemporary discourses of race, culture, and identity?' This popular musical was assembled by a team of inter-cultural artists and led by a woman with an anti-oppression orientation; yet the show was sponsored by an entertainment corporation known for its seductive yet imperialist and, at times, oppressive cultural products. How, then, could a musical that is a capitalist juggernaut, so dominant in mainstream culture and widely valued for its visual and sonic pleasures, provide something useful to us in this current, volatile, political moment in the early twenty-first century – a moment when public opinion seems so deeply fragmented on perceptions of, and meanings about, racial presence and civic belonging?

Problematizing the 'Universal' Musical

The hit song 'Hakuna Matata' from *The Lion King* film is one of a handful of songs that were featured in the source film and that survive in the stage adaptation. Never a fan of its catchy but cloying optimism, I was always bothered by its basic premise that keeping your mind free of troublesome thoughts is the best way to negotiate through one's life. Nevertheless, it is useful as a starting point in discussing the way that *The Lion King* on Broadway mirrors this era's double event of racial discourse through the double event of its own expressions of identity.

The Lion King on Broadway is a 'black musical', despite having a mostly Caucasian creative team and a Caucasian director. The narrowest definition of a cultural artefact that is deemed 'black' would be one in which the creator is black and the intended audience is black – a notion of culture emphasized by many throughout the history of United States cultural politics. There is utility in the politicized aims of this notion of culture, but it is unnecessarily limited around issues of ownership and power, and remains entangled in ever-complicated arguments around identity. When applied to the history of Broadway musicals, a definition this narrow ignores the now decades-worth of important critical theory on the performance of race and diverse conceptions of blackness and thus appears more than a little dishonest. If a musical theatre performance requires the presence of a black body to communicate its central meaning, then that show can and should be understood as a black musical. Furthermore, while *The Lion King* on Broadway has a Caucasian director, it succeeded because of a multiracial creative team, importantly including a black South African composer whose music gives the show its particular sonic personality – something that the show's familiar pop songs, written by the Caucasian main composer and retained from the animated film, could not have achieved on their own. *The Lion King* on Broadway plays to all audiences, sure, but the show was intentionally designed by its Caucasian director to have, and appeal to, black audiences as part of its larger reach.

My argument is that *The Lion King* on Broadway is a 'black musical', in that it is, like the larger 'black culture' it relies on and participates in, an imagined and imaginative construction; felt and perceived as real because it is performed; existing in some kind of relationship to the geographic space that is the African continent; made of an array of intercultural elements but dependent on African diaspora musical/rhythmic expressions; and requiring the (real or imagined) presence of performing black bodies in a communal/public space. *The Lion King* on Broadway is also, as a Broadway musical, an expression of that industry's imperialist, racialized aims. It is a 'white musical', too: led by a Caucasian director and a mostly Caucasian creative team; employing aesthetic elements based in European performance traditions; primitivist in its view of the geographic space that is the African continent; emphatic about establishing or returning to a rational sense of social order; infatuated with the notion of the individual; and eager to imagine a sanitized, imperial space of material bounty and power, where those in power and bounty are in perfect harmony with those who lack material resources and are not in power.

The show is meaningful and enjoyable to audiences, and I must emphasize that my statements here are not to disparage the progressive aims of the creative team members or the important anti-oppression work their *Lion King* on Broadway expresses. However, a more honest discussion would acknowledge that the show circulates complex ideas about society, race, gender, sex, place, and class. These ideas support and contradict each other in specific ways and do not merely implicate the people of colour who might be assumed to 'see' race at every turn. The creators of the show acknowledge its global sources (as in Taymor, 1998). Yet when the show's non-black creators insist on its universality, above any national or ethnic particularity, they and the aesthetic they present can sidestep the responsibility to address any number of political conflicts related to their theatrical choices, all simply by referencing back to the 'universality' the show affirms. Ultimately, the fragmentation in the perception of race within the *Lion King* musical produces a multiplication of images. This fragmentation is a profound mirror twin of the divide in civic discourse on identity that we saw in the 1990s. This discourse continues, unabated and ever-fragmented, in the early decades of the twenty-first century in the United States. Thus, Disney's *The Lion King* on Broadway can be better understood as a vital sign for our collective understanding of civic and racialized presence in the early twenty-first century. This Broadway show-as-sign operates through the most central, powerful, and organizing device of the musical: Taymor's *double event*.

Taymor's organizing design concept for *The Lion King* was developed from her work with puppetry techniques in Bali and Indonesia. She calls her Asian-inspired concept the 'double event' (Schechner, 1999). In this concept, the actors' leggings, costumes, face paint, and headdresses all indicate they belong to or are a part of the animal puppet they operate. Yet Taymor has designed each puppet so that some aspect or part of the human operator remains visible at all times. Rather than attempt a sense of magical escape by hiding the human aspect of the stage picture (as in a puppet in which the human operator is completely hidden from view behind a black screen),

Taymor's double event concept in *The Lion King* on Broadway is about showing the effort of theatre and seeks to make the human operator visible in the art. Taymor's design and directing choices offer more to the viewer than a live replica of a cartoon in this emphasis on human visibility.

Disney critics have long argued that the company's focus in their cultural products on the privileged, like the royal family depicted in *The Lion King* film and so many other Disney films, works to bury the image of the labouring body. For example, in 'Animating Hierarchy: Disney and the Globalization of Capitalism', Artz (2002) sees *The Lion King* film as an affirmation of the class-hierarchy and anti-social individualism that global capitalism encourages, since its images do not celebrate or even contain the producers and labourers of the society. This masking of labour by Disney in its mass entertainments is a critically important concern and is central to my argument elsewhere about the larger representation of labour and class in all Hollywood film musicals (see Granger, 2012). While Taymor's work in showing the human operator in a puppet emerges primarily from her own views on the power of theatre, that innovation is still worth applauding here in light of this particular body of Disney criticism. In contrast to what we often see in Disney musicals, Taymor's approach to staging the body in *The Lion King* on Broadway makes visible the labour of the actor that a typical Disney product would seek to hide.

American popular entertainment producers have for generations made respectable and respected black bodies invisible or inconsequential on stage. Because of this tradition of racially based diminishment, the sheer visibility of black bodies and their celebrated status as the central and heroic characters within the story of the *Lion King* musical, as well as within the sensory experience an audience has in the theatre space, serves as an anti-racist affirmation of a Broadway *supportive* of racial and ethnic diversity. Furthermore, the presence of black bodies being 'black' – signified through black musical gestures, through movement of racially marked bodies in space, through the display of costume patterns, face paints, hairstyles and simple skin tones that read as 'African' (particularly because they appear on performing black bodies) – amplifies and marks each double event as racially doubled. These performances are 'universal' (and, thus, unmarked and 'white' performances) in their apparent mythic quality, but they are also, in the same instance, black performances. Taymor's double event is most subversively effective during the mid-show performance of community by the bird chorus with the number 'One by One'. This performance contains provocative explanatory power around the notion of civic and racial presence, precisely because the doubled looking, which is necessary for Taymor's double event device to function successfully as a theatrical tool, is also in that same moment the site of *The Lion King* on Broadway's fragmented readings of race, culture, and belonging.

Activist Black Community on Stage

This brief and small but significant moment of black affirmation in 'One by One', enacted through Taymor's double event staging of anthropomorphic characters in *The Lion King* on Broadway, occurs at the end of the intermission between acts and during the entr'acte before the start of Act Two. A chorus of African humans (not heavily or even partially costumed with animal puppet extensions) enter singing a celebratory, acappella song with lyrics in an African language that, it can be assumed, remains unintelligible to most of the audience, since no translation of the lyrics appears in the programme or as super-titles projected in the theatre space.

Although a few of the performers enter with bird puppet-kites in hand, and the chorus is dressed in bright-coloured, 'tribal print' robes that tie them by design to the bird puppets, not all the chorus members carry bird puppet-kites. While the logic of the piece suggests to the audience that these very human-looking actors are representing birds through the presence of bird kites and their matching costume fabrics, the double event here nearly dissolves and the actors primarily appear to be wholly human and themselves, and appear comfortably black as well. This is the only time in the musical, other than the opening and closing moments, when the audience will clearly see a group of recognizably brown-skinned adult actors gathering in joy and harmony.

Thanks to the visual recognition of the chorus onstage as a human chorus, in addition to the bird chorus hinted at, the number literally becomes a song performed at a community gathering. This gathering is both imagined as a community coming together and is physically perceived as the literal manifestion of one onstage, and it grows in power through Taymor's double event. First, this sense of community expands through the gathering of the human actors who are representing characters in the fictional storytelling space; second, the sense of community expands through the gathering of all audience members as well as performers within the shared theatre space. It was a challenge, initially, to identify the African language, since Lebo M.'s lyrics for *The Lion King* as a whole include a mix of IsiXhosa, IsiZulu, SeSotho, KiSwahili, Congolese, and SetSwana (Cerniglia and Lynch, 2011). The typescript for the entire show that I have seen does not distinguish when one language versus another is being used. Eventually, however, I was able to discover that the lyrics of 'One by One' are in Zulu. Lebo M.'s choice in using lyrics most of the Broadway audience would not understand, aside from the English phrase 'One by One', which repeats through the number, could be potentially problematic since it could support a notion of an exotic African Other. However, when we examine the song lyrics in English, we can see the moment's more subversive, anti-racist and very black performance.

The first male vocalist sings a phrase in Zulu, which the typescript explains means, 'Hold on tight my people/Don't get weary.' The weariness of the audience could in this case be a joking reference to the pace or effectiveness of the show up to that point, or to an emotional weariness or anxiety in having reached a point of crisis for the main characters. While these levels of 'weary' can be suggested musically, the fact that the lyrics are in a foreign language point us to a different kind, or context, for this weariness. The singer is joined by other voices as they sing a repeating phrase in Zulu, and the typescript tells us that this new line repeats the word 'proud' (John, 1998).

Here, the link between the anthropomorphized animals and the humans they represent is broken. While birds can be said to be 'proud' in the sense that many bird species have colours they choose to display, the expression of pride in one's darkness is specifically an African diasporic/black consciousness political gesture and not at all related to the imagined 'Disney Africa' the first act has presented, or to the 'universal Africa' that non-black creative team members affirm in press interviews that the show is trying to represent. Furthermore, the song is performed in a melodic and vocal arrangement setting that is specifically South African Zulu, which suggests that it may be making a political statement that references the history of apartheid in that country.

South Africa removed the ban on black political parties and freed black leader Nelson Mandela in 1990. In 1994, when the film *The Lion King* was released, the African National Congress had won the country's first non-racial election only months before, and South Africa had sworn in the former political prisoner Mandela as the first black president in its history. By the time of *The Lion King* on Broadway's debut in 1997, South Africa's Truth and Reconciliation Commission had been underway for a year, and the racist National Party had withdrawn from government (Thompson, 2000). In light of this South African news and history the song 'One by One' becomes a subtle tribute to the progress that was achieved step by step and 'won' in one move forward at a time.

Taymor raises more questions than she knows when she comments publicly about the cultural contexts of the African elements in her show. In her book on *The Lion King* on Broadway, Taymor describes composer Lebo M.'s process of bringing African sonic elements into the show. She explains that she wanted to keep his songs in Zulu in order to retain the evocative and beautiful (in other words, 'authentic' and 'African') sound of that language. She was not worried about her Broadway audiences generally not understanding Zulu because, according to Taymor's own words, '*it is totally unimportant to understand the literal meaning*' of that language throughout the show (emphasis added; Taymor, 1998, p. 27).

When Taymor makes such claims about what is important in her representations and asserts she both understands fully and has control over their meanings, one might marvel at the degree of disconnect between these claims and the reality expressed, explicitly, by her black creative team members and cast. For example, Taymor claims in the book that the Zulu song 'One by One', written by Lebo M., bears no relation to anything in the Lion King story (Taymor, 1998, p. 26), implying that the Lion King story is not an African story, at least not directly. Later in the very same book, Lebo M. explains that all his music written for the musical is, in fact, directly based on his own life story and his identity as a black South African artist (Taymor, 1998, p. 157). Yet this fragmented perception is precisely where we are in our current civic moment on racial presence. The fact that the truth of the words, their literal meaning, is both accessible to the audience and hidden or masked from them by Taymor's directorial choices also speaks symbolically to our contemporary moment in the early twenty-first century.

Finally, the chorus sings the final lines of the song in English, praising Africa by emphasizing the word 'beautiful' (John, 1998). Without knowing African languages, most of the American audience members will interpret the ending lyric in English as a non-confrontational, non-political, and non-racial gloss on the aesthetic scene of beauty enacted by the physical sound of the singing and the costumes parading the stage. But the lyrics, in light of South Africa's recent history, point sharply to the notion of Africa as a racialized political space: Africa is beautiful because dark people can be proud within it. This pride does not preclude other races from also being proud within the African space constructed here. Again, I want to emphasize the reality that *The Lion King* on Broadway can be both figuratively 'universal' and culturally 'black', but it can never be not-black. The presence of these prideful lyrics, even if not clearly heard or understood by the audience unfamiliar with Zulu, only naturalizes the presence of dark people and their dark language (in this case, the beautiful, but unintelligible to most Broadway audience members, Zulu language) within the space.

The family tree of critics, working from Wickstrom, who dismiss *The Lion King* on Broadway as preserving the film for the stage by merely presenting a more creative, more lucrative, and more culturally influential version of the film's problematic cultural representations, miss Taymor's important anti-racist and anti-sexist deconstructions. Taymor's work is far better understood as a specific theatrical response to the racist and sexist problems of the original film. When considered against the animated film, Taymor's most significant theatrical choices – those moments that showcase her double event concept in action, such as the deceptively simple watering hole number 'One by One' – make *The Lion King* on Broadway a critically different experience.

Conclusion: Back to the Beginning, Circle-of-Life Style

I am sitting in the theatre, trying not to embarrass myself by crying too much at the sight of the elephant puppet that has stopped right next to my seat. Its tail is being supported and operated by a young African American girl, no older than six years of age by her looks. Her lips move just so slightly and her eyes maintain a tremendous focus ahead of her: she is counting and listening for her signal to move forward! I imagine her concentration in performing her elephant's tail role to be a source of great pride; then I imagine a wider circle of attention around her, such as her parents, and all the black parents watching this black child, so young yet displaying such professionalism and dedication, who can see that she is embraced and adored in this room. I sense this moment – this show, all the bodies and the sounds caressing my ears, my own breath and skin, all of it – as a black moment. I'm here, feeling a part of history, of this experience Broadway has not previously had – not quite like this. And yet the feeling expands in more circles, extending outside of but not dispelling race and the metaphors of colour, continuing. At once I see an audience eager to embrace a boundaryless but harmonious 'universal'. At the same time and in the same space, no less palpable, I also see an audience being recognized (or called into being?) as a community and responding to some power that attends these performing black bodies in our theatrical, communal space. We are here, all different and alike variations of us, loving it all. In the midst of such a spectacle of black performance, something close to what is meant by 'universal', in the experience of pleasure across race, class, biological sex, age, and gender lines, is perhaps being accomplished.

On the afternoon I watch, 'The Circle of Life' ends to extended applause. Just underneath the clapping I can hear the man seated behind me say, 'That was fucking awesome.' Later, as I float down the street, in love again with the power of theatre and feeling sort of proud of Broadway again, I don't think I will find a way to express that shared sentiment in critical, academic language any more effectively than he had in that moment.

Explanatory Note

My study of *The Lion King* on Broadway draws on my observations of the show at a matinee performance at its Minskoff Theatre location in New York City, and is also informed by an interview I conducted the following day with cast member Jim Ferris, who played the 'standby' or alternate actor for the bird Zazu and who performed that role the day

I attended the show. In addition to these experiential sources of information, I rely on reviews of the film and stage show published at the time of
their debuts, the text of the musical's book and its song lyrics, and scholarly criticism published during the subsequent years of the film's mainstream distribution and the stage show's more than 20-year Broadway run.

References

Artz, L. (2002) Animating Hierarchy: Disney and the Globalization of Capitalism. *Global Media Journal*, 1 (Fall).

Batiste, S.L. (2011) *Darkening Mirrors: Imperial Representation in Depression-Era African American Performance*. Durham and London: Duke University Press.

Cerniglia, K. & Lynch, A. (2011, April) Embodying Animal, Racial, Theatrical, and Commercial Power in The Lion King. In *Congress on Research in Dance* (Vol. 2011, pp. 3–9). Cambridge: Cambridge University Press.

Granger, B. (2012) Whistle While We Work: Working-Class Labor in Hollywood Film Musicals from Snow White and the Seven Dwarfs to Newsies. In Booker, M.K. (ed.), *Blue-Collar Pop Culture: From NASCAR to Jersey Shore* (Vol. 1, pp. 197–213). Santa Barbara: ABC-CLIO, LLC.

Hoppe, K.A. (2005) Simulated Safaris: Reading African Landscapes in the US. In Benesch, K., Schmidt, K. (eds.), *Space in America: Theory, History, Culture* (pp. 179–192). New York: Rodopi.

John, E. (1998) *The Lion King: Typescript*. New York: New York Public Library.

'PLAYBILL' (2013) *The Lion King on Broadway*. New York: Playbill, Inc. Available at: www.playbill.com. Accessed 27 July 2013.

Schechner, R. (1999) Julie Taymor: From Jacques Lecoq to The Lion King. *TDR/The Drama Review*, 43(3), 36–55.

States, B.O. (1987) *Great Reckonings in Little Rooms: On the Phenomenology of Theater*. Berkeley, CA: University of California Press.

Taymor, J. (1998) *The Lion King: Pride Rock on Broadway*. New York: Disney editions.

The Lion King Playbill (2011) New York: Playbill, Inc.

Thompson, L.M. (2000) *A History of South Africa*, 3rd edition. New Haven, CT: Yale University Press.

Wickstrom, M. (1999) Commodities, Mimesis, and The Lion King: Retail Theatre for the 1990s. *Theatre Journal*, 51(3), 285–298.

Part II

Challenging Historiographies

4

Beyond the Rue Pigalle: Recovering Ada 'Bricktop' Smith as 'Muse', Mentor and Maker of Transatlantic Musical Theatre

Maya Cantu

A Myth at the Margins: Modernism and Musical Theatre

With her brazen red hair and bolder presence, the expatriate African American nightclub hostess and performer Ada 'Bricktop' Smith has occupied a distinctive place in chronicles of Lost Generation Paris. During the 1920s, Bricktop's eponymous Montmartre nightclub attracted the legendary likes of T.S. Eliot, Man Ray, F. Scott Fitzgerald, and John Steinbeck. At 'Bricktop's', Smith – born in 1894 in Alderson, West Virginia – entertained both 'high' and café society. European aristocracy, Broadway celebrities, and luminaries of the Harlem Renaissance alike flocked to a club that was at once democratic and exclusive. As Tyler Stovall notes, 'By 1932, Bricktop had become not just a Parisian institution, but the darling of the international elite. The pages of her autobiography read like a *Who's Who* of the leading wealthy, famous and dissolute individuals of the Western world.' (1996, p. 87)

Yet, for much of the twentieth century, Bricktop has remained a myth at the margins of modernism: her club is memorialized by Fitzgerald in *Babylon Revisited* as the irresistible nightspot where protagonist Charlie Wales 'had parted with so many hours and so much money' ([1931] 2011, n.p.). While remembering Bricktop as one of the era's most fabulous hostesses, many twentieth-century accounts of Paris's 'moveable feast', by Fitzgerald, Woody Allen, and others, have minimized her role in creating the cultural banquet itself. As Tracy Denean Sharpley-Whiting comments, 'American cultural and intellectual history of this period seems riveted on maleness and whiteness' (2015, p. 8). In 1983's *Zelig*, Allen summoned Bricktop as a magnetic, yet peripheral, living legend. In the film, Bricktop (as an 89-year-old woman) comments on Leonard Zelig's occasional appearances at her democratically exclusive club: 'Everyone used to be at my place; that is, everyone who was someone.' (Allen, [1983] 2006) After her 30-second-long spot, the film's focus returns squarely to the shape-shifting, world-famous Zelig.

Recent scholarship, including Stovall's *Paris Noir: African Americans in the City of Light* (1996) and Sharpley-Whiting's *Bricktop's Paris: African American Women in Paris between the Two World Wars* (2015), has persuasively shifted Bricktop's role from a glittering footnote to a central force of 1920s modernism. As Sharpley-Whiting observes, 'Bricktop served as both anchor and magnet for an expatriate community of African American women' (2015, p. 12) that included Josephine Baker, Elisabeth Welch, and Ethel Waters, and artists and writers such as Gwendolyn Bennett and Eslanda Goode Robeson. Though playing host to a predominantly white cultural elite, Bricktop carved an enduring career as an entertainer and entrepreneur, while creating a powerful sense of professional and communal solidarity among dozens of African American artists, musicians, and entertainers in Paris between the two World Wars.

Yet even as Bricktop gains prominence in histories of modernism, she remains an overlooked presence in histories of musical theatre, to which she made significant contributions as a maker, mentor, and agent of artistic inspiration (traditionally constructed in the passive, female-gendered terms of the 'muse'). Her relative omission from musical theatre studies demonstrates the exclusion of many figures who have contributed to shaping the form, even while working outside traditional models of musical theatre performance. Additionally, Bricktop eluded easy categorizations due to a complex mix of factors. These include her transatlantic career performing in vaudeville and nightclubs rather than on Broadway or the West End; the complex nature of her identity as a nightclub hostess rather than a performer on the 'legitimate' stage; and the marginalization of African American performers in many twentieth-century, historical narratives of the stage and screen musical.

Bricktop herself acknowledged she was difficult to categorize. Loved by Cole Porter and others for her ineffable charm and charisma at her nightclubs on the Rue Pigalle, she confounded New Yorkers after leaving Paris for Manhattan in 1939. She suggested that New Yorkers didn't comprehend the model of the hostess-entertainer: 'I baffled the audience. I wasn't a torch singer, a funny girl, or a blues singer. I wasn't even a singer.' (Smith, with Haskins, 1983, p. 214) A figure of Parisian café society who sang Broadway showtunes and Harlem jazz numbers, and an American who immersed herself in French culture (with later, long interludes in Italy and Mexico), Bricktop drew upon a stylistic and cultural eclecticism that may have distanced American audiences in her native country. A series of Broadway and Hollywood crossover attempts in the 1960s, 1970s and 1980s failed to introduce Bricktop to wider audiences, and also contributed to her relative obscurity within the discipline of musical theatre studies.

In this essay, I'll focus upon three aspects of Bricktop's career in, and contributions to, transatlantic musical theatre. As a performer, she embarked upon a lengthy career in American vaudeville and nightclubs from 1908 to 1924, culminating in her work with the Panama Trio: a group that also included Cora Green and Florence Mills. As a mentor, Bricktop played a significant role in the lives and careers of Mills, for whom she arranged the replacement second lead role in *Shuffle Along* (1921); Josephine Baker, to whom she provided guidance and support as Baker transitioned into a superstar; and cabaret legend Mabel Mercer, whose career Bricktop launched. Finally, I consider Bricktop's cultivation of not only musical theatre performance, but songwriting, as an influential close friend to Cole Porter. Bricktop inspired one of the Broadway composer-lyricist's most iconic songs, 'Miss Otis Regrets', during a period in which Porter – as a Jazz Age expatriate – engaged in complex emotional and professional relationships with African American artists. Over the course of over seven decades – upon American vaudeville stages and in nightclubs throughout Chicago, New York, Paris, Mexico City and Rome – Bricktop built an extraordinary performance career defined by acts of racial, cultural, and national border-crossing.

Bricktop as Maker

Endowed with the remarkable name Ada Beatrice Queen Victoria Louise Virginia Smith – a family concession to multiple officious relatives – Bricktop was born in Alderson, West Virginia on 14 August 1894. Later describing herself as a 'one-hundred percent American Negro with a trigger-Irish temper' (Smith, with Haskins, 1983, p. xv), Ada Smith was the youngest child of Thomas Smith, a barber who served a segregated white clientele, and his independent-spirited wife, Harriet. In her memoir, Smith vividly described her early years, the emotional support that her mother provided in encouraging her in her ambitions, and her keen awareness of racial difference (1983, p. 23).

> My father had dark brown skin [...] My mother was seven-eighths white [...] Then along I came with white, white skin like my mother's, and red-gold hair.
>
> (Smith, with Haskins, 1983, p. 4)

Bricktop developed another distinctive physical characteristic at the age of three: the freckles and red hair for which she became known (Smith, with Haskins, 1983, p. 5).

While navigating the complexities of her racial identity, Bricktop became saloon-struck. At the age of six, after Thomas's death, Harriet moved the family to Chicago, where she operated a boarding-house – and where young Ada avidly explored the city and its attractions. Ada gravitated towards State Street's many saloons, where she peeked her head under doors to see the crowds and musicians (Smith, with Haskins, 1983, p. 19). When her sister, Ethel, had the chance to perform, she was envious. However, at this point, Ada was more interested in being in the audience of the saloons than performing (p. 19).

Instead, Bricktop turned her attentions to Chicago's varied and bustling theatre scene, and particularly to the Pekin Theatre (Smith, with Haskins, 1983, p. 19). At the Pekin, Chicago's first African American professional stock company, Ada 'dragged' her mother and siblings to the Sunday matinees, while reserving her greatest enthusiasm for African American superstars Bert Williams and George Walker, and Aida Overton Walker, as well as for the Jewish American 'Last of the Red Hot Mamas', Sophie

Tucker, a favourite of hers to whom she would later be compared (p. 23). Now determined to enter show business herself, Ada and a number of school friends heard rumours of a need for children for a new show. Cast in the ensemble, Ada was soon pulled out of the Pekin show by a truancy officer (p. 21).

After turning 16, Ada professionally entered show business, embarking upon a career in American vaudeville and nightclubs that lasted until her move to Paris in May of 1924. Learning that the comedy team of Flournoy Miller and Aubrey Lyles, then Pekin Theatre regulars, needed children for the chorus, the 16-year-old Ada prepared to go on the road with Miller and Lyles's new show. As Bricktop remembered in her 1983 memoir, their act, performed in blackface with dance and a fight scene, was imitated by other vaudeville acts (Smith, with Haskins, 1983, p. 24). While Bricktop didn't identify the title of the Miller and Lyles act in her memoir, this show may have been 1909's *The Colored Aristocrats*, a musical comedy set in Jackson, Tennessee. According to Henry T. Sampson, it was in this show that Miller and Lyles 'first introduced the characters of Steve Jenkins (Miller) and Sam Peck (Lyles) that would become famous a decade later in their Broadway hit production of *Shuffle Along*' (Sampson, 2013, p. 72). Sylvester Russell's *Indianapolis Freeman* review of *The Colored Aristocrats* refers not only to a 'chorus of very young people especially proficient in dancing', but to 'Miss Ada Smith, who sang "Pleading Eyes," [but] was not mentioned on the program' (Russell, 1909, p. 706).

Over the next few years, Ada Smith performed consistently in vaudeville, primarily on the Theatre Owners Booking Association (TOBA) circuit, and sometimes crossing over into semi-integrated vaudeville circuits that played to predominantly white audiences. Like the Miller and Lyles show in which she made her debut, the vaudeville acts in which Ada Smith appeared shared much with the 'black musical comedies in the first forty years of the twentieth century [that] had their roots in the early minstrel shows of the postbellum period', as described by Sampson (2013, p. 1). Yet even while these shows, on the surface, conformed to demeaning white stereotypes of African American culture, they also offered sizeable professional opportunities to black performers. Many subtly subverted and undermined textual stereotypes through the 'sardonic subterfuge' of performance, as Daphne Brooks describes Bert Williams and George Walker's work as, respectively, Shylock Homestead and Rareback Pinkerton in 1903's *In Dahomey* (2006, p. 210). *In Dahomey* joined other early black musicals that 'played with both re-inscribing and undoing racist tropes while also bearing the burden of their contiguity with a bygone (white) minstrelsy era' (Brooks, 2006, p. 211). It is likely that Smith's vaudeville acts shared some of these strategies.

As recounted in her memoir, Smith followed the Miller and Lyles show with, successively, performances with McCabe's Georgia Troubadours, the Oma Crosby Trio (billed in the early 1910s as 'Oma Crosby's Kinkies'), the Ten Georgia Campers, and the Kinky-Doo Trio. Touring 'around Illinois and the neighboring states' (Smith, with Haskins, 1983, p. 25) with the popular black minstrel troupe McCabe's Georgia Troubadours, Smith – who regarded herself as a natural dancer (p. 26) – drew enthusiastic notice from newspaper reviewers. On 16 December 1909, the *New York Age*'s Lester A. Walton observed:

> Ada Smith is the life and joy of the company, always bringing sunshine whenever there seems a cloud of discontent. She is the pet of the first part, and is doing a red-hot double turn with Jack Windbush in the olio.
>
> (Walton, 1909)

Touring on the TOBA circuit in 1910 with a trio headed by Oma Crosby, one of the original members of the Pekin Theatre stock company, Smith also attracted reviewers' praise: 'Miss Crosby's partner, Ada Smith, makes a good teammate, and both girls are very pretty and dress nicely, both in their singing, dancing and jungle scenes' (Russell, 1910, p. 191).[1] During her time playing a booking at New York's Gibson Theater, Smith paid a visit to one of Harlem's most famous nightspots, Barron Wilkins' Exclusive Club, where the titular Barron, admiring Smith's red hair, dubbed her with a new professional identity: 'I think I'll call you Bricktop.' (Smith, with Haskins, 1983, p. 34) While touring with Oma Crosby, Bricktop also experienced doubts about the direction of her performing career – and decided to leave vaudeville. Far from a glamorous life, she saw it as 'a world of dingy theaters, sudden cancellations, and [...] getting stranded' (p. 25).

Still a vaudeville trouper, Bricktop left the Oma Crosby Trio and joined the Ten Georgia Campers, another singing and dancing group. After performing with the Ten Georgia Campers on the 'big-time' Pantages Circuit (Smith, with Haskins, 1983, p. 35), Bricktop then, in 1911, joined a final vaudeville troupe: the Kinky-Doo Trio, made up of Madeline Cooper, Lola Wicks and herself, who toured predominantly on the TOBA circuit (1983, p. 37).

Realizing her early dream to become a professional 'saloon singer', Bricktop spent the next 10 years performing in nightclubs throughout Chicago and in Harlem. According to Bricktop, her nightclub career – which she initiated in the back room of Roy Jones's smart saloon at 21st Street and Wabash Avenue (Smith, with Haskins, 1983, p. 39) – brought her both a higher salary and greater creative freedom. Here, Bricktop sang and danced to solo piano accompaniment – often for large tips that would be shared between performers and the band (p. 40). At Roy Jones's, Bricktop was noticed by Jack Johnson, then internationally famous as the first African American world heavyweight boxing champion after defeating white boxer Jim Jeffries in a 1910 'fight of the century'. In 1912, Johnson hired Bricktop for his Café de Champion (shortened to Café Champ). Remembering the athlete-entrepreneur with great fondness in her memoir, Bricktop praised Johnson for giving Chicago an elegant saloon that was racially integrated (Smith, with Haskins, 1983, p. 44). Yet Café Champ's liberalism as an integrated nightclub – and Johnson's interracial romances with Etta Duryea and Lucille Cameron – drew animus from white authorities. A 1912 crime of passion enabled a shut-down of the club when one of Johnson's spurned lovers shot him; its liquor licence was withdrawn and business closed (p. 49).

Bricktop's next major Chicago nightclub engagement, at the Panama Club, marked a new professional pinnacle. In 1914, she joined the Panama Trio alongside Cora Green and Florence Mills. Bricktop noted that this was one of best in the city, and again played to integrated audiences (Smith, with Haskins, 1983, p. 53). Teaming up with Cora Green after meeting her at Gertie Jackson's Theatrical Boardinghouse, Bricktop also recounted her discovery of Florence Mills as the third member of the trio. Mills was tired of the multiple shows a day in vaudeville, and asked Bricktop to help her get a cabaret job (p. 54). The Panama Club's owner

Isadore 'Izzy' Levine expressed reservations that the lithe, silvery-voiced Mills was 'too skinny' and a soprano (something he wasn't keen on). However, Bricktop persuaded him, proudly seeing it as her contribution to Mills' escape from vaudeville (p. 54).

The Panama Trio is significant to the history of the American musical not only for nurturing three of the most prominent black women performers of the Harlem Renaissance era, but for the collective performance innovations of Mills, Smith, and Green. While Florence Mills would become a legend as 'Harlem's Little Blackbird' after her 1921 breakout performance in *Shuffle Along* (a casting in which Bricktop also played a substantial role), Cora Green also established a notable career in vaudeville and on Broadway (in 1922's *Strut, Miss Lizzie* and 1924's *Dixie to Broadway,* also with Mills), and gave a dynamic lead performance as Mandy Jenkins in Oscar Micheaux's landmark, backstage musical *Swing!* (1938). As Bricktop recalled, the Panama Trio were early adaptors of close-harmony vocal techniques before other groups popularized the style (Smith, with Haskins, 1983, p. 55). Playing the Pantages Circuit in 1919, the Panama Trio received billing as the 'Syncopated Maids', and praise as 'very good jazz singers […] they are a hit' (Josephs, 1919, p. 22). However, by now, Bricktop had definitively made up her mind to pursue her career in nightclubs, because she wanted to be able to interact with and see her audience (Smith, with Haskins, 1983, p. 61).

Leaving the Panama Trio in 1917, as the United States entered World War I, Bricktop concluded her American nightclub career in New York at two of Harlem's most famous nightclubs (Smith, with Haskins, 1983, p. 75). Fresh from gigs at speakeasies in Los Angeles, San Francisco, and Atlantic City, Smith was hired in 1922 at Barron Wilkins' Exclusive Club, the nightclub run by the same colourful figure who had dubbed her Bricktop. Unlike the Café Champ, the Panama Club, and Bricktop's own Parisian nightclubs later, Barron's was not racially integrated (she recalled that only 'light-skinned Negroes' and celebrities for whom exceptions were made, such as Jack Johnson or Bert Williams, were able to attend (p. 75)). In 1923, Bricktop received a call from Connie Immermann, the owner of Connie's Inn, who invited her to appear as a soubrette. Dancing in as a 'red rose' at the end of a revue flower number, she was soon promoted to headliner (p. 81).

While performing at Connie's Inn, Bricktop received a career-changing request from Sammy Richardson, one of the few African Americans to have already established a performing career in Paris. Richardson relayed an offer for Smith to replace the singer-dancer Florence Jones as the headliner of Le Grand Duc nightclub in Paris. Bricktop recalled that Palmer, Florence's husband, suggested her to the manager, Gene Bullard, as a replacement, on the basis that she was not a great singer, but had 'the damndest personality, and she can dance. She'll be a big success over here' (Smith, with Haskins, 1983, p. 82).[2] In May of 1924, Bricktop arrived in Paris. On the raffish Montmartre street of the Rue Pigalle, she then embarked upon the fabled second chapter of her performing career as the hostess of Le Grand Duc, and then the hostess and manager of *Bricktop's*, a role in which mentoring would play a significant part.

Bricktop as Mentor

A 1961 proposal for a television programme to be entitled 'Bricktop's Ball' described the entertainer as 'the top-talent picker of her time, bringing the best new artists and comedians to television screens' (Prospectus for 'Bricktop's Ball', 1961). While 'Bricktop's Ball' wasn't picked up for TV, she was nevertheless keenly attuned to the guidance and promotion of talented peers, particularly other African American women. As Sharpley-Whiting observes, Bricktop's mentorship ranged from offering communal camaraderie at her nightclub to one-on-one professional assistance to a diverse network of expatriate and visiting African American women artists, musicians, writers, and performers in Paris:

> For many, such as the poet-painter Gwendolyn Bennett and portrait artist Laura Wheeler, Bricktop's was the last stop on a night out. Composer and singer Nora Holt and performance artist Florence Mills frequently dined with the saloonkeeper during their time in the city. Bricktop counseled Josephine Baker in her early days in Paris, helping her to read and write, and offered refuge to a homesick Ethel Waters who, tired of croissants and beurre blanc, desperately wanted a place to cook.
>
> (Sharpley-Whiting, 2015, p. 12)

For Florence Mills, Josephine Baker, and Mabel Mercer, Bricktop's mentorship would be particularly significant in contributing to the history of both musical theatre and American cabaret. With all three women, but particularly Mills and Mercer, Bricktop can be viewed as a collaborative factor in their professional success, despite never being formally involved on a Broadway or West End producing team.

On a number of occasions, Bricktop provided direct career advancement to Florence Mills. Most momentously, Bricktop's assistance led to the latter's star-is-born casting in *Shuffle Along*. While briefly performing with Bricktop at Barron Wilkins' Exclusive Club in 1921, Mills benefited not only from Bricktop's initiative and generosity as a 'talent picker' but the latter's expanding professional network, which drew together brilliant colleagues from both Bricktop's first vaudeville tour and the Panama Trio. Bricktop recommended Mills to Harriet Sissle (composer Noble Sissle's wife) of *Shuffle Along* when its lead, Gertrude Saunders, went into burlesque to make more money (Smith, with Haskins, 1983, p. 79). Concerned that Mills 'was not the right type' for the ingénue second lead of Ruth Little, Noble Sissle saw Mills through a long series of auditions. On the strength of Bricktop's recommendation, Harriet Sissle continued to advocate for Mills, and on her first performance in the role she had 'seventeen encores' (p. 79). As Zakiya R. Adair observes, Mills' sensational successes in London and Paris revues such as *Dover Street to Dixie* (1923) and the 1926 edition of *Blackbirds* (*Les oiseaux noirs*) 'helped open the door for subsequent trans-Atlantic African American women performers like Josephine Baker and Adelaide Hall' (2013, p. 21).

While Bricktop facilitated Mills in her professional opportunities, resulting in the latter's *Shuffle Along* stardom, she worked with Baker from a different angle. With Baker having already exploded upon Paris's consciousness in 1925's epochal *La Revue Nègre*, Bricktop took the sensitive young woman under her wing. She helped Baker negotiate her rapidly growing, intensely eroticized celebrity during the period that Bricktop described as *Le Tumulte Noir*. In her memoir, Bricktop observed how young Baker was when she became famous, and that the reputation she gained for performing in the nude obscured her actual talent as a performer (Smith, with Haskins, 1983, pp. 107–108). While Bricktop recounts helping Baker with some specific matters of personal etiquette (i.e. concealing her early lack of schooling with an autograph stamp; teaching her 'how to take care of nice things', including Baker's Poiret gowns), the older woman also made herself available for more encompassing emotional support: 'I became her big sister. [...] She'd say, "Bricky, tell me what to do." She wouldn't go around the corner without asking my advice.' (p. 108)

Bricktop's mentoring friendship of Baker soured significantly with the entrance of Pepito Abatino. Spurious in his impersonation of an Italian aristocrat (Bricktop famously referred to him as the 'no-account count' (Smith, with Haskins, 1983, p. 109)), Abatino was nonetheless a shrewd businessman who succeeded Bricktop as Baker's mentor. At the same time, he assumed new roles as her manager and husband – though one of controlling, Pygmalionesque tendencies. Bricktop recalled that while Abatino played a role in re-establishing Baker's fame, and tried to give her an education, Baker could have accomplished this by herself (p. 110).[3] While Bricktop and Baker did not resume the closeness of their former friendship, the two remained on sufficiently admiring terms for Bricktop to introduce Baker at the latter's legendary 1973 concert at Carnegie Hall.

While Bricktop provided Mills with professional connections, and Baker with emotional guidance and support, she engaged in her most equitable and mutual mentorship with Mabel Mercer. One of the founding mothers of American cabaret, and the namesake of the Mabel Mercer Foundation (sponsoring the New York Cabaret Convention), Mercer was born in Staffordshire, England in 1900, the daughter of a white chorus girl and a black musician. Once again, Bricktop drew upon her keen sense of 'talent-picking' to hire Mercer at her new location of a larger *Bricktop's* location at 66 Rue Pigalle.[4] Opening the new Bricktop's in November 1931, Bricktop recalled she needed assistance and turned to Mabel Mercer, one of the few black women she recalled seeing in Paris (Smith, with Haskins, 1983, p. 159). Drawn to Mercer's alluring poise – complementing her own entrepreneurial hustle – Bricktop took Mercer on as featured singer and partner.

At 66 Rue Pigalle, Mercer began her own rise to cabaret stardom under the aegis of Bricktop. While Mercer had performed in vaudeville, small nightclubs, and in the chorus of Paris revues (as well as in the 'Negro chorus' of the 1928 London production of *Show Boat*), Mercer's hiring by Bricktop proved pivotal to the former's career. As Bricktop recalled, with her customary pride, the two helped each other: Mercer with her audience-pleasing elegance, and Bricktop in her coaxing of Mercer as a star (Smith, with Haskins, 1983, p. 160). At *Bricktop's*, Mercer excelled in performing the songs of Cole Porter, and also introduced 'Love for Sale' to Parisians shortly after its debut in 1930's *The New Yorkers* (p. 179).

If Bricktop mentored the vulnerable 17-year-old Josephine Baker on a personal and emotional level, while leaving Baker to her own spectacular onstage devices, she helped Mercer in more performance-oriented ways. Working with Bricktop, Mercer gained both assertion and intimacy in her engagement with a cabaret audience, skills that would prove invaluable when, in 1938, Mercer moved to New York, and started singing at the 'first of a series of New York supper clubs over which she reigned over the next thirty years', as Ben Yagoda notes (2015, p. 224). Despite the initial disappointment that Mercer's vocal style – an elegantly clipped soprano – was not immediately popular with audiences (Smith, with Haskins, 1983, p. 161), Bricktop guided Mercer to chat and mingle with her audiences, and also assuaged Mercer's self-doubts about her abilities (p. 161).

While Mercer, like Bricktop, later focused on cabarets and nightclubs rather than the Broadway or West End musical stage, she went on to play a crucial role in the canonization of the 'Great American Songbook', and of many interwar Broadway showtunes by Porter, Rodgers and Hart, and the Gershwins, among others. 'Will Friedwald writes that Mercer and similar singers "were virtually the only artists to keep performing the great songs of the twenties and thirties into the forties and fifties, like monks hiding manuscripts in the Dark Ages"', Yagoda (2015, p. 225) writes of Mercer's under-the-radar, yet immensely influential appeal as a mid-century cabaret stylist who influenced a generation of singers of the American Songbook.

> Being a devotee of hers was like being a member of an exclusive club; she became famous for being unknown. One prominent member of the club was Frank Sinatra, who in 1955 was quoted in Walter Winchell's column in the *New York Mirror*: 'Everything I learned I owe to Mabel Mercer.'
>
> (Yagoda, 2015, pp. 224–225)

At the same time, Mercer learned much from her mentor. Bricktop wrote in her memoir, 'Mabel will tell you even today, "If I know anything about taking care of people, I got it from Brick"' (Smith, with Haskins, 1983, p. 161). Meanwhile, the nightclub hostess also served as inspiration to several artists – in particular, Cole Porter.

Bricktop – And *Bricktop's* – As 'Muse'

While Bricktop became an inspiring presence to her close friend Cole Porter, her nightclub itself provided creative fuel for the many Broadway and Harlem talents who carved out transatlantic careers – or merely visited Paris – between the two World Wars. If Bricktop herself called her nightclub a 'combination mail-drop, bank, rehearsal hall, clubhouse – even a neighborhood bar' (Smith, with Haskins, 1983, p. 125), the rehearsal hall element often took precedence. Le Grand Duc, and then *Bricktop's*, sparked performances and new songs from dozens of visiting stars and songwriters, of both Broadway and Harlem stages (overlapping if distinct social worlds throughout the 1920s). While *Bricktop's* entertained visits by Ethel Waters, Paul Robeson, Florence Mills, and the latter's *Shuffle Along* co-star Lottie Gee,[5] Broadway and West End theatre celebrities both sought entertainment and entertained at *Bricktop's*, at which Smith herself played hostess-headliner. Bricktop counted performers Fred and Adele Astaire, Helen Morgan, and Marilyn Miller, as well as producers Dwight Deere Wiman and J.J. Shubert, among her regulars, along with Irving Berlin and Noël Coward. Indeed, she remembered Coward trying out new songs at the club (Smith, with Haskins, 1983, p. 122).

Yet if composer-lyricists like Berlin and Coward favoured Bricktop, the hostess was most deeply and closely associated with Cole Porter during her time in Paris. If Bricktop would later serve as Porter's inspiration, he was also her most influential patron. F. Scott Fitzgerald had already popularized Bricktop's earlier performance venue, Le Grand Duc, as a destination for the jazz-craving Montparnasse set.[6] Yet it was Porter's promotion of Smith and Le Grand Duc that established the latter as the rage of Parisian nightlife, due to the parade of European aristocrats and Broadway and Hollywood celebrities that Cole and Linda Lee Porter attracted to the club. At their first meeting in the winter of 1925 – when a 'slight, immaculately dressed man' (Smith, with Haskins, 1983, p. 100) eating corned-beef hash with a poached egg revealed himself to be Cole Porter – the songwriter and hostess immediately established a rapport. Impressed by Bricktop's performance of his 'I'm in Love Again', unwittingly sung before the song's composer, Porter asked Bricktop if she could dance the Charleston. As Bricktop recounted, the dance had not made it to Europe, but she had already learned it in the US. After Bricktop performed the Charleston for Porter, the songwriter told her that she had 'talking feet and legs', and assured her they would meet again (p. 101).

Before long, Porter enlisted Bricktop to teach the dance – and soon after, the Black Bottom – at 'Charleston parties' at his spectacular house on 13 Rue Monsieur. The Parisian and New York press avidly chronicled Bricktop teaching the Charleston to Lady Mendl (the former Elsie de Wolfe), the Duke of York, and the Aga Khan, among others. Bricktop recounted that the Charleston launched her as a 'saloonkeeper [...] It caught on and I caught on, Cole Porter standing right there behind me and never leaving me, until I became Bricktop, the one and only' (Smith, with Haskins, 1983, p. 102).

In her memoir, Bricktop characterized her relationship with Cole Porter as one of deep mutual love and respect. She recalled that he was a good friend, 'one of the best I ever had' (Smith, with Haskins, 1983, p. 112). At the same time, her affectionate memories of Porter hint at complex racial undertones – and inequitable power dynamics – in the relationship. During a Jazz Age in which Paris and Venice – arguably more than New York – served as Cole Porter's home-bases, the composer-lyricist forged a number of beneficial and meaningful friendships and professional relationships with black European, and expatriate black American, performers and musicians who spurred his songwriting craft: most notably, the American-born Elisabeth Welch (who played a featured role in Porter's racy 1933 London musical *Nymph Errant*), as well as cabaret/nightclub performers Leslie 'Hutch' Hutchinson, Mabel Mercer, and Bricktop. The latter's nightclub served as a songwriting workshop space for Porter, as well as Noël Coward. Bricktop suggested that 'Night and Day', 'Begin the Beguine', and 'Love for Sale' all started at the nightclub

(Smith, with Haskins, 1983, p. 179). Journalist Eslanda Goode Robeson, too, recounted going to *Bricktop's*, where she took in 'Cole Porter's pre-viewing of the song "Mr. and Mrs. Fitch" accompanied by Bricktop' (Sharpley-Whiting, 2015, p. 151). Only later, in November 1932, did the song debut on Broadway in *Gay Divorce*.

At the same time, Bricktop's memoir leaves little doubt that she served not only as a musical inspiration, but as a professional asset to the aristo-cratic, Midwestern WASP Porter. Through her Charleston lessons and the pair's friendship, Bricktop conferred upon Porter cultural capital and cool during a Parisian Jazz Age of '*Négromanie*', in which 'the Negro was in vogue' (in the words of Langston Hughes, [1940] 2002, p. 175), and many of Broadway's songwriters – including George Gershwin and Porter – worked to import the rhythms of jazz into their stage hits. When Bricktop, in 1939, was forced by the Nazi invasion of Paris to depart her beloved adopted city, Cole Porter could only offer limited assistance, as a patron to Bricktop, within the context of a deeply segregated American society. As Sharpley-Whiting observes: 'Porter, too, known to be gracious but equally persnickety, may have realized that the social barriers crossed in Europe did not apply in America.' (2015, p. 34) In her memoir, Bricktop recounted her first taste of racism in New York in 1939, and being coldly snubbed by Cole Porter's receptionist at the Waldorf Towers. Porter's minimizing of the incident disappointed her; he regretfully advised that Bricktop would continue 'to see more of that' in the United States (Smith, with Haskins, 1983, p. 209).

If the relationship between Porter and Bricktop was shaped by exter-nal forces of structural racism, as well as abiding mutual admiration and respect, both aspects of the friendship expressed themselves in the song for which Bricktop famously served as Porter's inspiration: 'Miss Otis Regrets'. Famous as a cabaret number, though introduced on stage in the 1934 London revue *Hi Diddle Diddle*, 'Miss Otis Regrets' is famous as a murder-ballad about a scorned society woman: 'Miss Otis regrets she's unable to lunch today.' After shooting her unfaithful lover with a gun from 'under her velvet gown', Miss Otis is then dragged away by a mob, and 'strung up on the willow across the way' (quoted in McBrien, 2011, p. 239).

Though the song has become associated with a wide array of both black and white performers – from Ella Fitzgerald and Ethel Waters to

Marlene Dietrich and Bette Midler – Bricktop discussed the song's submerged racial subtext as an anti-lynching narrative. In 1932, as Bricktop recounted, Porter walked into *Bricktop's* and told her he had a song for her. On hearing the name, Bricktop recalled asking Porter, 'Where on earth did you get that title?' He replied:

> 'From you. Don't you remember the other day we were talking about a lynching down South, and you said, "Well that man won't lunch tomorrow."'
>
> (Smith, with Haskins, 1983, p. 178)

Porter told her he had returned to his apartment and written his song that evening. This exchange might indicate a glib interpretation of Jim Crow violence in the American South, given the song's ultimate context as a soigné cabaret standard. Yet Bricktop recounted that she took very seriously her frequent performances of the song with which she became closely associated for the remainder of her career. Of 'Miss Otis Regrets', which Porter composed in a more bluesy style than many of his songs, Bricktop noted that the song is a tragic one, and is rarely properly performed: 'The pronunciation, the pauses and things are very important.' (Smith, with Haskins, 1983, p. 178) Noting that Porter preferred for Bricktop, and other singers, to 'use our imaginations' in interpretation and delivery of his songs, Bricktop remembered that she felt the singer was a maid, and inserted a bow at the end of the song, and then 'raised my hand in a cut across the neck to suggest a lynching' (p. 178). 'Miss Otis Regrets' portrays the actions of a high-society woman along the lines of Porter's aristocratic social set. Yet, in choosing to draw focus upon the narration of a character she identified as Miss Otis's maid, Bricktop may have intended to blur the lines of the audience's identification, and the lines between a conventionalized, high-society crime of passion and the very real racial violence in the American South. That the song remained such a staple of Bricktop's repertoire suggests not only the care and skill with which she performed it, but also its multivalence of interpretation.[7]

Along with 'Miss Otis Regrets', Bricktop continued to perform numerous songs of Cole Porter, and relive their fond friendship, at her eponymous nightclubs in Mexico City (where she resided from 1943 through 1949) and Rome (where she operated a *Bricktop's* on the Via Veneto from

1951 through 1964). Bricktop performed a repertoire of dozens of songs that included Porter's 'Easy to Love', 'Just One of Those Things', 'Get Out of Town', and 'It's Alright with Me', along with jazz standards (i.e. 'Saint. Louis Blues' and 'Sweet Georgia Brown') and camp parodies (i.e. the Gershwins' 'The Man I Love', transformed into 'The Man We Love', a duet with Gimi Beni ('Annotated list of song repertoire, c. 1976–1977)).

Bricktop's Legacy: Race and Identity

In her work as a nightclub performer and hostess, Bricktop not only crossed boundaries among musical genres, and the 'legitimate' and 'illegitimate' stage, but also troubled culturally constructed categories of race and performance. Bricktop functioned as a powerful source of solidarity and support to expatriate African American artists in Paris. Harlem nightclubs, such as the Cotton Club and Barron Wilkins' Exclusive Club, offered spectacles of black performance to largely well-heeled white audiences. By contrast, *Bricktop's* audiences were racially integrated, if economically restricted by the nightclub's steep prices, though she 'reserved her warmest welcomes for African American celebrities like Paul Robeson and Jack Johnson' (Stovall 2005, p. 232).

While creating a welcoming community for African Americans in Paris, Bricktop created a performance persona that was uniquely her own. As Tyler Stovall notes, Bricktop carefully negotiated the demands that many African Americans in 1920s Paris faced in balancing 'black community' with 'black spectacle' oriented to the white gaze. Stovall writes that, while Bricktop might have played host to 'a series of white aristocrats', she, Josephine Baker, and other peers 'also resisted the pressures of performance as spectacle, striving to perform their art on their own terms' (2005, p. 232). Bricktop committed cultural acts of resistance not only in the racial integration of her nightclub, but in the eclecticism and cosmopolitanism of her performances. While famous for songs like 'Miss Otis Regrets', Bricktop drew upon the Broadway musical stage, French cabaret, jazz and blues traditions, and the black vaudeville circuit in which she had learned her craft.

Bricktop's verbal resistance to her home country's poor treatment of African Americans must also be considered in assessing her performance legacy. While not directly involved in political activism during her career, Bricktop spoke candidly and powerfully about racism in the United States. In one 1960 interview, given after her return to Europe from the United States (and embracing a new home in Rome), Bricktop told the *New York Post* that Miss Otis, indeed, had some regrets about her home country:

> I always say that there are only two real Americans – the Indians because they owned the joint, and the Negroes, because they were invited here, and those that didn't want to accept the invitation and were *brought*. But freedom is anywhere you find it. We're making strides and even though it's taking too many tomorrows, I'm glad to say I'm an American until I die.
>
> (Smith, with Haskins, 1960, p. 41)[8]

Unfortunately, Bricktop – who moved back to the United States in the early 1970s – failed to cross over into large-scale American success, one of multiple factors that may have contributed to her marginalization in histories of musical theatre, despite her reclamation as a central figure in African American and modernist studies.

Bricktop in Musical Theatre History

The 1983 publication of Smith's memoir, *Bricktop*, crested a late-career renaissance in the 1970s and 1980s. However, Bricktop never reached mainstream American celebrity. With her Carnegie Hall and other Broadway appearances, Josephine Baker would become a legend back in the United States in the 1960s and 1970s. By contrast, Bricktop struggled to cross over into mainstream American success. She made few song recordings, never appeared in a Broadway (or West End) musical, and remained indelibly associated with her nightclub hostess career to those who knew of her work in Paris, Mexico City, and Rome. Ed Sullivan (1961) mentioned in *The New York Daily News*, 'Back home, in the United States [...] the Negro entertainer and nightclub singer isn't very well-known.'

Yet, in the later years of her career, Bricktop did attempt crossover into high-profile American show business, as well as film and television, to limited success. A planned 1962 Carnegie Hall benefit concert dissolved due to inaction from the pledged co-sponsor, the Duchess of Windsor (Smith, with Haskins, 1983, p. 274). Similarly, a proposed movie biopic (in which Bricktop hoped for Pearl Bailey to play her) did not come to fruition (Hoefer, 1960). Television networks also failed to pick up two TV variety show proposals. These were 1961's 'Bricktop's Ball' and a self-titled 1977 programme that might have shifted Bricktop's stature from that of a cult figure to a household name.

The proposal for the latter programme presents a tantalizing alternative history in which Bricktop had introduced herself to a much larger, mass American audience – and possibly become more visibly and centrally represented in historical narratives of musical theatre. Housed at Bricktop's papers at the Schomburg Center for Research in Black Culture, the proposal touted Bricktop as an 'international social potentate' and the programme as 'one of the hottest variety programs of the year'. As produced by Oracle Productions Group, the show was intended to feature a mix of entertainment by Bricktop and her guests, choreography by Alvin Ailey and sketches by the comedy ensemble Disclaimer, as well an 'unprecedented repertoire of electronically produced graphic and animated images'. A cross-generational mix of entertainers was also proposed, with Frank Sinatra, Carol Channing, Lena Horne, Fred Astaire, Eubie Blake, Sammy Davis, Jr., Richard Pryor, Stevie Wonder, Cher, Liza Minnelli, and Michael Jackson listed among over four dozen guest stars (Prospectus for 'Bricktop's' television program, c. 1977).

At the same time, she became increasingly memorialized as a mythic symbol of Lost Generation nostalgia. The National Urban League Guild honoured 'The Legendary Bricktop' at a Beaux Arts Ball gala entitled *Broadway '76–77 – The Great Black Way*, celebrating a season that included *for colored girls who have considered suicide/when the rainbow is enuf*, *Your Arms Too Short to Box with God*, and an all-black revival of *Guys and Dolls*, among others (Programme for *Broadway '76–77*, 1977). Yet other representations of Bricktop focused on her Parisian nightclub as a backdrop for white, literary, and theatrical legends. While Smith appeared as one of the multiple 'talking heads' reminiscing about the protean Leonard Zelig in Allen's 1983 film, she also appeared as a supporting character (played by Jonelle Allen) in Randy Strawderman's 1979 revue, *Red, Hot, and Cole*, at the Variety Arts Theatre in Los Angeles. Here, the fictional Bricktop recounts her memories of meeting Cole and Linda Porter in Paris, and leads a medley of 'Anything Goes' and other Porter songs. Although Allen drew praise for her 'electric presence' (Hunter, 1979), Smith's remarkable life and varied performing career suggest her story as subject matter for a spectacular 'Bricktop' musical of her own. Given her transatlantic trajectory from Chicago vaudeville and Harlem nightclubs, and from Paris to Mexico City and Rome, this imagined *Bricktop! The Musical* might not necessarily debut on the mainstages of New York or London.

In its cosmopolitan span and fluidity, the career of Ada 'Bricktop' Smith suggests rich possibilities for reframing models of musical theatre scholarship, and in rendering its history more expansively mobile. Radiating from the bohemian enclaves of Paris, Bricktop's career challenges notions of musical theatre history as anchored in the United States and England; as confined primarily behind the proscenium stages of the 'legitimate' musical stage; and – given Smith's distinctive role as a 'hostess-entertainer' – as synonymous with the performances of traditional Broadway-style 'triple threats'. Tapping into contemporary understandings of the musical in 'a global context' (Wolf, 2016, p. 1), Bricktop's performances invite scholars to continue investigating musical theatre history not only beyond the geographical centralities of Broadway and the West End, but as part of a wider circuit of spatial multiplicities. These include the nightclubs and cabarets that ranged in the 1920s and 1930s from Harlem to Greenwich Village, and from Montmartre to Berlin's Kurfürstendamm.

At the same time, Smith's life and work centralize the agency of African American women as not only performers, but enterprising producers and creative catalysts, within a musical theatre historiography that has often marginalized their innovations. In her work at *Bricktop's*, and in her collaborations with artists like Florence Mills, Josephine Baker, Mabel Mercer, and Cole Porter, Smith broadened the representational strategies, and professional opportunities, available to African American performers. She contributed a powerful performance legacy drawing upon a fluid navigation of racial, cultural, and national identities. Significant to musical theatre history – if unknown to the stages of Broadway – Ada 'Bricktop' Smith sets a model of border-leaping that resonates well beyond the Rue Pigalle.

Notes

1. Such 'jungle scenes' reflected white, primitivist constructs of blackness rooted in the stereotypes of American minstrelsy – which commonly restricted African American performers and characters to such locations as Southern plantations and African jungles. The 1924 Lew Leslie-produced revue, *Dixie to Broadway*, conflated the two locales, as Florence Mills, dressed 'in an elaborate feathered costume as a Zulu dancer', performed 'Jungle Nights in Dixieland' (Egan, 2004, p. 110).

2. According to Tracy Denean Sharpley-Whiting (quoting Taylor, with Cook, *Alberta Hunter: A Celebration in Blues*, 1988), Bricktop may not have recounted the story of her call from the Grand Duc, and Gene Bullard, truthfully in her memoir. Sharpley-Whiting discusses speculation that the telegram was intended for stage performer and blues singer Alberta Hunter, though sent care of Eve Blanche when Hunter was on the road: 'Bricktop picked up [from Blanche] the telegram for Alberta, saying she was going to deliver it, read it instead and took off immediately for Paris. As Harry [Watkins] said, "In those days, you had to survive. You got a job wherever you could, however you could"' (2015, p. 23).

3. Abatino also wrote the film scenario for the 1935 Baker star vehicle *Princess Tam-Tam*, illustrating the Pygmalion narrative of a Tunisian shepherdess, Alwina (Baker), who is coached and transformed by a white French novelist, Max de Mirecourt, into the glamorous aristocrat of the title – a metamorphosis that turns out, by the film's end, to have been a fantasy sequence from Max's novel, *Civilization.*

4. Starting at Le Grand Duc, at 52 Rue Pigalle in 1924, Bricktop then operated the Music Box nightclub in 1926, before managing her own *Bricktop's* nightclub in 1927, and then moving to a larger location, at 66 Rue Pigalle, in 1931.

5. Artist and writer Gwendolyn Bennett described the community-building nature of Gee's performance at the nightclub: 'Then at 4:15 A.M. to dear old Bricktop's .... and Lottie Gee sings for Brick her hit from *Shuffle Along*, "I'm Just Wild About Harry." Her voice is not what it might have been and she had too much champaign (sic), but still there was something very personal and dear about her singing it and we colored folks just applauded like mad.' (Sharpley-Whiting, 2015, p. 99)

6. Bricktop quoted Fitzgerald: 'My greatest claim to fame is that I discovered Bricktop before Cole Porter.' (Smith, with Haskins, 1983, p. 98)

7. Bricktop's definitive account of Porter writing 'Miss Otis Regrets' for her is disputed by Porter's biographer, William McBrien. McBrien cites several alternate origin theories for the song, including one newspaper cutting that 'claimed "Miss Otis" was inspired by a bad cowboy lament he heard at a party at a private home' (2011, pp. 239–240). While considering other accounts of the writing of 'Miss Otis', Bricktop's close relationship with Porter, and the trust she placed in their friendship, suggests the persuasiveness of her own story, and its credibility as a song with an anti-lynching subtext.
8. According to producer Jack Jordan, James Baldwin briefly considered Bricktop as the subject of a prospective book, but the project never materialized (Jordan, 1979).

References

Adair, Z.R. (2013) 'Respectable Vamp': A Black Feminist Analysis of Florence Mills' Career in Early Vaudeville Theatre. *Journal of African American Studies*, 17(1), 21.

Allen, W. ([1983] 2006) *Zelig*, *DVD*. Los Angeles, CA: MGM.

Annotated list of song repertoire (c. 1976–1977). Ada 'Bricktop' Smith DuConge (1894–1984) Papers, Schomburg Center for Research in Black Culture, New York Public Library, Harlem, New York, Box 5, Folder 21.

Brooks, D. (2006) *Bodies in Dissent: Spectacular Performances of Race and Freedom, 1850–1910*. Durham, NC: Duke University Press.

Egan, B. (2004) *Florence Mills: Harlem Jazz Queen*. Lanham, MD: Scarecrow Press.

Fitzgerald, F.S. ([1931] 2011) *Babylon Revisited*. London: Penguin UK, Google Books.

Haskins, J. (1983) Introduction. In Smith, Ada 'Bricktop', with Haskins, J., *Bricktop*. New York: Atheneum Press.

Hoefer, G. (1960) The Hot Box. *Downbeat*, 23 June. Ada 'Bricktop' Smith DuConge (1894–1984) Papers, Schomburg Center for Research in Black Culture, Harlem, New York, Box 7, Folder 4.

Hughes, L. (1940) When the Negro Was in Vogue. *Autobiography: The Big Sea*. In McLaren, J. (ed.) (2002), *The Collected Works of Langston Hughes* (Vol. 13, pp. 175–182). Columbus, MO: University of Missouri Press.

Hunter, G. (1979) A Hot Attraction. *The Burbank Daily News*, 9 May. Ada 'Bricktop' Smith DuConge (1894–1984) Papers, Schomburg Center for Research in Black Culture, Harlem, New York, Box 2, Folder 2.

Jordan, J. (1979) Letter to Bricktop, 4 August. Ada 'Bricktop' Smith DuConge (1894–1984) Papers, Schomburg Center for Research in Black Culture, Harlem, New York, Box 2, Folder 21.

Josephs, J. (1919) Show Reviews: Pantages, San Francisco. *Variety*, 8 October, p. 22.

McBrien, W. (2011) *Cole Porter*. New York: Knopf Doubleday Publishing Group.

Programme for '*Broadway '76–77 – The Great Black* Way' (1977), National Urban League Guild, 4 February, Ada 'Bricktop' Smith DuConge (1894–1984) Papers, Schomburg Center for Research in Black Culture, Harlem, New York, Box 5, Folder 4.

Prospectus for 'Bricktop's Ball' (1961) Ada 'Bricktop' Smith DuConge (1894–1984) Papers, Schomburg Center for Research in Black Culture, Harlem, New York, Box 7, Folder 3.

Prospectus for 'Bricktop's' television program (c. 1977) Ada 'Bricktop' Smith DuConge (1894–1984) Papers, Schomburg Center for Research in Black Culture, Harlem, New York, Box 5, Folder 4.

Russell, S. (1909) *The Colored Aristocrats* Review. *Indianapolis Freeman*, 4 September. In Sampson, Henry T. (2013), *Blacks in Blackface: A Sourcebook on Early Black Musical Shows* (p. 706). Lanham, MD: Scarecrow Press.

Russell, S. (1910) Oma Crosby's Kinkies Review. *Indianapolis Freeman*, 17 December. In Sampson, H.T. (2013), *Blacks in Blackface: A Sourcebook on Early Black Musical Shows* (p. 191). Lanham, MD: Scarecrow Press.

Sampson, H.T. (2013) *Blacks in Blackface: A Sourcebook on Early Black Musical Shows*. Lanham, MD: Scarecrow Press.

Sharpley-Whiting, T.D. (2015) *Bricktop's Paris: African American Women in Paris between the Two World Wars*. Albany, NY: SUNY University Press.

Smith, Ada 'Bricktop', with Haskins, J. (1960) The life and times of Bricktop: 'Miss Otis' has no regrets. *The New York Post*, 8 May, p. 41. Ada 'Bricktop' Smith DuConge (1894–1984) Papers, Schomburg Center for Research in Black Culture, Harlem, New York, Box 7, Folder 4.

Smith, Ada 'Bricktop', with Haskins, J. (1983) *Bricktop*. New York: Atheneum Press.

Stovall, T. (1996) *Paris Noir: African Americans in the City of Light*. New York: Houghton Mifflin.

Stovall, T. (2005) Black Community, Black Spectacle: Performance and Race in Transatlantic Perspective. In Elam, H.J., Jr & Jackson, K. (eds.), *Black Cultural Traffic: Crossroads in Global Performance and Popular Culture* (pp. 221–241). Ann Arbor, MI: University of Michigan Press.

Sullivan, E. (1961) Little Old New York. *The New York Daily News*, 24 July. Ada 'Bricktop' Smith DuConge (1894–1984) Papers, Schomburg Center for Research in Black Culture, Harlem, New York, Box 7, Folder 5.

Taylor, F.C. with Cook, Gerald (1988) *Alberta Hunter: A Celebration in Blues*. New York: McGraw-Hill.

Walton, L.A. (1909) Music and the Stage: Georgia Troubadours. *The New York Age*, 16 November, n.p.

Wolf, S. (2016) Musical Theatre Studies. *The Journal of American Drama and Theatre*, Winter 28(1), 1.

Yagoda, B. (2015) *The B Side: The Death of Tin Pan Alley and the Rebirth of the Great American Song*. New York: Penguin Books.

5

Identity and Representation in a Theatrical Dynasty: Examining Oscar Hammerstein II's Legacy in Britain

Arianne Johnson Quinn

Oscar Hammerstein II has long been revered as one of the foremost figures in American musical theatre, both in the United States and abroad. Hammerstein played a key role in the representation of the post-war American political onstage, often challenging assumptions about race and identity in his plays and combining a strong sense of equality and progressive values (Most, 2000). Although scholars such as Andrea Most have examined the extent of his political activities and affiliations as they affected his presence in the United States, the enormity of Hammerstein's influence in a global context has yet to be explored (Block, 2003; Knapp, 2005). Hammerstein's work also played into the British affinity for American culture in the post-war period that was often seen as a nostalgia for the Old American South, while it confronted aspects of American culture which the British found troubling, such as the blatant racism towards and mistreatment of African Americans (Bailey, 2007). Along with his collaborators, including Richard Rodgers and Jerome Kern, Hammerstein was able to navigate the post-war social and political climate of Britain more effectively than any other American librettist (Fordin, 1977). This in turn led to frequent revivals by both professional and amateur companies throughout Britain.[1]

As a result, Hammerstein's legacy in Britain is a complex one. On the one hand his works represent American social liberalism and progress, particularly in works such as *South Pacific*. However, these works are also fraught with problematic representations of non-Western culture and racial minorities, presenting a challenge for modern directors, actors and audiences. This chapter explores Oscar Hammerstein's legacy in Britain as an ambassador for progressive American political ideology and the ways in which his family reputation and social connections allowed him to act as a political spokesman. I explore two productions that were produced in post-World War II London: *South Pacific* (1951) and *Carmen Jones* (1991). The ready acceptance of these works by the British public not only shaped audience expectations for Hammerstein's work, but influenced British musical theatre by fuelling an already present affinity for American musical theatre in post-war London. Moreover, the reception and production history for both of these shows demonstrates the ways in which British audiences responded to issues of race and identity in the American musical, while at the same time perhaps turning a blind eye to homegrown racial conflicts (Turner, 2009; Black, 2010).

By considering two productions that took place 40 years apart, we see the longevity of Hammerstein's popularity in London and the nostalgia not just for his works, but for Hammerstein himself and the post-war idealism that he represented. The reception history for *South Pacific* raises questions about the influence of Rodgers and Hammerstein in London, particularly as the critical response demonstrates the unique and privileged position that Hammerstein occupied in London as they cast a critical eye on both the war and the failed racial politics of American life in the 1940s. *Carmen Jones* is a production that attempts to narrate the experiences of African Americans, demonstrates the crystallized sense of nostalgia for the pre-war Hammerstein and the myth of progressive theatre (Bennett, 1996, p. 5). As narrated from the perspective of director Simon Callow, this production also highlights the challenges of recreating interpretations of African American culture through the lens of white musical culture onstage.

Both *South Pacific* and *Carmen Jones* point to the dichotomy between Hammerstein's political ideals and the challenges of presenting and replicating these values onstage in such a way as to take into account the lived experiences of those the productions seek to represent. The perceived liberalism of both *South Pacific* and *Carmen Jones* is narrated through the contrived images of Black stereotypes or the experiences of white characters that are ultimately seeking absolution from their own failings. Thus the very issues of race and equality that Hammerstein attempted to tackle in both of these librettos unintentionally reified attitudes of race and difference through the mythos of progressive theatre.

Staging the White Saviour Myth

Hammerstein's own commitment to racial equality was tempered by the same business acumen that led him to foster useful connections and a deliberate public persona in Britain along with his collaborators. The success of his ability to craft the image of ambassador of American progress and equality and white liberal saviour who rescues the stories of racial minorities is reflected in the pervasive narratives surrounding his work. These narratives, such as the myths of American progress and racial and cultural authenticity, are often unwittingly retold by modern directors, audiences and producers (Ma, 2003; Kim, 2013).

Both *Carmen Jones* and *South Pacific* attempt to present narratives of racial equality from the perspective of white, mainstream culture without actually taking into account the lived narratives and experiences of the oppressed, particularly as Hammerstein perceived it in the 1940s. Hammerstein, who was an advocate for organizations such as the National Association for the Advancement of Colored People (NAACP) and was also censured by the United States government for overt political statements in the book for *South Pacific*, was keenly aware of racial prejudice. However, he was also seemingly unaware of the stereotypes which his works perpetuated, with *The King and I* being a prime example. As Andrea Most states with regard to Rodgers and Hammerstein's blindness towards stereotypes in *South Pacific*: 'just as a good liberal like Hammerstein can write songs against stereotype and not see the ways in which his own work perpetuates the very problems he laments, so [the protagonist] Emile props up the system he claims to abhor' (Most, 2000, p. 331). Hammerstein, like countless other playwrights before and after him, relied upon his sense of progressive goodwill, which in turn granted him an immunity from any accusations involving representation or authenticity.

In terms of global politics offstage this intervention into the power dynamics of another race has long been justified as a necessity because the oppressed subaltern is frequently cast as being incapable of resolving conflicts without intervention. Theorist J. Maggio argues that:

> [w]hereas the West marches forward in the temporal world, the colonial world is always fixed, regardless of the 'movement' of time. 'Civilization', 'progress' and even 'self-identity' itself always eludes the subaltern. In other words, the West is defined by its differentiation between the 'present', 'past', and 'future', as well as a sense of the other. The colonial world has no such self-identity, at least as the Western viewer perceives it.
>
> (Maggio, 2007, p. 423)

Thus the narrative of the colonized, the oppressed or the invisible is crafted by the ruling society. In a theatrical context, staging the racial conflicts of another nation allowed British audiences to maintain a position of superiority without interrogating domestic conflicts. This is similar to feminist theorist bell hooks's argument, as she states: 'Frequently, white feminists act as if black women did not know sexist oppression existed until they voiced feminist sentiment. They believe they are providing black women with "the" analysis and "the" program for liberation.' (hooks, 1984, p. 11)

Many of these so-called progressive liberal works, including shows such as *Finian's Rainbow* (1947), relied on the presence of strong, white heroes who often rescued the oppressed from their own culture, in what Gayatri Chakravorty Spivak characterized as 'White men [...] saving the brown women from brown men' (Spivak, 2003, p. 93). Theatrical representations of progressive society presenting white culture as a sort of white saviour who intervenes in the struggles of other races are often seen onstage, with Oscar Hammerstein's work being but one example. Spivak suggests: 'The colonizer constructs himself as he constructs the colony.' (In Maggio, 2007, p. 423) The colonizer in this case is also read through the eyes of an American public, eager to create a sense of national identity that is supportive of a larger cultural agenda. Within these works the white saviour remains intact and the subaltern is left with powerless visibility (Oja, 2009, p. 25).

Although the study of the white saviour myth has rarely been explored in the context of musical theatre scholarship, similar work in film studies provides a useful framework for post-war theatre. Matthew Hughey's arguments, in particular, regarding race in film provide a mechanism for understanding the complexity of racial representation in artworks that claim to adhere to progressive values. Hughey argues that the white saviour myth is continually replicated in films precisely because of the narration of social liberalism from the perspective of whiteness. Films that present these narratives of liberal whiteness tend to contain specific but contradictory characteristics, including, as he states, 'a prevalent hope and desire for a societal change to an authentically egalitarian society absent racial prejudice and discrimination' (Hughey, 2014, p. 165). This principle is particularly relevant in understanding Hammerstein's work.

In *South Pacific* this hope is presented directly in musical numbers such as 'You've Got To Be Carefully Taught', as Nellie Forbush and Lt. Cable are forced to confront their prejudice from a privileged position. In *Carmen Jones*, it is presented in what director Simon Callow has called a 'self-enclosed black world' in which the characters of the opera-turned-realist-musical-play respond to the strictures around them (Callow, 2017). The problem with the formulation of racial representation in Hammerstein's post-war works, particularly *Carmen Jones* and *South Pacific*, is that they attempt to represent the oppressed without taking into account actual lived narratives and experiences. Hammerstein's ability to market these stereotypes abroad resulted from his long-standing connections to British theatre.

Strategic Political Connections

Perhaps unsurprisingly, given his political associations in the States, Hammerstein also had connections to left-leaning British politicians (Most, 2000, p. 309). By utilizing these political connections, Hammerstein deliberately maintained a stronghold on British theatre in a way other American figures could not, although not without consequence. As William Hyland notes, Hammerstein was involved with the United World Federalists and was only granted a restricted passport in

1953 due to his support of left-wing causes, possibly a reason why he only made limited trips to Britain during this period (Hyland, 1998, p. 192).

These connections led to mutually beneficial arrangements, particularly as opening nights for a new Hammerstein production were frequently used to raise money for specific political causes under the guise of charity. Although this was a common tactic in British musical theatre, Hammerstein's approach to charity is revealing. The opening night of *Carousel* was in fact organized as a benefit for the Margaret McMillan Memorial Fund, which was a socialist nursing organization. Hammerstein wrote to theatre manager Prince Littler at Drury Lane on behalf of his friend Gilbert McAllister, who was a member of the left-leaning Labour Party, in order to facilitate this. This is certainly an interesting connection for Hammerstein to have had, and demonstrates the extent of his political connections in London. Further correspondence back and forth between Hammerstein's wife, Dorothy, and McAllister discusses the possibility of the Royal Family being in attendance for the benefit. Not only would a charitable event have bolstered Hammerstein's reputation but the presence of the monarchs at a musical theatre production virtually guaranteed that because of the additional press coverage the opening night of the play would be a success.

Despite the usefulness of certain political connections, Hammerstein was careful to avoid taking direct political stances in London, often denying requests from organizations that were too far in either direction. A request from Sigmund Gestetner, head of a Zionist Group called the Jewish National Fund, for a benefit performance was denied. Hammerstein was diplomatic in his reply, arguing that there would be no special performance of *South Pacific*, despite numerous requests, because he did not want to show favouritism. However, what is more likely is that Hammerstein was attempting to avoid any political backlash to an already controversial play.

By all accounts, Hammerstein balanced a concern for charitable causes with a protective approach to his work. When the Royal National Hospital requested that they be allowed to perform *South Pacific* for patients in the hospital using the then unpublished libretto, Hammerstein denied the request for a libretto, but stated that they could send someone to attend the play and then copy it without him knowing. Interactions such as this also demonstrate that Hammerstein – and his business associates in London – attempted to maintain the positive impression of American entertainers who performed in Britain during the Second World War. It was likely that these political connections allowed him to promote and control the performance of his work out of the reach of government censorship.[2]

South Pacific in London

Because *South Pacific* presented the most controversial plot to British audiences of any of their works, Rodgers and Hammerstein were extremely cautious about its method of production. Much like the star vehicles of the 1930s and 1940s, Rodgers and Hammerstein relied heavily on the reputation of Mary Martin, who was much loved in Britain. Martin had appeared in several productions in London, including Noël Coward's *Pacific 1860* which reopened on Drury Lane at the end of the war in 1946, referred to by an anonymous critic as 'that other Pacific show [...] which flopped' (Anon., 1951a, 2 November 1951). According to critics, Martin was indeed the only remarkable aspect of Coward's show, which had a brief run and has never been revived. Between the combination of Rodgers and Hammerstein's reputation and Martin's 'star power', *South Pacific* was set to be a great success. Rodgers and Hammerstein produced several non-musical plays in London, even after the failure of two plays they had produced, *The Heart of the Matter* by Graham Greene and *Burning Bright* by John Steinbeck, which had led to the decision to stop producing non-musical plays in the States. Documents in the *South Pacific* folder held in the Hammerstein collection at the Library of Congress indicated that one such play, *The Happy Time*, was plagued by censorship issues and was initially denied licence by the Lord Chamberlain's Office. This setback was surely a source of frustration for Hammerstein (Hyland, 1998, p. 192).

The show was indeed a success thanks to heavy advertisement, advanced theatre bookings with raised ticket prices, Martin's reputation, the timely publication of James A. Michener's book *Tales of the South Pacific*, and musical recordings (Anon., 1951b, *The Sketch*, 21 November 1951). Critics marvelled; as one stated:

> There never was such a build-up for a dollar import; there never was such advance salesmanship; even the raised prices raised more excitement... The First Night to make all other First Nights look like the opening of a concert party in a zinc shed at Shrimpton-on-Sea.

The same critic also noted the lamentable lack of Agnes de Mille's dances, arguing that the story should have had complex 'fantastic native rites' to accompany songs such Bali Hai (*The Times*, 4 November 1951). Indeed it had the third largest run of any show at Drury Lane in the 1950s, running for two and a half years before embarking on a national tour.

Despite the advanced press, critics felt that Rodgers and Hammerstein took a risk by bringing *South Pacific* to London because it not only presented a simplistic portrait of the Second World War from an American perspective, but the political nature of the production had created a great deal of controversy in the States (Most, 2000, p. 228). Further, these same critics felt the show presented a superficial and naive portrait of wartime politics. Harold Hobson complained that the plot lacked the reality of the harshness of war, stating: '[...] the story's heroics are such as used to delight us in the days when we played with toy soldiers [...]' (Hobson, 1951). Even the portrayal of racial politics fell flat, as Nellie and the other Americans were perceived as being superficial 'happy-go-lucky' characters.

British audiences felt that this was a poor reflection of the complexities of race relations in the United States. Critic John Barber argued that what was relevant for American audiences – the Pacific war, the race issue and technical wizardry – was simply not relatable for the British public: 'we can't forget that it's not our men fighting' (Barber, 1951).

Director Joshua Logan clearly anticipated the problems with the show's presentation of the war and race, and had advised Hammerstein to make several changes to the production in order to make it more suitable for British audiences. He argued that Cable should be played by an American actor rather than a British one, because his weakness in terms of sexual immorality and race relations would make his character seem an insult to the British public. He also suggested they change the part of Emile's Polynesian wife to that of a housekeeper in order to situate the relationship within expected bounds. In Logan's opinion it was perfectly acceptable for a British man to engage in sexual relations for 'practical reasons' with a colonized woman, while marrying someone from a different race was unacceptable. As Logan argued: 'though the British practise [sic] race prejudice in the colonies, they think of themselves as knights in armor where America is concerned and do not go along with us or sympathize with our race problems at all' (Logan, 1951). The hypocrisy on the part of the British in terms of gender and race likely baffled Rodgers and Hammerstein. Instead of reworking the play, they chose to ignore these suggestions and stage the play as it had been performed in the States.

Mary Martin's 'Star Appeal' as Political Currency

As part of a deliberate campaign to overcome negative perception, Rodgers and Hammerstein, along with Jerome Whyte, framed critical discussions of the play around Martin's popularity. Martin spoke to the press several times, often addressing issues of racial politics (Whyte, 1951). An article in the *Daily Express* went so far as to claim that the show was the reason why even a Southerner such as Martin who had been raised not to question racial prejudice had a change of heart. Martin stated:

> When he [Hammerstein] wrote *South Pacific* with the part of the girl who is prejudiced against coloured people, and changes her mind, he sent it to me. And he reminded me of that talk years before. That is why I feel I know Nellie so well. You see – I was so like her.
>
> (Anon., 1951c, *The Daily Express*, 31 October 1951)

Similar articles further persuaded London audiences to attend the show and also likely influenced the British perception of American life and politics. While it is unclear whether or not Hammerstein's political views directly impacted the reception of his work in Britain, Kenneth Tynan – and other critics as well – were careful to frame the political issues of

South Pacific as being uniquely American. Tynan, for one, only made a passing reference to Hammerstein's liberal views when he stated that Hammerstein 'makes no secret of his sympathy for the idea of a federated world government' (Tynan, 1956).

Martin's appeal managed to circumvent any misgivings the audience may have had, particularly because she exemplified perceptions of the 'typical' American woman: simple, homespun, as well as being a wife and mother. As was typical of the gendered representations of women in theatrical press from the post-war period, Martin was presented as a mother and wife first and foremost and an American artist second. Moreover, as a cultural outsider, Martin's appeal allowed her to escape much of the typical criticism aimed at American actors and created a favourable impression of Rodgers and Hammerstein's work.

John Barber reveals that, on meeting Princess Margaret, Mary Martin 'blurt[ed] out, with no trace of a Ma'am, "Do tell your sister how sorry I am that she couldn't see me tonight"' (Barber, 1951). Rather than being seen as an insult to national pride, Martin's flippant approach to the Royal Family was seen as a reflection on the simplicity of good-natured Americans. Hammerstein capitalized on this along with his collaborators as a means of furthering their reputation as American progressives, and downplaying their own Jewishness in the process (Most, 2000, p. 328). By the time *Carmen Jones* arrived in 1991, Hammerstein's work had become an integral part of the British musical theatre canon, and along with this came the mythology of Hammerstein as being the pre-eminent progressive storyteller.

Carmen Jones and the Nostalgia for the Old South

Although certainly Hammerstein was more progressive than his contemporaries, he in many ways simply repackaged stereotypes of non-white characters in his librettos. *Carmen Jones* is no different. His retelling of Bizet's operatic triumph shifts the exoticism onto a different racial group – in a similar way to *Porgy and Bess* (Locke, 2007, p. 431). The reception of the 1991 production of *Carmen Jones* reflects the love and nostalgia for Hammerstein with its dialogue and representations of Black sensuality onstage.

As demonstrated by the many revivals of productions such as *Show Boat*, most recently in 2016 in London, a recurring theme of the Imagined South permeates British notions of America's race and identity struggles on stage and that allows for the continual reconstruction of false Black American existence on stage. This same nostalgia allows for shows such as *Show Boat* and *Carmen Jones* – which would be problematic to stage in the States to say the least – to be reconstructed onstage. Brian Ward argues that post-war British audiences 'often blurred' distinctions between South and Black, creating a multilayered exoticism (Ward, 2014, p. 41). This is in part because British audiences had experienced jazz performers and Black revues beginning in the 1920s with the Original Dixieland Jazzband, in what Ward called 'Dixiephilia' (Ward, 2014, p. 41).

Production Background

Carmen Jones opened at the Broadway Theatre in 1943 and was later made into a film in 1954 with Harry Belafonte and Dorothy Dandridge. Because the initial run was a success on Broadway, producer Billy Rose suggested the possibility of an eight-week run of the play at Covent Garden in the summer, with a suggestion to move from Covent Garden to another London theatre if successful. He then proposed a tour of the provinces followed by a transfer of a translated production to Paris. This production never took place, likely because of financial complications (Hammerstein, 1949).

Hammerstein was hesitant, stating that the pound devaluation would hurt the production and indeed was hurting the *Oklahoma!* run (Hammerstein, 1949). A statement from Whyte dated 27 September 1947 indicates the ways in which the massive fluctuations in the value of the pound affected funding for American productions (Hammerstein, 1949).

Thus it wasn't until 1991 that Simon Callow's production opened at the Old Vic (the first British production of this work), challenging expectations for musical theatre and opera. Callow's production is intriguing for many reasons – the production methods, casting, and the treatment of American musical theatre as an operatic work. This production took place during a period of frequent revivals of American Golden Age book musicals in the late 1980s and 1990s, spurred by the public nostalgia for post-war American culture (Bennett, 1996, p. 5). These nostalgia productions, such as Ian Marshall Fisher's 'Lost Musicals' project, attempted to recreate the original productions in their entirety.

This production of *Carmen Jones* reflects the dual sense of nostalgia for the Old American South and for the Golden Age musical represented by Oscar Hammerstein II. The original work comprises multiple layers of gender and racial portrayals, in what scholar Annegret Fauser refers to as a 'complex chain of performativity' in which race and gender adhere to 1940s societal expectations (Fauser, 2010, p. 136). Callow himself stated that the impulse behind this production arose from Hammerstein's desire to translate an operatic work into the world of American musical theatre, arguing:

> being as alert as he [Hammerstein] was to everything that was going on in the world he took this tremendously radical decision to do it in an all-black community... it was a most creative response to making opera accessible to the millions.
>
> (Callow, 2017)

The production attempted to represent the 'smart black world' versus the setting of the traditional Deep South, which was represented in the original play. Callow stated that 'we made all of these things as vividly as we could', drawing on African American singers as well as British singers who had recently been part of Trevor Nunn's *Porgy and Bess* cast at Glyndebourne, and African American conductor Henry Lewis (Callow, 2017). This casting choice is significant because it demonstrates Callow's desire for historical accuracy in the representation of the African American characters onstage.

Callow employed two different casts in the production in order to balance the challenges of operatic singing with the abilities of performers who were trained in musical theatre, personally coaching singers in musical theatre performance styles. He stated: 'I'm very proud of that [...] when it started two thirds of the cast were from America because we didn't have enough people in this country who could sing this stuff'; as he states, over the course of the run the American cast was largely replaced (Callow, 2017). Although the casting of American performers was initially due to a lack of British performers who were able to perform the operatic singing style of the work, the gradual replacement of an American cast by a British one may have bolstered a sense of cultural familiarity for the audience that allowed them to view these complex racial presentations in relatable ways. These casting and production decisions highlight Callow's desire to stage a rendition of *Carmen Jones* that adhered to notions of post-war American culture. Callow's production maintained the original dialogue, including what called Warren Hoffman called the 'faux negro speech, similar to the dialect that he [Hammerstein] crafted for the black characters in *Show Boat*' (Hoffman, 2014, p. 115). Callow wanted to maintain the sense of the 'self-contained black world' by conducting extensive research into the world of the Tuskegee airmen and other African American aspects of World War II history. In doing so he was able to manufacture a world onstage that adhered to the expectations of modern audiences as to what an African American world should look and sound like.

Despite the attempts at historical authenticity, the play replicated Black culture that was interpreted through what critic Michael Coveney (1991) called: 'White musical culture'. Other critics such as Charles Osborne felt that regardless of the lack of historical representation, the work was a testament to Hammerstein himself. He argued: 'The advantage of Carmen Jones [...] lies surely, in the fact that, in spirit, Oscar Hammerstein's creation remains close to the original work. Much more violence is done nowadays to operas by directors than was inflicted by Hammerstein' (in Coveney, 1991). Thus Hammerstein's legacy superseded any concerns about representation onstage. Not all critics agreed with the approach of the self-contained, all-Black world onstage, arguing that Hammerstein's work itself transcended notions of race and colour. Critic Benedict Nightingale argued that the all-Black cast was in itself a novel idea, even in 1991: 'had Bizet seen what the Viennese and other revisionists did with *Carmen* soon after his death, he might have been grateful for what, in both senses of the word, is Hammerstein's freshness' (Nightingale, 1991). Nightingale's comments highlight the dichotomy between the realist world and theatrical fantasy that both Hammerstein and Callow wanted to portray by employing an all-Black cast and using historically accurate scenery. However, from the perspective of several critics and British audiences, the racial representation in this work was no different than in the days of racial stereotypes in Ruritanian operetta and was therefore as far removed from the experience of the modern audience as the original opera *Carmen*.[3]

Callow pushed back against accusations of political incorrectness by pointing out that other prominent works featuring African American culture were more directly exploitative, including *Porgy and Bess* with its 'corrosive use of black language' (2017). The restaging of this work further positioned the musical as a white and not a Black art form, reinterpreting race through nostalgic eyes. Part of this nostalgia stemmed from the creative process which Callow and others employed. Moreover, it represents a sort of reclamation of certain ideas in Hammerstein's work – such as the brazen sexuality of Carmen that was portrayed by critics as being a feminist expression. Rather than perceiving the recycled aspects of the play, critics interpreted Carmen as commandeering her own sexuality in order to control her destiny. The exception was critic Michael Billington's harsh dismissal of this work as being too much a product of white musical culture and a reinforcement of tired cultural and ethnic stereotypes (Billington, 1991). Critic Maureen Paton stated: 'The sexually aggressive Carmen is the prototype of the modern superwoman. She takes the initiative in everything and she slaps her poor men around as if tenderizing meat.' (Paton, 1991) This perception was by no means unique to Britain; in fact, Callow recounts his experience of taking this production on tour in Japan. As he tells it, several critics responded positively to what they saw as the strong, powerful figure of Carmen who used her sexuality to free herself from the clutches of men (Callow, 2017).

Understanding Hammerstein's Legacy Today

Ultimately, the conflicted response to this production points to Hammerstein's lasting popularity in London. As Simon Callow stated:

> I think it's because Oscar Hammerstein had such a cast iron sense of dramatic form. That they are always musical plays. He had such a vivid sense

of character. Such [a] largely infallible sense of dramatic momentum and [he] personifies more than any other librettist book writing that I know. The basic function of the scene is to bring it to a point where nothing satisfies it but a song. It's just skill. It's just sheer craftsmanship. And I think we like that very much. I think we like our musical shows to be very organic in character.

(Callow, 2017)

Hammerstein's popularity rests on his ability to circumvent the thorny aspects of racial representation and portray progressive ideals onstage through highly crafted narratives.

The fact that *Carmen Jones* was produced in Britain in the 1990s at all stems from the love of Hammerstein as a cultural icon. In a similar manner, *South Pacific* has become a classic in Britain, performed by light opera and amateur theatre companies several times since its original Drury Lane run. Thus the mythos surrounding his work continues to be replicated on the London stage, creating challenges for modern directors, performers and audiences. What do we make of these two productions? Do we dismiss them because they project tired stereotypes and diminish works by Black artists? Or do we reframe these discussions and find new ways of reclaiming authenticity and identity? I suggest that, as Callow and others have done, we retranslate these works for modern audiences, bearing in mind the multiple layers of representation and identity that come into play.

Notions of progressivism and authenticity in British musical theatre shift over time, but what has remained is the perception of Hammerstein's role in shaping British theatre as the master storyteller. While his work has been contested, tested, reframed and subjected to scrutiny, it has survived in Britain because of the nostalgia surrounding Hammerstein himself. Much like other cultural outsiders such as Handel and Mendelssohn before him, Hammerstein holds a key place in the British cultural imagination. But what exactly is this place and how should we respond to flawed notions of race and equality in his works? This is for future generations of performers and audiences to decide. To paraphrase *South Pacific*'s Nellie Forbush: 'We've got to be carefully taught.'

Notes

1. Several light opera companies throughout Britain have performed *South Pacific,* including the Glasgow Theatre Guild who first performed it in 1960 as the very first production at the Theatre Royal, Glasgow.
2. The original copy of *South Pacific* that was submitted to the Lord Chamberlain's Office can be found in the Lord Chamberlain's play collection held in the British Library. (See the Lord Chamberlain's Play Collection held at the British Library, LCP 1951/4.)
3. Ruritanization refers to the common practice of setting a musical play in fictional Austro-Germanic countries. British playwrights frequently used this practice to neutralize politically charged themes and avoid the censors. For more on post-war Ruritanian musical theatre see John Snelson, Chapter 4, '*King's Rhapsody*: Novello, Ruritania and European Tradition' in *The West End Musical 1947–1954: British Identity and the 'American Invasion'* (Unpublished Ph.D. thesis, University of Birmingham, 2002).

References

Anon. (1951a) *Daily Express*, 2 November.

Anon. (1951b) *The Sketch*, 21 November.

Bailey, P. (2007) Fats Waller Meets Harry Champion: Americanization, National Identity and Sexual Politics in Inter-War British Music Hall. *Cultural and Social History*, 4(4), 495–509.

Barber, J. (1951) Alas, Some Not Entirely Enchanted Evenings: 'South Pacific' Has Melody, Ideas – But No Wonder Touch. *Daily Express*, 2 November.

Bennett, S. (1996) *Performing Nostalgia: Shifting Shakespeare and the Contemporary Past*. London. New York: Routledge.

Billington, M. (1991) Putting on the Old Hat and Doing up the Details. *The Guardian*, 10 April.

Black, L. (2010) *Redefining British Politics: Culture, Consumerism and Participation, 1954–70*. Houndmills, Basingstoke: Palgrave Macmillan.

Block, G.H. (2003) *Richard Rodgers*. New Haven, CN: Yale University Press.

Callow, S. (2017) Interview with author. 7 July 2017.

Coveney, M. (1991). A Juicy Main Squeeze. *The Observer*, 14 April, p. 61.

Depardieu, B. (2008) Carmen Jones: A Carmen 'À La Afro-American'. Published in *Studies in Musical Theatre*, 2(3), 223–234.

Ewen, D. (1957) *Richard Rodgers*, 1st edition. New York: Holt.

Fauser, A. (2010) 'Dixie Carmen': War, Race, and Identity in Oscar Hammerstein's 'Carmen Jones' (1943). *Journal of the Society for American Music*, 4(2), 127–174.

Fordin, H. (1977) *Getting to Know Him: A Biography of Oscar Hammerstein II*. New York: Random House.

Hammerstein, D. (1950) Letter to Gilbert McAllister, 5 April 1950. Oscar Hammerstein correspondence files, 'London *South Pacific*' folder, box 8/9, Library of Congress.

Hammerstein, O. (1949) Letter to Billy Rose, 31 October 1949. Oscar Hammerstein collection, 'London *Oklahoma!*' box 8/9, Performing Arts Reading Room, Library of Congress.

Hobson, H. (1951) Of South Pacific. *Sunday Times*, 4 November.

Hoffman, W. (2014) *The Great White Way: Race and the Broadway Musical*. New Brunswick, NJ and London: Rutger University Press.

hooks, b. (1984) *Feminist Theory from Margin to Center*. Boston, MA: South End Press.

Hughey, M.W. (2014) *The White Savior Film: Content, Critics, and Consumption*. Philadelphia, PA: Temple University Press.

Hyland, W.G. (1998) *Rodgers*. New Haven, CT: Yale University Press.

Kim, C. (2013) Asian Performance on the Stage of American Empire in Flower Drum Song. *Cultural Critique*, 85(85), 1–37.

Knapp, R. (2005) *The American Musical and the Formation of National Identity*. Princeton, NJ: Princeton University Press.

Locke, R. (2007) A Broader View of Musical Exoticism. *The Journal of Musicology*, 24(4), 477–521.

Logan, J. (1951). Letter to Oscar Hammerstein, 30 July 1951. Oscar Hammerstein collection, '*South Pacific* England' folder, box 7/9, Library of Congress.

Lord Chamberlain's Play Collection, British Library, LCP 1951/4 (2017).

Ma, S. (2003) Rodgers and Hammerstein's 'Chopsticks' Musicals. *Literature/Film Quarterly*, 31(1), 17–26.

Maggio, J. (2007, Oct–Dec) 'Can the Subaltern Be Heard?': Political Theory, Translation, Representation, and Gayatri Chakravorty Spivak. *Alternatives: Global, Local, Political*, 32(4), 419–443.

Merriman, A. (2013) *Greasepaint and Cordite: The Story of ENSA and Concert Party Entertainment during the Second World War*. London: Aurum Press Ltd.

Michener, J.A. (1952) *Tales of the South Pacific*. New York: Macmillan.

Most, A. (2000) 'You've Got to Be Carefully Taught': The Politics of Race in Rodgers and Hammerstein's South Pacific. *Theatre Journal*, 52(3), 307–337.

Most, A. (2013) *Theatrical Liberalism: Jews and Popular Entertainment in America*. New York: New York University Press.

Nightingale, B. (1991) Touch of Class in West End. *The Times*, 9 April.

Oja, C. (2009) *West Side Story* and *the Music Man*: Whiteness, Immigration, and Race in the US during the Late 1950s. *Studies in Musical Theatre*, 3(1), 13–30.

Paton, M. (1991) Supergirl Carmen Slaps £4 m Show into Shape. *The Telegraph*, 11 April.

Snelson, J. (2002) *The West End Musical 1947–1954: British Identity and the 'American Invasion'*. Unpublished Ph.D. thesis, University of Birmingham.

Spivak, G.C. (2003) Can the Subaltern Speak? *Die Philosophin*, 14(27), 42–58.

Turner, M.J. (2009) *British Power and International Relations during the 1950s: A Tenable Position?* Lanham, MD: Lexington Books.

Tynan, K. (1956) Rhyme & Time Millionaires. *Everybody's Magazine*, 22 May.

Ward, B. (2014) Music, Musical Theater, and the Imagined South in Interwar Britain. *Journal of Southern History*, 80(1), 39–72.

Waters, R. (2016) Thinking Black: Peter Fryer's Staying Power and the Politics of Writing Black British History in the 1980s. *History Workshop Journal*, 82(1), 104–120.

Whyte, J. (1951) Letter from Jerry Whyte to Dick and Oc, 15 September 1951. Oscar Hammerstein collection, '*South Pacific* England' folder, box 7/9, Library of Congress.

6

Black Conductors Make History on the Great 'White' Way: The Lost Labours of the Music Director in Musical Theatre

Sean Mayes

Musical theatre at its nucleus is a fully collaborative art form: it requires collaborative efforts of creators across the disciplines of dance, drama, and music. Music is elemental to the whole, and one would think that the labour behind its engineering and orchestration would illicit greater acknowledgement for those responsible for its implementation. Regrettably, this is not the case. From a historical perspective, the names and faces of music directors responsible for the literal realization of the tunes and recordings we love so well are all but forgotten. Processes and documentation of music directors are all but consigned to oblivion with no active pursuance of chronicling. Moreover, those with whom the music director shares the platform of leadership are exalted and raised to higher importance and recollection – we recall and laud the contributions to the art of directors and choreographers alike, but are hard pressed to name even five music directors throughout its history – let alone see their names in larger print on a poster or a marquee.

This dilemma is exacerbated by considering music directors' limitations from a further perspective: as minorities. In 2014, an online article claimed 'Black Conductors Make History on Broadway', declaring that, for the first time in history, New York was privileged to have four conductors of colour at the helm of orchestras in Broadway shows (Pittsburgh Courier, 2014). Considering the 44 productions that occupied Broadway in the 2013–2014 season, this minute percentage of representation stands to serve as reminder that minority practitioners seek to find greater opportunity within the theatre. I challenge you to pause for a moment and list five musical directors of musical theatre. Now, if this is still too easy a task, consider how many of the following foundational names you could identify: Eubie Blake, Everett Lee, Will Marion Cook, Harold Wheeler, Joyce Brown.

Why has the contribution and the significance of the music director gone unrecognized? Furthermore, why has this disregard of the music director further limited the work of minority practitioners? This chapter will examine, reflect on, and illuminate the work of the music director through what I identify as 'lost labours'. In this chapter, I open dialogue and glance at the expansive work the music director has laid in the archive of musical theatre. This chapter seeks to broadly uncover the kinds of work that have previously been obscured. It looks to acknowledge and unearth those who were instrumental to the success of musical theatre due to their diverse capabilities. It aims to examine the work and efforts of those active today who tirelessly strive to add to the art in production, even when behind curtains or in a pit under a stage. The chapter draws on critical race theories of liminality from Brandi Wilkins Catanese (2014) and of intersectionality from Kimberlé Crenshaw (1991). As a practitioner, I seek to represent and illuminate the work done by these labouring artists, and as a Black practitioner, shed distinct light on how this has particularly afflicted practitioners of colour while also acknowledging the problems that all minority practitioners experience.

The Development of the Music Director's Role

One can consider the evolution of the musical director (MD) throughout assorted phases in its history to address how the role has changed since its inception. As John Graziano outlines, the early role of the music director was often fluid – theatre orchestras were an expanding concept in the 1860s, and quite frequently the music director (dubbed the 'leader') was the 'composer, conductor, and arranger', either conducting by baton or often being the principal violinist as a member of the orchestra themselves (Graziano, 2014, p. 112). With this fluidity, a diversity of conducting and leadership responsibilities is evident even at this early stage. This fluctuation of role definition has largely defined the music director not only as a leader through rehearsals but often also as the show's conductor – the terms of 'MD' and 'conductor' which will interchange through this chapter.

As music has developed, a conducting style appropriate to the requirement of each show has accompanied it. Into the twentieth century, further stylistic evolution of American theatre demonstrates a maturity of the conductor in performance. Musicals of the early twentieth century through to the Golden Age were reminiscent of music ranging anywhere from the orchestral grandeur of classical rooting to rhythmic and emphatic styles of new 'distinctly' American styles such as jazz and ragtime, all penned by composers and orchestrators of an era that embraced a matured fusion of this European style and American vaudeville in eventually defining a 'Broadway' sound (Symonds, 2011). As the musical progresses, a stark change in stylistic employment changes the needs of the music director: the genesis of the rock era mid-twentieth century provokes new exemplar musicals, and moves the music director between the pit orchestra and the pit *band*. Further tracing of this trajectory emphasizes the transition of the music director into a role more entrenched in theatrical labour, versus one of higher eminence as seen in neighbouring genres such as opera – the modern keyboard conductor holds less artistic gravitas than a conductor presiding over an orchestra via baton.

The musical has ebbed and flowed from its traditionalist sound of the brassy Broadway show tune, and has embraced numerous genres in execution. With this, the music director has experienced a diverse cycle in which their duties and leaderships have matured and interchanged. The case studies which follow give some indication as to the multiplicity and diversity within the encompassing umbrella of the MD's role.

Pathfinders of Music Direction

I would like to offer a few names of music directors, both historical and recent, who exhibit the immense variety of role and capacity of the typical music director, yet, in contrast to the fame and identifiable eminence of directors and choreographers, have often dissolved out of recognition.

Music Director as Performer

In affirming the duality of the conductor as conductor-performer, there are numerous names on which the honour of 'first' could be bestowed. Upon inspection, there appears to be uncertainty in previous academic work in pinpointing the first Black (or minority, to be comprehensive) music director of a modern show. Harvard musicologist Carol J. Oja writes in *Bernstein Meets Broadway: Collaborative Art in a Time of War* (2014) that this can be accredited to African American conductor Everett Lee in 1945, when composer Leonard Bernstein approached him nine months into production of *On The Town* to ask if he would lead the orchestra, making this grand gesture the first time an accolade of this stature was bestowed upon a minority in any semblance (Oja, 2014). However, earlier practitioners had attained this accomplishment. There is evidence to indicate that *Shuffle Along* (1921), a foundational pillar in musical theatre history of African American parentage, might have an exemplar in helping deconstruct this false benchmark, serving amidst evidence of even earlier practitioners. Despite its controversy in academic circles as a truly progressive representation of African Americans, there is little denying that Blake and Sissle's *Shuffle Along* is an influential staple of the canon. The show not only holds distinction in being a formative piece of theatre in assisting transition of the musical from revue to the 'book musical' we know today, it also assisted the legitimization of Black performers. It develops the representation of African Americans as a construct within musical theatre: in rejecting the hierarchical design of the time, the show 'rejected the standard blackface makeup, ragged minstrel attire, and "comic darky" behavior expected of African American performers' (Wintz and Finkelman, 2004a, p. 152).

Shuffle Along's creative inception can be traced and credited to numerous creatives of Black heritage, most notably through the show's composer, musical director, and conductor Eubie Blake (1883–1983). An American composer and exceptionally talented pianist, Blake was well known for his work both in ragtime and musical theatre, with a compositional style reflective of his ease in playing highly intricate and syncopated figures not dissimilar to the stylistic convention heard in *Shuffle Along*. Differentiated accounts mark Eubie Blake as a fearless piano-conductor in the show's opening. In liner notes for the show's recording, co-composer Noble Sissle recounts the writers' trepidation of opening night, affirming Blake's contribution: 'We thought of [Eubie] Blake, stuck out there in front, leading the orchestra – his bald head would get the brunt of the tomatoes and the rotten eggs.' (Sissle, 2002) Blake's exceptional ability forces an acknowledgement of greatness in execution, and in transcendence of racial limitations of the time. Blake paved a route as a creative patriarch of the show, in which he was not only composer, conductor and musical director, but also featured as pianist in performances. Eubie Blake can be considered one of the formative musical directors of his time, musically responsible for rejecting customs of liminality both as a musical director and through racial convention as a Black practitioner.

Music Director as Dramaturg

A testament to the truly *visible* oversight of the music director, Lehman Engel (1910–1982) is fondly commemorated in his obituary as being 'perhaps best known to theatergoers from the back of his baldish head as he conducted [as] musical director for "Showboat," "Brigadoon," "Annie Get Your Gun," "Fanny," "Guys and Dolls," "Carousel" and many other productions' (Barbanel, 1982). Perhaps one of the most familiar names of music direction in the Golden Age, Engel is credited as a music director and conductor of numerous theatre shows and films of his time, as well as a composer of shows and films. A Tony Award-winning music director, he is particularly notable for two paramount aspects of his legacy: his work encompassed publications recounting his experiences and the role of the practitioner in developing the functional libretto; and he embraced the mentoring of future generations of music directors through his inaugurated *BMI Lehman Engel Musical Theatre Workshop*, in which numerous music directors and composers, not limited to Stephen Flaherty, Maury Yeston, and Alan Menken, have sought tutelage from the 1960s to present day (Suskin, 2010, pp. 356, 371, 376). Correspondingly, his work demonstrates the often disregarded contribution of the music director as dramaturg in developing and governing any production. Engel penned two vital texts of the art, validating the need for contribution from practitioners: *Words and Music: Creating the Broadway Musical Libretto* (1972) and *The American Musical Theatre* (1975). As a white male, Engel was not overtly revealing of his own status as a minority in being gay: an undoubted parallel conflict of lost identity in both his personal and professional life. Nonetheless, his work exemplifies the incredible contribution of the music director (Harbin et al., 2005).

Music Director as Orchestrator

The versatility of the music director in assimilating numerous roles not limited to accompanist, vocal director, and often arranger and orchestrator, is often embraced. One often forgotten individual is the remarkably prolific music director, arranger, orchestrator, and composer Luther Henderson (1919–2003). A graduate of the Juilliard School of Music and an orchestrator for Duke Ellington, Henderson's reputation in theatre began through involvement as dance arranger on Rodgers and Hammerstein's *Flower Drum Song* (1958) (Suskin, 2009, p. 143). His work expanded and stretched through five decades in shows including *Funny Girl* (1964), *No, No, Nanette* (1971), and *Jelly's Last Jam* (1992). Nevertheless, his most characteristic stamp is perhaps on the iconic Black musical of the 1970s, *Ain't Misbehavin'* (1978), for which Henderson bore the exhaustive titles of orchestrator, arranger, music supervisor, and, during select years, music director. With remarkable effort, Henderson arranged the stride jazz music reminiscent of preceding composer Fats Waller, while conducting the jazz combo responsible for aural realization of his orchestrations from the piano. As a Black practitioner, Luther Henderson is frequently unknown to purveyors of musical theatre in both face and name, but is largely accountable for the sound and style so known to the attuned ear.

Music Director as Collaborator

Perhaps one of the most well-represented music directors in theatre today – perhaps ever – is Alex Lacamoire. A Cuban American Latino MD equally comfortable as arranger-orchestrator, Lacamoire has risen to significant fame through his involvement with two pieces in which he functioned equally as a collaborator in the rehearsal room and as music director: *In the Heights* (2008) and, of more recent distinction, *Hamilton* (2016) (Manley, 2016). In pairing with actor-writer-creator of both shows Lin-Manuel Miranda, Lacamoire has effectively secured an identity within theatre circles as the template collaborator, serving as orchestrator, arranger, conductor, keyboardist, and inceptive music director on both productions. In doing so, Lacamoire proves with astonishing craft – and borderline stardom – that the labours of the music director are not easily swept under the rug. Often a collaborator in the rehearsal room, the music director customarily and tirelessly works behind the scenes alongside the director, choreographer and, in some instances, composer, not only in steering the ship musically, but often providing indispensably formative advice and design in creating what routinely emerges as the final likeness of the show.

Lost Labours of Music Direction

These trailblazers affirm the contribution of the music director as expansive and requisite. Despite this, the music director, as artist and labourer, has been subject to what I term *lost labours* – the evidence of their creation and maintenance has been predominantly all but lost, a shadow of the discourse explored when surveying a vast history. How does the input of the one practitioner charged with arguably the most central premise of the art – music – become disregarded?

Formal role identification and delineation is one area where the music director has suffered. Part of pinpointing where identity is squandered must be in outlining concretely what music directors do. In any given production, the MD may be required for a multitude of tasks, not exclusive to any of the following, from pre-production to closing night: sitting in discussion with director and choreographer on artistic vision; evaluating performers for suitability; recruiting and contracting instrumentalists for the production; teaching vocals to the cast during rehearsals; serving as accompanist during staging and dance rehearsals; liaising with sound, stage management, and tech for audio requirements; orchestrating; arranging new music in conjunction (or not) with the composer; programming for electronic instruments; assisting instrumentalists in integration mid-process; baton-conducting or piano-conducting performances; editing music and collaborating for dramaturgical and musical content and form; updating and distributing new additions to and editions of scores for vocal and instrumental changes; maintaining cast morale during a run; serving as the single triumvirate practitioner from the creative team, which is still required and active after opening; monitoring vocal health ... any need for more? (See Church, 2015, p. 335.)

Certainly, among all these labours, it is understandable if only in part how some working processes may slip through consideration. The title of the 'music director' has traditionally served as an umbrella term encompassing all of these auxiliary, yet important, pieces of the musical puzzle. Despite this multiplicity, music directors have not historically received certification for the diversity of their role and work. The paramount work can often be considered comparable to that of a good theatre orchestra – if the job is being done well, one will not notice the labour, it being inconspicuous and only heard rather than seen. Pioneering orchestrator Robert Russell Bennett stresses that 'when an ineffective musical director is on the job nothing can sound good; the finest bands, the greatest productions, the most charming music, the most brilliant arrangements all go down the sink when the [one] in the middle hasn't "got rhythm"' (Bennett and Ferencz, 1999, p. 281).

A lack of recognition, aside from obligatory noted credit among colleagues or to the public, shows a quite stark contrast with musical theatre's older cousin, opera, where music directors are given full billing. How often is it that one sees the music director with full billing in visibility printed alongside the director or director-choreographer of a musical? How many years must pass before the value of the discharged Tony Award for Music Direction is recalled, reinstated alongside comparative praise? Music director David Alan Bunn, a protégé of Luther Henderson and one of the first Black music directors at the advent of the twenty-first century in New York City, describes comprehensible disbelief in the lack of visual display of the music director:

I do notice on the marquee, they will list the director, they will list the choreographer, but they will not list the music director. And that's for a musical. I've never understood that. You couldn't do a musical without a music director, but you don't list the music director.

(Bunn, 2017)

It is staggering that more attention has not been given to the documentation of the MD's approach, methodology, and arduous practice. With providential planning, these processes have the potential to reach chronicles from conscious thought. In reviewing first source archival material, Luther Henderson gives detailed accounts of much of his work in colloquially brief yet insightful notes on audition processes for *Ain't Misbehavin'* (Henderson, 1987). Although incremental, methodical conservation of documentation process such as this will provide insight for theatre historians and dedicated patrons alike in future exploration of procedural methodology, casting decisions, artistic decisions, changes to music with edits and keys, and much more. Joe Church expands on one potential example of this in considering the preservation of the rehearsal score in his book:

By nature, productions cannot be reproduced exactly, just as no two performances can be alike. With additional productions of a show [...], the written score is one of the ways that a production can be preserved and repeated with the same intent in music direction (and, to some extent, the stage direction). The written score may be the best [...] tangible and enduring testaments to a music director's considerable efforts.

(Church, 2015, pp. 347, 358)

In similar vein, perhaps one of the most crucial labours of the music director worth further scrutiny is the role of the MD as sole creative practitioner who remains with a production until its culmination. Despite the abundant recognition they receive, from the beginning of the process to the end, a director and choreographer seldom remain with a production past opening. The music director is responsible for maintaining the integrity and form of a show past the opening by providing musical and technical clarity as the foremost relation between the music and the cast:

As music director, [they] are among the only members of the creative staff who remains in site after opening night. [...] In [their] presence and attitude as a leading member of the company, and on the podium with [their] conducting, [they] maintain the music, carry the creative torch, and uphold the production's vision. [...] [They] will have some tangible role in its ongoing quality control.

(Church, 2015, p. 335)

It is worth considering the information that gets lost without documentation from the MD after opening, particularly when a show emerges on tours with new practitioners. Numerous approaches to execution deserve documentation or we face the risk of misplacing invaluable counsel in our longer term understanding of musicals, and in how future practice is informed.

Role versus Race – Artist versus Labourer: Comparing Liminality and Intersectionality in Music Direction

The music director has stood as a martyr of the neglect and dissolution of memory within the musical theatre: habitually forgotten and historically unrecognized, the music director has stood as the least remembered practitioner in a contemptible display of disregard towards momentous contribution. Not only has this disseminated to the entirety of music direction but, unfortunately, it has also reared its head when enabling the full inclusivity of directors: inclusive of the African diaspora, women, LGBTQ+, and other minoritized groups. In this, we currently face what I put forth as a comparative authenticity between role discrimination and race discrimination. It is useful to consider the similarities between the plight of the music director and the narrative of Black practitioners and artists. I offer that both the music director and minority practitioners have suffered from transgression in arriving at what can be collaterally compared as performative liminality. In her book *The Problem of the Color[Blind]: Racial Transgression and the Politics of Black Performance*, Brandi Wilkins Catanese describes the construct of liminality in relation to blackness and performance, which she offers are 'ineluctably linked' (2014, p. 1): 'on both institutional and cultural levels, performance has become the medium through which American anxieties about race (and in particular, blackness) are pondered, articulated, managed, and challenged' (Wilkins Catanese, 2014, p. 3).

In this notion around liminality, I offer that music directors have found themselves at a transitional stage: required within the art, yet continually self-asserting behind the threshold of recognition for an identity that has resulted in being both un-asserted and undefined. In addition, this has left minorities within this role susceptible to discrimination within their own realm. This duality of facing discrimination both via role and via race can also be comparatively linked to the offerings of critical race theorist Kimberlé Crenshaw in her concept of intersectionality. In her seminal article 'Mapping the Margins: Intersectionality, Identity Politics, and Violence Against Women of Color', Crenshaw depicts the notion of intersectionality through the lens of the Black woman: minorities who find themselves at the crossroads of two paths of discrimination they traverse are found in discriminatory isolation. Not only must they affirm their worth against two constructs of bias, but the idiosyncrasy of their selfhood also creates a framework of identity which is not understood by those in any position of power. As a result, those who need the firmest understanding of their essential exposure fall short of comprehension – creating situations where the need for preferential treatment is underplayed by the knowledge that both constructs individually are exposed to opportunity (for example, being hired as Black or as a woman, but not as both), and therefore the liminal access intersectional individuals face does not truly exist (Crenshaw, 1991).

Place this within the framework of the minority music director: minority both within our art and within societal class structure. In comparatively extracting Crenshaw's models, the music director is understood as its own role – validating one construct. The minority active within musical theatre is understood as its own role – validating another. This is perceived affirmation of a comfortable minority access. What we do not appraise, however, is the desperate need for these two arenas to intersect, and how, in doing so, we may see the liminal access that has been granted to those who stand at the crossroads thus far. Consider Crenshaw's words on the lack of framework and how this affects exposure for these groups: 'Without frames that allow us to see how social problems impact all the members of a targeted group, many will fall through the cracks of our movements, left to suffer in virtual isolation.' (Crenshaw, 2016)

It is less than ideal at the time of writing to have to propose that there is still ground to be covered in advocating full assimilation of minority music directors into a current professional scene. However, it is inarguable that the lines and boundaries within race that we seek to dissolve and mesh in approaching theatre are completely extinct: our current society is guilty of periodically embracing an overly ambitious model absent of institutionalized racism, and of being more progressive than our current landscape proves. Wilkins Catanese aptly quips that 'the twenty-first century [...] has forged its own relationship to the still-unresolved controversies over race, culture, and national character' (2014, p. 148). In further anecdotal consideration, discussion with numerous active and retired Black music directors provides an internal viewpoint for consideration of the lack of practitioners from minority groups. Consider the select anonymous thoughts of established practitioners about embracing contention. One music director stresses the need for embracing the contribution of the African diaspora through musical genres in theatre:

> African American MDs are generally not acknowledged at all, and that's important as there is an amazing contribution that African American MDs brought to Broadway – they brought [styles such as] jazz [... and] gospel, et cetera.

Further discussion of visible experienced trends unearths pivotal questions on access and inclusivity for leading practitioners, with one music director asking: 'Out of [thousands] of musicians in New York, how many on Broadway are Black?' Furthermore, there are questions about how minority music directors are received in duties of leadership, with one music director bravely recounting:

> I conducted a production [...] which [was] predominantly a White show, and I felt alone. And though people are progressive, some musicians may not want to see a Black conductor, particularly when they think a Black conductor is conducting what is their work.

The comment highlights questions of the history of this in theatre. Music director Linda Twine, Broadway conductor of *Jelly's Last Jam* and *The Color Purple* and a former conductor for Lena Horne, discusses her thoughts in early stages of her career in an early 1980s interview with *Ebony* magazine:

> There is discrimination against African Americans. Look in the pits, and you see mostly White faces, although it is slightly better now than a few years ago.
>
> (Stein, 1982, p. 50)

Twine continues on to describe her fervent aspirations and efforts towards expanding these opportunities to both people of colour and women, whom she remarks may not have had the same circumstances for exposure. Evidently, these thoughts demonstrate frustration and evidential value in considering any lack of involvement of Black music directors on Broadway today. Note again the 2014 newspaper article I mentioned earlier, 'Black Conductors Make History on Broadway' (Pittsburgh Courier, 2014): an issue with the celebration of a disintegrated model of the disallowance of minorities into leadership roles is worth noting. Wilkins Catanese further affirms this as a prime exemplification of what I would like to propose as a constructed institutional permanence – a state where music directors through virtue of systematic organization and continued institutionalized constructs, both via role and race, have not only found themselves in a stagnant condition of being unrecognized, but furthermore as a minority find themselves trapped within the work and construct of their own identity and existence.

Consider Music Director Linda Twine's thoughts in the early 1980s: she continues on in her *Ebony* interview to affirm that Black practitioners and creatives often end up involved with almost exclusively Black-centralized works. Upon first inspection, this appears to be an ideal and honourably equitable mandate: Black artists are working and performing in works that represent them and that they are most able to fundamentally represent. Conversely, this paradigm only further perpetuates the institutional permanence faced perhaps most staunchly by the Black community. We recognize the unpleasantness of embracing the idea of discrepancy in treatment. However, Wilkins Catanese does embrace this, juxtaposing W.E.B. Du Bois' thoughts with a perceived progressive twenty-first-century mindset:

> DuBois's concerns could now be reframed to assert that the problem of the twenty-first century is the problem of the color-blind: those who wish to disavow the continued material manifestations of race in our society: For reasons both well intentioned and sinister, a significant number [...] believe that a total ignorance of race is the obvious, and only, solution to the problems that an acute attention to race has brought to our society.
>
> (Wilkins Catanese, 2014, p. 6)

Astoundingly, the very manufactured notions we revile and seek to dissolve are the ones we inadvertently preserve: 'ironically, color blindness, through its efforts to dematerialize racial difference, offers itself as the structural vehicle through which material racialized differences and discrimination will be overcome' (Wilkins Catanese, 2014, p. 6). Playwright August Wilson sought to further express this dissatisfying hypothesis in his work with Black actors and in doing exclusively Black works for Black theatre companies. In Wilson's view, the conditional absorption of Black cultural resources into these institutions (commercial theatres) diluted rather than reinforced the strength of Black culture, not because of the undesirability of cross-racial collaboration, but because of the intermittent rather than sustained nature of these mainstream theatres' engagement with Black culture, and through the disproportionate number of opportunities extended to Black actors in which they could 'transcend' rather than engage with their racial and cultural specificity. (Wilkins Catanese, 2014, p. 47)

We Shall Overcome: Moving Forward

Through surveillance of role versus race, artist versus labourer, we consider, given our histories, how we seek to move forward. What is the music director's role in the history of musical theatre? How are we benefiting and serving our art in preserving it? And how can this be accomplished?

In beginning to answer these questions, I would propose that anyone who is ignorant of their past is in proper form to repeat it. Examining the historical relevancy and providing additional survey on the people who are responsible for designing the function of the music director is crucial in uncovering how they worked, and what individual contributions to the field were provided. As seen earlier, accolades can be frequently tossed out with a pat on the back in accomplishing integration – for example, many individuals have been in turns cast as 'the first' African American music director or conductor: variously William Accooee in 1896; Will Marion Cook in 1903; Everett Lee for *Carmen Jones* (1943); Cornelius Tate for *Hair* (1969); and Dr Joyce Brown as the first woman for *Purlie* (1970). The inconsistency within identification allows for these names to slip through the cracks, along with many others not mentioned at length in this chapter but eager for unearthing: Shelton Becton, Joesph Joubert, Zane Mark, Daryl Waters, Linda Twine, Joyce Brown, Chapman Roberts, Neal Tate, Thom Bridwell, Leah Richardson, Margaret Harris, Danny Holgate, Harold Wheeler, Frank Owens, Hank Jones, J. Leonard Oxley. All of these people, despite discovery sometimes only within buried archives, have laid a pathway worth exploration. As those whose names are forgotten are unearthed, we discover in their methodologies how their work was developed.

An insight into processes on past productions may help to devise a system by which future music directors can find inspiration and assistance – an absence frequently experienced by people going into this industry. As a staunch advocate of practice as research, to me this could not be more relevant than in the practice of music direction. As the role of the music director is of a fluid nature, the requirement of flexibility often brings uncertainty of executional framework. Background structure will provide stability, both to the craft and the art. In revisiting methodology and practice as research, I emphasize the importance of developing a practice and form of notation in which the trajectory of the music director may be tracked: including thoughts, ideas and actions taken during pre-production, in conducting and leading rehearsals, up to and including dissemination of the role to collegial pit musicians and subsequent directors on tour or in other productions.

Ultimately, the reconstruction of lost labours – both in role and in race – must be embraced for what it needs to be: a reconstruction. The acknowledgement of the shortfalls within our theatre community in fully acknowledging the music director in all its realms, whether in recognition in performance to the public via greater prominence, in equal appreciation through our own circles (reinstating that 'Tony Award for Music Direction'?) or by sheer higher virtue in embracing greater ownership in the rehearsal space. Not only must we embrace this within the role, but we must accept the history of a standardized approach towards the liminal nature of this role, and by doing so, reject the closed institutionalized tendencies of the colour-blind past in opening up opportunity to leaders of all multiplicities. This could hold no more truth than within the periphery of the theatre practitioner community. Black practitioners must seek to lead musicals that sit outside of a Black-centralized idiom, while the theatre community must actively seek to employ practitioners of all minority standings in all shows, regardless of casting, setting or profile. Exploration of Black works by Black practitioners is impactful but not enough; transparency throughout the entire community is key in the synthesis of dissolving current constraints of liminality, intersectionality and institutional permanence for not only minority music directors but music direction at large. Institutionalized permanence of expectations within role and race must be rejected, as homogeneity of approach to style and content is discarded and all practitioners are guided into projects across all spectrums. The impetus points in a promising direction, but the road is long, and we must be wary of taking our hands from the steering wheel. This chapter calls for academics and students to carry on exploring the works and people beyond the scope of this chapter that will illuminate the history of the music director; considering the numerous practitioners involved in works like *Shuffle Along* or earlier works such as *In Dahomey* (1903), or seeking the insights into the role of practitioners and minorities that await discovery within the rich history of British musical theatre and its music directors.

Bibliography

Barbanel, J. (1982) Lehman Engel, 71, Conductor of Broadway Musicals, Dead. *New York Times*, 30 August. Available at: www.nytimes.com. Accessed 16 June 2017.

Bennett, R.R. & Ferencz, G.J. (1999) *The Broadway Sound: The Autobiography and Selected Essays of Robert Russell Bennett*. Rochester, NY: University of Rochester Press.

Bowen, J.A. (ed.) (2007) *The Cambridge Companion to Conducting*. Cambridge: Cambridge University Press.

Bunn, D.A. (2017) Interview by the author, 2 June 2017.

Church, J. (2015) *Music Direction for the Stage: A View from the Podium*. New York: Oxford University Press.

Colbert, S.D. (2017) *Black Movements: Performance and Cultural Politics*. New Brunswick, NJ: Rutgers University Press.

Crenshaw, K. (1991) Mapping the Margins: Intersectionality, Identity Politics, and Violence against Women of Color. *Stanford Law Review*, 43(6), 1241–1299.

Crenshaw, K. (2016). The Urgency of Intersectionality [Video file]. Retrieved from www.ted.com/talks/kimberle_crenshaw_the_urgency_of_intersectionality. Accessed 20 June 2017.

Dicker/Sun, G. (2008) *African American Theater: A Cultural Companion*. Cambridge: Polity Press.

Engel, L. (1974) *This Bright Day: An Autobiography*. New York: Macmillan.

Gottschild, B.D. (1998) *Digging the Africanist Presence in American Performance: Dance and Other Contexts*. Westport, CT: Praeger.

Graziano, J. (2014) Invisible Instruments: Theater Orchestras in New York, 1850–1900. In Spitzer, J. (ed.), *American Orchestras in the Nineteenth Century* (pp. 109–129). Chicago, IL: University of Chicago Press.

Harbin, B.J., Marra, K. & Schanke, R.A. (eds.) (2005) *The Gay and Lesbian Theatrical Legacy: A Biographical Dictionary of Major Figures in American Stage History in the pre-Stonewall Era*. Ann Arbor, MI: University of Michigan Press.

Henderson, L. (1987) Audition Notes [Document] Schomburg Center for Research in Black Culture, Manuscripts, Archives and Rare Books Division, New York Public Library, Luther Henderson Papers, 1909–1985.

Hill, E. (1987) *The Theater of Black Americans: A Collection of Critical Essays*. New York: Applause.

Jackson, R. (2005) *Performance Practice: A Dictionary-Guide for Musicians*. London: Routledge.

Johnson, E.P. (2009) *Appropriating Blackness: Performance and the Politics of Authenticity*. Durham, NC: Duke University Press.

Johnson, J.W. & Wilson, S.K. (1995) *The Selected Writings of James Weldon Johnson*. New York: Oxford University Press.

Lane, S. (2015) *Black Broadway: African Americans on the Great White Way*. Garden City Park, NY: Square One Publishers.

Manley, M. (2016) Making Musical History with Alex Lacamoire. *International Musician: Official Journal of the American Federation of Musicians of the United States and Canada*, 114(11), 18–19.

Mordden, E. (2013) *Anything Goes: A History of the American Musical Theatre*. New York: Oxford University Press.

Oja, C.J. (2014) *Bernstein Meets Broadway: Collaborative Art in a Time of War*. New York, NY: Oxford University Press.

Pittsburgh Courier (2014) Black Conductors Make History on Broadway, 20 July. Available at: www.newpittsburghcourieronline.com. Accessed 17 June 2017.

Sissle, N. (2002). [Liner Notes]. In Sissle & Blake's *Shuffle Along* [CD]. New York: New World Records.

Stein, R. (1982) Lena's Conductor, *Ebony*, 38(2), 46, 50.

Sullivan, J.J. (2016) 'Shuffle Along' and the Lost History of Black Performance in America. *New York Times*, 24 March. Available at: www.nytimes.com/2016/03/27/magazine/shuffle-along-and-the-painful-history-of-black-performance-in-america.html?mcubz=0. Accessed 23 June 2017.

Suskin, S. (2009) *The Sound of Broadway Music: A Book of Orchestrators and Orchestrations*. New York: Oxford University Press.

Suskin, S. (2010) *Show Tunes: The Songs, Shows, and Careers of Broadway's Major Composers*, 4th edition. New York: Oxford University Press.

Symonds, D. (2011) Orchestration and Arrangement: Creating the Broadway Sound. In Knapp, R., Morris, M. & Wolf, S. (eds.), *Oxford Handbook of the American Musical* (pp. 266–280). New York: Oxford University Press.

Valencia, B. (2014) A Method for Musical Theatre Dramaturgy. In Romanska, M. (ed.), *The Routledge Companion to Dramaturgy* (pp. 342–347). Abingdon: Routledge.

Wilkins Catanese, B.W. (2014) (2014) *Problem of the Color[Blind]: Racial Transgression and the Politics of Black Performance*. Ann Arbor, MI: University of Michigan Press.

Wintz, C.D. & Finkelman, P. (2004a) *Encyclopedia of the Harlem Renaissance* (Vol. 1 A–J). New York: Routledge.

Wintz, C.D. & Finkelman, P. (2004b) *Encyclopedia of the Harlem Renaissance* (Vol. 2 K–Y). New York: Routledge.

7

The Evolution of Musical Theatre in Spain Throughout the Twentieth and Twenty-First Centuries

Alejandro Postigo

Over the last few decades, Spain has been subject to imports of mega-musicals – globalized musical theatre shows that replicate the original production anywhere in the world, although often in different languages. While these shows have revitalized the Spanish musico-theatrical industry of the twenty-first century, the narratives and idiosyncrasy of mega-musical imports has also eclipsed or ignored the cultural and historical frameworks of the Spanish musical. This chapter will explore the trajectory and influences of musical theatre forms developed in Spain with aims to understand the financial and socio-political contexts that have led to the present cultural landscape and the identity crisis that currently characterizes the Spanish musical.

Musical theatre in Spain, as in many other places around the world, has developed interculturally. The first manifestations of musical theatre found in Spain date back to the Middle Ages, when music accompanied religious worship with a tendency towards theatricality. Liturgical acts and representations like the popular *Canto de la Pasión* (*Easter Passion Cantata*), dating from the sixteenth century, might be considered forerunners in the combined use of music and drama, but the main exemplar of Spanish musical theatre history is the *zarzuela*, a representative Spanish musical theatre genre initially under the influence of foreign imports such as Italian opera or French comic opera, and popularized by the mid-nineteenth century as a response to the monarchic impositions of foreign genres during previous centuries (for more on the origins of musical theatre in Spain see Fernández-Cid, 1975).

In the twentieth century, Spain experienced a series of key political episodes, the most decisive being the Spanish Civil War (1936–1939) that transformed the progressive left-wing Republican government of 1932 into a fascist dictatorship that lasted for almost 40 years. This change impacted all aspects of society, including the arts, and the old-fashioned *zarzuela* became quickly replaced by indigenous and ideologically influenced pro-Franco revues. These revues enjoyed a prolific existence throughout the first few decades of the fascist dictatorship but suffered a decline from the late 1960s, aggravated further in the 1970s and 1980s, which led the genre to near extinction. This exhaustion of the musical theatre genre in Spain left a vacuum in the entertainment industry quickly filled by Anglo-American blockbuster imports like *Jesus Christ Superstar* or *Man of la Mancha*.

The replacement of decadent Spanish revues by foreign mega-musicals has created a commercial trend now difficult to reverse, as these shows attract spectators in far more copious numbers than the autochthonous musicals ever managed. This begs the question of whether the cultural identity of the Spanish musical will be forever jeopardized by capitalist principles or if there is a way forward for the Spanish musical to re-emerge. Throughout the chapter, I will look in detail at this cultural evolution with aims to throw some light over the identity crisis of the Spanish musical and analyse its present and future alternatives.

The *Zarzuela*: Forerunner of the Spanish Musical

The *zarzuela* is a lyric-dramatic genre that has married music and theatre in Spain for over 365 years, and has widely represented Spanish cultural patrimony abroad. The *zarzuela* combines operatic and popular song and dance with spoken word and evolved from the mid-seventeenth century, known as the Baroque period of *zarzuela*, to the early twentieth century, the Romantic period of *zarzuela* (Fernández-Cid, 1975). The *zarzuela* originated from the inclusion of musical numbers into what was known as *teatro breve* (short theatre pieces) during the kingdom of

Felipe IV (1621–1665), and with the favour of Spanish nobility it became an established convention in Spain. The first *zarzuelas* were 'intended as court entertainments [...] and seem to have included more comedy than other court plays' (Stein 1993, p. 261, in MacCarthy, 2007, p. 28). With the setting to music of *sainetes* (comic sketches) and *entremeses* (short farces) that combined sung and spoken sections and musical interludes, *zarzuelas* took their name from King Felipe IV's *Zarzuela* palace in Madrid where they were initially performed (Lamas, 2012, p. 195). *Zarzuela* then moved into public theatres, with song and dance fused into a sort of variety show (for more on the origins of the *zarzuela* see Lamas, 2012).

At the beginning of the nineteenth century, various tendencies in musical theatre coexisted in Spain: Spanish translations of Italian and French operas; Spanish scores attached to foreign texts; and the development of new musical theatre materials directly in Spanish. By the mid-nineteenth century, the word *zarzuela* had acquired common currency and high-profile composers like Barbieri wrote and popularized what are now recognized as masterpiece *zarzuelas* like *Pan y toros* (*Bread and bullfighting*, 1864) and *El barberillo de Lavapiés* (*The Little Barber of Lavapiés*, 1874), mainly three-act pieces with complex music and libretti inspired by eighteenth-century Spanish history. The *zarzuela* soon became the primary music theatre genre in Spain, experiencing a golden age in the period between 1875 and 1910. During the twentieth century, *sainetes* (short farces) and *revistas* (revues) replaced most *zarzuelas*, which lost popularity and momentum. The decline of *zarzuela* coincided with the rise of cinema, which in Spain began with the filming of *zarzuelas* by Segundo de Chomón (1871–1929) in 1910. Film prompted a shift from live performance to recordings of *zarzuelas* (Lamas, 2012, p. 207). *Zarzuela* had difficulties gaining a place in theatre companies' repertoires, given the complexity and high cost of their productions. In 1946, Matilde Muñoz considered that *zarzuela* was destined to oblivion; librettists at that time were focusing on simpler forms like modern comedy sketches, with easier productions and cheaper modest costumes (Muñoz, 1946, p. 159). As Muñoz predicted, *zarzuela* did not find a way to reinvent itself as a means of survival and eventually faded away, making room for new forms of entertainment. At present, *zarzuela* is treated as 'high art', which creates a disconnection with the idea of popular entertainment and social impact that once differentiated it from opera. The only performance space that offers full-year seasons of *zarzuela* is Teatro de la Zarzuela in Madrid; Barcelona's Gran Teatre del Liceu features occasional performances but Madrid's Teatro Real opts largely for an opera programme. Although there have been no new *zarzuelas* composed since the mid-twentieth century, some directors, like Calixto Bieito and Lluís Pasqual, have provided innovative productions, showing how the genre can be dramaturgically pruned and re-contextualized to offer theatrically innovative social commentaries for the contemporary age (Lamas, 2012, p. 209).

Zarzuela is now considered a highly representative Spanish genre. It differs from opera through the inclusion of spoken scenes, but mainly through populist themes that historically attracted a lower-class audience. However, authors like Arrieta considered that the name '*zarzuela*' deeply hurt the development of comic opera in Spain:

> *Zarzuela* is just opera with spoken scenes, what in France is called Comic Opera and has been cultivated throughout many years, without the French lamenting about this sort of spectacle that in Spain is qualified as hybrid and unworthy by those who should respect it.
>
> (Arrieta, in Fernández-Cid, 1975, p. 51)[1]

The rise of *zarzuela* needs to be seen in relation to the position of opera in Spain, for *zarzuela* drew on and was nourished by its competition with opera. Each art form was associated with a different audience demographic: opera in the nineteenth century was viewed as an upper-class entertainment where nobility gathered to be seen, while *zarzuela* with its urban tales of popular folk triumphing over adversity animated lower-class audiences. While opera's influence waned in Madrid in the early twentieth century, leading to the close of the Teatro Real in 1925, *zarzuela* was celebrated as an indigenous art form and enjoyed a cultural capital in Madrid which continued through the early decades of the Franco regime, for the dictatorship was keen to promote a vision of Spain rooted in national art forms like the *zarzuela*. Its adaptability and its ability to spawn smaller siblings, like the *género chico*, helped it adapt in ways that opera could not. The roots of the *revista* owe much to the forms of musical theatre pioneered by *zarzuela*. *Zarzuela* is currently considered a Spanish traditional genre that requires government support and preservation – with the Teatro de la Zarzuela being one of its most generously subsidised theatres: Lamas argues that 'the genre has exhausted its own creative means and now remains a historical relic' (Lamas, 2012, p. 193). However, it originated interculturally as a response to Italian and French operatic imports and bears the imprints of a range of theatrical and musical styles.

The *Revista*: Spanish Revues

In 1886, a *zarzuela* called *La Gran Vía* propelled a renovation of the Spanish genre, making a transition towards what we widely regard as 'musical theatre'. Its authors defined it as *'revista-lírico-fantástica-callejera'* (lyrical-fantastical-streetwise revue). The four words contained in this title anticipated the new upcoming genre (revue), but still clarified the preservation of style (lyrical) and reaffirmed its popular orientation (streetwise). The 1880s witnessed a veritable increase in popularity of the so-called minor theatre forms (*género chico*, *sainetes*, vaudevilles and other farces and sketches set to music). The *revista* (revue) was born in Spain in the late 1880s as a genre featuring political and social news in a caricatured way; these were comical vaudeville plays with musical numbers that often had little relation to the plot of the piece. Revues and operettas with their zappier, pacier rhythm became the favourite type of show of audiences who were tiring of the long, repetitive plots of *zarzuela*. Musical theatre became a source of income for many authors and composers alternating the writing of *zarzuela*s with *revistas*.

In the late nineteenth century, Barcelona audiences showed little interest in the Madrilenian 'born-and-bred' revues. So Catalan artists developed their own particular style that resembled the Parisian model and style of variety, incorporating female nudity and extravaganzas. The early revues were thus born with influences from the French *género ínfimo* (racy genre), taking place at smaller cabaret clubs before slowly expanding into larger-scale theatre venues. By that time, the *zarzuela* was in clear decline, its audience opting instead for the incipient revues. The *género ínfimo* pieces had a different format and non-linear narratives, and featured diverse artists from different disciplines (singers, dancers, and actors). As the genre developed, connecting plots between the musical numbers were written; these were light and of minor importance since the popularity of these shows was based around the spectacular nature of new musical numbers, involving extravagant choreographies and lavish effects.

In post-Civil War Spain, racy revues had replaced the big romantic *zarzuelas* in popularity; however, they had to confront the obstacle of the new regime's censorship that opposed any sexual innuendos or political mockery of the new government and its rules. The erotic *cuplé*, wildly popular in the 1910s and 1920s, gradually gave way to more 'respectable' variety shows. In an inspired business initiative, lead actress and impresario (sympathetic to the new regime) Celia Gámez proposed a new musical comedy formula that she defined as *zarzuelas cómicas modernas* (modern-comical *zarzuela*) in order to keep both censors and audiences happy. Her initiative was in part a response to the proliferation of musical comedies, considered to be 'something American' and a real threat in times of political and cultural autarchy (Patterson, 2010, p. 18). *La Cenicienta del Palace* (*Hotel Palace's Cinderella*, 1940) was considered by some to be the first musical comedy with characteristics from the Spanish revues from before the Civil War such as *Las Leandras* (1931) or *La pipa de oro* (*The Golden Pipe*, 1932). The borrowed characteristics included *costumbrista* themes and folkloric tunes. The new approach was determined by a sense of spectacle and solemnity inherited from other European and American productions of the time (Montijano Ruiz, 2010, p. 129).

The censorship introduced at the end of the Civil War prohibited any reference to these works as 'revues' because of the political associations of the term – the regime had concerns about the potential of racy jokes to ridicule the regime and so authors renamed them to avoid potential problems. As such, they came to be known as '*humorada cómico-lírica, pasatiempo cómico-lírico, zarzuela cómica-moderna, operetta cómica*', etc. (modern *zarzuela*, lyrical-comic entertainment, comic operetta…) – just a few of the many combinations of terms that defined this increasingly popular genre (Montijano Ruiz, 2010, p. 129). With the new imposition of the fascist dictatorship and the censorship imposed upon the *revista*, a new cultural movement in the 1940s known as the 'empire of folklore' came to encompass all theatre shows that included folkloric numbers such as flamenco and *copla* songs.

Despite the socio-economic difficulties of the time, new revue companies emerged during these years, providing diversion to suffering audiences who had survived the war.[2] These companies both reprised conservative classics of the genre and staged new and successful revues like *Yola* (1941) and *La Blanca doble* (*The Double Blanca*, 1947) that coexisted with the newly fashionable *copla* and folkloric spectacles. The 1950s saw a proliferation of the revue productions of the 1940s with little innovation; by the 1960s, with the rise of television and the retirement of established stars of the time, lyric performance was undergoing a crisis of identity. The main revue companies kept touring and new composers and librettists appeared, but the quality of the materials decreased progressively. The genre relied on big names but audiences got tired of the *revista*, which in that period 'seemed doomed to disappear' (Montijano Ruiz, 2010, p. 208).

Indeed, the 1960s were critical for musical theatre in Spain: there were practically no openings of new shows, no new *zarzuelas*, and operas were primarily restricted to Barcelona's Teatre Liceu. Revues did not have the impact they had enjoyed in previous decades and even folkloric shows experienced a decline. In this music theatre crisis, modern singers, music hall artists and comical actors compensated for their lack of musical technique with some vernacular and populist attitudes that replicated the stereotypical attitudes and ways of speaking of the lower classes; this marked a shift in the stardom so far attributed to gifted singers but now associated with these performative qualities. Just as with some contemporary mega-musicals, orchestras were reduced in number and electrically amplified with pre-recordings, interpolations, microphones and loudspeakers; and concert galas by popular artists that took the barren ground left from previous national music theatre manifestations.

With the arrival of democracy in 1975, a time of great social change took place in Spain: censorship was abolished in 1977; adultery, homosexuality and the sale of contraception decriminalized in 1978; divorce legalized in 1981; and abortion legalized in 1984. The disappearance of censorship affected once again the development of the revues: female nudity was permitted on stage, plots became predictable in that they repeated the same patterns, even though still funny, and new scores recycled hits from the past (Montijano Ruiz, 2010, p. 221). According to critic Lorenzo López Sáncho, the Spanish revue became:

> a book in between the *sainete* (sketch) and a comical toy, musical numbers interpolated without coherence with a plot or narrative, happy music (and modern if possible), girls' and – for a number of years now – boys' ballet ensembles.
>
> (in Montijano Ruiz, 2010, p. 238)[3]

In 1975, Fernández-Cid complained about the scarcity of new Spanish musical theatre works, and expressed a concern about the potential disappearance of Spanish musical theatre.[4] *Zarzuela* and *revista* experienced life cycles that evolved with the societies of the times in which they were first performed and popularized but they did not regenerate as those societies underwent transformation. These genres were linked to a populist reflection of societal archetypes, and being framed by political contexts such as censorship were unable to evolve beyond their imposed restrictions. However, whereas some genres experienced longer lives and developed along with the evolving society (as with *zarzuela* which survived over a number of centuries), others only lasted a few decades (*revista* and folkloric shows).

With the demise of local musical genres and the new openings offered by democracy in the period after 1975, Spanish producers looked to the US and the rest of the European continent for musical products, identifying an opportunity to catch up with the world which turned into a relationship of dependence on imported culture that has proved such a hallmark of Spain's artistic cultural development over the last 40 years. Patterson describes the first years of democracy as a period in which Anglophone musical theatre becomes a 'mandatory reference for those who want to invest in musical theatre'. The new foreign products effectively crippled Spanish musical theatre which was not able to compete with these works, as producers were unwilling to take the risk of investing in local musicals of a particular scope or scale (Patterson, 2010, p. 24).[5]

By the 1980s very few revue artists remained; revues had moved to discos, casinos and gay clubs, which altered the form towards an overtly 'queer' aesthetic including political parody, fewer musical numbers, and more choreography. *Revistas* were viewed as passé. As nudity and permissiveness became a feature of the culture of the transition, these shows could no longer claim *risqué* as a unique selling point. Audiences lost interest and composers, showgirls and comedians moved to other forms of entertainment. The genre effectively disappeared from the Spanish stages (Montijano Ruiz, 2010, p. 242).

The decline of *zarzuelas* and revues called for a different type of show, but the influence of the Anglo-American musical had not really fed into the work of Spanish composers as Spanish musical theatre had historically been fed from regional and popular folklore and never established a link with the American stage musical. Even though the first American musical import took place in Spain in 1955 when director José Tamayo directed a version of *South Pacific* at Teatro de la Zarzuela, the shift only fully materialized in democracy through what we know as pop music, a style that appeals to a new, younger generation of spectators that has bought into the idea of the global musical (Patterson, 2010, p. 27).[6]

The (Global) Musical

The new constitution of 1978 moved away from the centralization policies pursued by Franco's regime and implemented a policy of political autonomy. Difference was more readily recognized. Spain opened its doors to foreign influences, and this deeply affected the development of musical theatre. British and American musicals were translated into Spanish versions, progressively establishing themselves with audiences and so serving as growing commercial enterprises. According to philologist Marta Mateo, the first mega-musical import production to Spain was *Jesus Christ Superstar* (Madrid, 1975). This became a big success followed by other hits: *Les Misérables* (1992, produced by José Tamayo, Plácido Domingo and Cameron Macintosh), *El diluvio que viene* (*After Me the Deluge*, 1996), *West Side Story* (1997) and also a few flops, such as *A Chorus Line* (1984) which competed with a few revues and *zarzuela* repositions that were still very much in the collective memory, such as *Vaya par de gemelas* (*What a Pair of Twins*, featuring popular artist Lina Morgan, 1981–1983) and anthology *Mamá, quiero ser artista* (*Mom, I Want to be an Artist*, featuring popular artist Concha Velasco, 1986). These were revue successes of the decade before the genre completely disappeared from the Spanish stages, leaving compilations as the only remains (Montijano Ruiz, 2010, p. 259).

The background in which musical imports proliferated was not always favourable as musicals were initially seen as 'americanadas' (typical American things). 1974 saw the creation of Dagoll Dagom, a Catalan company (and first theatre company in Spain) almost entirely dedicated to the creation and production of musical theatre. Its own productions of *Antaviana* (1978) and *Mar i Cel* (*Sea and Sky*, 1989) enjoyed good audience support, and positioned the company as a reference point in the creation of Spain's autochthonous musical theatre. But the company combined the production of new musicals with some imports such as *Evita* (1981) and *The Mikado* (1986).

A milestone in the importation of musical theatre in Spain was *Man of La Mancha* produced by Luis Ramírez at the Teatro Lope de Vega in Madrid in 1997. It became a phenomenal success, with an average daily audience of 1400 people and an estimated box office profit of 400 million pesetas (approximately €2.5 million) in the first six weeks of its run. Because of popular demand, the musical was brought back to Madrid in 2004 and toured in 2005. Following this success, producer Ramírez acquired the rights to produce the Broadway hit *Grease* in 1999, disproving the popular saying that Spain 'could not do musicals' (Mateo, 2008, p. 324). Other producers like José Tamayo also attempted to bring mega-musicals to Spain by dedicating some theatre venues like Teatro Apolo to the exclusive production of musicals. This idea did not quite work during the 1980s, but it has now become a reality as theatre venues such as Lope de Vega, Coliseum, Rialto, Calderón and Nuevo Alcalá are almost entirely turned over to the production of stage musicals. At the turn of the twenty-first century, a group of producers intended to turn Madrid's Gran Vía into a reproduction of New York's Broadway. Since then, Madrid has become the second European capital in terms of the production of musicals, only surpassed by London

(Mateo, 2008, p. 327). This has involved the upgrading of venues such as the expansion of Lope de Vega and the Coliseum to be able to host the complex sets that are part of the visual thrills of the mega-musical.[7] Nevertheless, only a very limited number of foreign productions reach the Spanish stages compared to the development of musicals in London and New York, partly due to the lack of infrastructure and technology, and partly because Spanish audiences are still somehow new to this musical theatre tradition.

Following the globalization trend that has ruled musical theatre in the twenty-first century, Spanish productions have increasingly resembled their Anglo-American originals. Since 2003, with the Spanish production of *Cabaret* at the Nuevo Teatro Alcalá in Madrid, many of the creative teams from musicals in London and New York have travelled to Spain to recreate their original productions. In the case of some musicals such as *Victor Victoria* (2005) and *The Producers* (2006), translations of the scripts were altered to appeal to local audiences. The gap between the productions' original year of production and their transfer to Spain started to shorten as with John Rando's Broadway hit *The Wedding Singer* (2006); Rando himself directed the Madrid production in Nuevo Teatro Alcalá in 2007, one year after its Broadway premiere. The musical vogue in Spain reflected the return of the popularity of 'spectacle' which had been such a part of *zarzuela*'s appeal. Other factors to take into consideration are the recognition of these musicals as previous hit movies, the collaboration of celebrity singers and actors (such as Raphael, who starred in 2000 in the Spanish musical version of *Jekyll & Hyde*). A big name can help with initial sales and interest, but once a musical is firmly established, less famous actors or singers may take over, as happens on Broadway and in the West End. It is interesting to note that some factors that help build the popularity of musicals abroad, such as the Tony Awards, are not regarded as universal and do not have a direct effect on the scheduling of musicals in Spain (Mateo, 2008, p. 333).

Broadway musicals came to fill the gap left from other previously popular genres such as *revista* or *zarzuela*. The new and imported musicals provided light entertainment, an emotional experience and technical and artistic quality, presenting stories that were not associated with traditional Spanish life (Mateo, 2008, p. 332). As had happened in the late 1970s and early 1980s, Spanish autochthonous productions found growing difficulties in competing with the increasingly well-established international imports. Impresarios increasingly pursued the adaptation of foreign shows instead of investing in the development of national materials (Patterson, 2010, p. 24). Contrary to what happened at the beginning of the nineteenth century with the rise of *zarzuela* in a rebellion against operatic imports from France and Italy, Spain's youth demanded new styles of music and theatre coming from abroad, effectively wanting to forget about anything related to the long years of the dictatorship.

Data from 2005 reveals that more musicals opened in the first five years of the twenty-first century than throughout the entire twentieth century: musicals are becoming a cultural and tourism asset to Spain's largest cities (Patterson, 2010, p. 26). The decline of *zarzuela* was due its lack of innovation under the Franco dictatorship. Instead, early developments of Spanish musical theatre fed from regional types of folklore and from popular music with influences from Latin America and central Europe. But Spanish stage music was rarely influenced by jazz, pop or rock (as Anglo-American musicals are). These styles entered the Spanish cultural spectrum through the discographic rather than the theatre industry. However, a takeover has now materialized through the popularization of jukebox musicals that follow the formula of successful imports like *Mamma Mia*, playing in Spain since 2004, in which the audience identified with the songs and bought into the spectacle as a result of this process of identification. This has led onto a further step in the history of the Spanish musical: the creation of Spanish jukebox musicals, pioneered in 2005 by *Hoy no me puedo levantar* (*Today I Can't Get Up*) that features the songs of 1980s iconic band Mecano.

Hoy No Me Puedo Levantar: Challenging Dominance of Imported Musicals

Hoy no me puedo levantar was a game-changer, the first musical to challenge the dominance of imported musicals at the Spanish theatre box office, and the trailblazer for a new collection of Spanish jukebox musicals that have emerged and continue to find audiences. With an initial budget of 8 million euros, it was able to compete with the imported musicals with its high production values. Its success can be mapped in commercial terms: a million spectators saw it in its first four seasons, with shows playing to a capacity of 85 per cent or above. The success encouraged the production company, Drive, to produce a children's version of the musical, *En tu fiesta me colé* (*I Sneaked into Your Party* 2005), which also brought commercial success with over 70,000 spectators, performing only one matinee per week. This followed the lead of a recent boom for musicals for young people such as the also autochthonous *Antígona tiene un plan* (*Antigone has a Plan*, 2004) or the foreign imports *Annie* (2000) and *101 Dalmatians* (2002). The production of *Hoy no me puedo levantar* was identified as a national response to the success of other international jukebox musicals in Spain like *Mamma Mia* (2004) and was successfully advertised as 'finally a musical in which you'll be able to sing all songs'[8] (Fouz Hernández, 2009, p. 174). The casting processes for this show were widely advertised in all media, generating a high level of expectation. Tickets were sold at 70 euros, a price well above average at the time in Spain, and the formula proved so resonant that *Hoy no me puedo levantar* was exported to Latin America, becoming a huge success in Mexico with more than 400 shows in 2006 and revivals in 2014 and 2017. A 2007 Mexican tour expanded to other Latin American countries and later to the USA and Northern Europe, making it the first contemporary Spanish musical theatre production to be transferred abroad (Fouz Hernández, 2009, p. 173).

Risk and lack of continuity in musical theatre initiatives are ongoing in Spain in the twenty-first century. Anglo-American imports have established their market and national attempts have arguably become experiments mostly reliant on nostalgia, as with *Hoy no me puedo levantar*. Like most Western audiences, Spanish audiences currently tend to attend theatre shows that anticipate commercial success through high-profile marketing campaigns and/or popular actors attached to the opening run. It is difficult for a show without these elements to be noticed by a big audience. Successful musicals in Spain are either produced by franchises in Madrid such as Stage Entertainment, currently responsible for the most conspicuous musical theatre success in Spain thus far, *El Rey León*, showing in Madrid since 2011 with over three million spectators, the longest running musical in Madrid's Gran Vía, or its principal competitor SOM Produce, a new company created from the merger of Drive and Vertigo. These companies now tend to focus on the production of musicals that have been tested abroad, or that have strong associations with Spanish popular culture, such as the Spanish jukebox musicals pioneered by *Hoy no me puedo levantar* and followed by: *Quisiera Ser* (*I'd Wish to Be*, 2007) with songs by Dúo Dinámico; *Es por ti* (*It's Because of You*, 2010) with songs by Cómplices; *Más De 100 Mentiras* (*More Than 100 Lies*, 2012), with songs by Joaquín Sabina; and *Marta tiene un marcapasos* (*Marta has a Pacemaker*, 2012) with songs by Hombres G. There are also smaller productions that have achieved a solid degree of success in Spain like Tricicle's adaptation of Monty Python's *Spamalot* (2008) or *The Diary of Anne Frank* (2008), the first Spanish musical theatre adaptation from a well-known literary source.

There have also been fringe autochthonous productions that have achieved a significant relevance through various runs in Spain, as with *Por los ojos de Raquel Meller* (*Through Raquel Meller's Eyes*, 2006–2013), and internationally, like *Pegados* (*Stuck*, 2010–2014). Also, many established Spanish theatre companies have produced shows in the twenty-first century that combine music and theatre, even though they are not always considered musical theatre by the most dogmatic definitions. A few examples are the revival of *Mamá quiero ser famoso* (*Mom I Want to Be Famous*, 2005) by La Cubana; *Pagagnini* (2007) by Yllana; *El Nacional* (*The National*, 2011) by Els Joglars; *Perséfone, Variaciones mortals* (*Persephone, Mortal Variatons*, 2011) by Els Comediants; and *Time al tiempo* (*Cheat the Time*, 2011) from newest company Ron La La.

The growing popularity of musical theatre led in 2007 to the creation of the Gran Vía Musical Theatre Awards to recognize the labour and excellence of musical theatre produced in Spain, even if largely from imported sources. The establishment of the British and American musical imports has shifted the focus in the Spanish production of musical theatre from composers and librettists to directors, but most especially to performers, who became increasingly recognized and very much in demand as many new imported musicals required all-round performers that could cope with the requirements (singing, dancing, acting) of the new shows. Therefore, a proliferation of drama schools offering a combination of training in these three areas also opened a competitive market for education in this discipline. Even national drama schools like RESAD (Royal Superior School of Dramatic Arts) have implemented a musical theatre strand, which has grown in demand year after year.

In summary, the coexistence of opera and *zarzuela* through centuries facilitated the intercultural influence of opera in the creation of a national Spanish musical theatre genre. The *zarzuela chica* transitioned into the *revista*, a genre that evolved throughout the twentieth century into a 'non-integrated' Spanish musical comedy. The *revista* ended up as a variety spectacle with political commentary and racy content that faded in the late 1990s due to loss of audience interest and disappearance of professionals. *Revista*, like *zarzuela*, are considered largely Spanish genres in content, created in response to the intercultural influences that existed in Spain at the time of their birth, but neither genre significantly incorporated foreign themes, elements or ideas. A shift took place with the arrival of the global musical in Spain. A series of imported shows have progressively conquered the Spanish market by bringing something not seen in Spain before: narratives integrated in music, escapist entertainment in tune with the current tastes of society, often based on powerful nostalgic draws. These have even provided a revolutionary formula for Spanish musicals to develop: the jukebox musical.

The musical is the most popular form of live theatre in America and Britain today, and increasingly in other countries such as Spain. Its success is measured by comparison with other live theatrical and musical genres in terms of commercial profit, as box office records prove. The commodification of Anglophone culture has played a central role in the spread of the musical. As Dan Rebellato explains in *Theatre and Globalization*, mega-musicals function through a franchise system that does not just involve acquiring the rights to a show but rather to the entire original production: the set, costumes, direction, poster, and all associated merchandizing (Rebellato, 2009, p. 41). This ensures that the same original production can be experienced anywhere in the world. Standardization, however, means that the possibilities for responding to place and time are compromised; these musicals cannot generally adapt to a specific cultural context, as alterations of the original production are not contemplated. Consequently, the international influence of Anglophone culture facilitates the exportation of musicals everywhere by somehow collapsing and replacing other cultural systems, which has been the case for Spain during the twenty-first century.

The musical in Spain has grown, introduced innovations and has ultimately secured a position as the theatre genre in most demand by a variety of spectators. Musicals have achieved considerable social relevance in Spain, which is not determined by how long a musical genre 'has lived' in a particular society but by whether it is 'lived socially' (Marti I Pérez, in Mateo, 2008, p. 338). Madrid has become the third capital of the production of musicals in the world today, boasting excellent quality and substantial box office takings, and now even starting to export some ideas or sets. However, there is still a long way to go for the musical here, compared to theatre hubs like London or New York, where musical productions have evolved since the early twentieth century. The considerable expansion of musical theatre in Spain is mainly limited to the twenty-first century, so there are many more foreign musicals yet to be discovered, produced and adapted. But even more importantly, it remains to be seen what the Spanish creators can do to build this genre. Will the rapid expansion of the genre inspire Spanish writers and artists to create sustainable Spanish works? To that extent, maybe the answer to the future lies in looking at the Spanish musical past.

Notes

1. 'La zarzuela es, ni más ni menos, que lo que en Francia se llama ópera cómica, es decir la ópera con escenas habladas, como se viene cultivando muchos lustros ha [...] sin que a nadie se le haya ocurrido lamentarse de esta clase de espectáculos, calificándolos de híbridos e indignos del arte, como aquí lo hacen los que más obligados están a respetarlo' (All translations by the author).
2. The Spanish Civil War (1936–1939) left Spain in desolated conditions of poverty, autarchy, and political persecution, with violent exclusion of the defeated Republicans.
3. Un libro entre el sainete y el juguete cómico, números musicales interpolados sin ninguna conexión con texto o argumento, música alegre y en lo posible, moderna, chicas de ballets y – hace ya bastantes años – boys.

4. A medida que pasa el tiempo y nos acercamos al presente, es difícil encontrar un solo título válido. De continuar este camino, llegará un día en que nuestro teatro cantado pertenezca de lleno a la historia y sólo a ella (Fernández-Cid, 1975, p. 196).

5. El modelo anglosajón va instalándose y convirtiéndose en referencia obligada para todo aquel empresario, autor o compositor que desee hacer una incursión en este género. Sin embargo, eso que a priori parece algo positivo se convierte a la larga en un hándicap importante, ya que algunos intentos de creación puramente nacionales no consiguen pasar el examen y se convierten en experimentos, en evidentes fracasos comerciales la mayoría de las veces, lo que obviamente frena el desarrollo normal de la posible demanda y genera baches que evidencian el temor del empresario a equivocarse y sufrir pérdidas irrecuperables.

6. El relevo se ha materializado a través de lo que llamamos música pop. Interesa a la juventud que, reconociendo canciones muy populares, se deja atraer por la magia del espectáculo.

7. Playwright and academic Dan Rebellato defines mega-musicals as 'visually spectacular, quasi-operatic musical theatre productions, many of them globally successful, performed thousands of times in front of millions of people in hundreds of productions in dozens of cities worldwide' (Rebellato 2006, p. 98).

8. Por fin un musical en el que podrás cantar todas las canciones.

References

Centro de Documentación Teatral (CDT) *Registros de recaudación de espectáculos de teatro musical en Madrid y Barcelona (1994–2008)*. SGAE Database, Spain.

Delgado, M.M. (2003) *'Other' Spanish Theatres*. Manchester and New York: Manchester University Press.

Fernández-Cid, A. (1975) *Cien años de teatro musical en España (1875–1975)*. Madrid: Real Musical, D.L.

Fouz Hernández, S. (2009) Me cuesta tanto olvidarte: Mecano and the Movida Remixed, Revisited and Repackaged. *Journal of Spanish Cultural Studies*, 10 (2), 167–187.

Lamas, R. (2012). *Zarzuela*: Prejudice and Mass Culture in Spain. In Delgado, M.M. & Thatcher, D. (eds.), *A History of Theatre in Spain* (pp. 193–210). Cambridge: Cambridge University Press.

MacCarthy, H.W. (2007) *Cuban Zarzuela and the (Neo)Colonial Imagination: A Subaltern Historiography of Music Theater in the Caribbean.* PhD Thesis, Ohio University, ProQuest.

Mateo, M. (2008) Anglo-American Musicals in Spanish Theatres. *The Translator,* 14 (2), 319–342 (Special Issue: Translation and Music, ed. by S. Susam-Sarajeva, Manchester).

Montijano Ruiz, J.J. (2010) *Historia del teatro frívolo español (1864–2010).* Madrid: Editorial Fundamentos.

Muñoz, M. (1946) *Historia de la zarzuela y el género chico.* Madrid: Editorial Tesoro.

Patterson, M. (2010) *75 años de historia del musical en España (1930–2005).* Madrid: Ediciones y Publicaciones Autor, SRL; Tramart.

Pérez, A. & Andrés, J. (2009) *El teatro musical en España. La Revista (1925–1962),* PhD thesis, Universitat de Valencia.

Rebellato, D. (2006) Playwriting and Globalisation: Towards a Site-Unspecific Theatre. *Contemporary Theatre Review,* 16 (1), 96–112.

Rebellato, D. (2009) *Theatre and Globalisation.* Basingstoke: Palgrave.

8

Reparation and Reanimation in Musical Theatre: Savion Glover's Choreography of *Shuffle Along – Or The Making Of The Musical Sensation of 1921 And All That Followed*

Phoebe Rumsey

In a dexterous moment of storytelling in the second act of the 2016 Broadway musical *Shuffle Along – Or The Making Of The Musical Sensation of 1921 And All That Followed*, composer Eubie Blake (played by Brandon Victor Dixon) steps forward and explains to the audience that three nights in a row, George Gershwin sat behind him not watching the stage but observing his conducting technique and a particular clarinet player, William Grant Still. The accusatory tale and song in the show 'Till Georgie Took 'Em Away' is told through a solo tap dancer 'playing' clarinet in a smoky spotlight, with the Harmony Kings singing and 'patting' downstage right.[1] The dancer begins with simple rhythms, and as the telling of the wrongdoings of the borrowing of Blake's music and style increases, the riffs of the dancing clarinetist grow in complexity, along with the body percussion of the Harmony Kings. The magnitude of the theft is felt through the commanding and forceful tap and rhythm styles. Though Blake's suggestions are done with a sly wink, the notion of appropriation is readily put forth. Certainly lyrics such as 'steal those black notes, steal that rhythm, write a hit song' emphasize the point (*Shuffle Along*, 2016). Importantly, the accentuation and building of tensions in regard to the appropriation of music is done through tap and body percussion, emphatically pointing towards the unashamed borrowing of movement as well as music.

Introduction

The 2016 Broadway musical *Shuffle Along – Or The Making Of The Musical Sensation of 1921 And All That Follows*, with direction and book by George C. Wolfe and choreography by Savion Glover, is a vital addition to the musical theatre canon. In continuance with Wolfe's practice of recovery as resistance, this production has a strong pedagogical and recuperative focus. By (re)telling the story of the making of a show, and reimagining the original artists and their labour, the bodies on stage in the 2016 *Shuffle Along* culturally and politically present the archive of the show, and uphold the legacy of the African American foundations of US musical theatre.

Glover's choreography for the production is a key element to this rebuilding process. His dance palette, heavy with an assortment of tap dance and early-twentieth-century social and popular dance techniques, has an exuberance to it with the intention of recapturing the dynamism and effervescence of the mounting of the original 1921 *Shuffle Along*. Glover not only populates the piece with African American movement signatures of the 1920s, such as shoulder shimmies and early iterations of the Charleston, but he also infuses the show with his characteristic contemporary tap dance expressions as way to connect the past to the present. Wolfe and Glover's dramaturgical reanimation of the original show's journey to Broadway foregrounds its significance in the contemporary moment. Kristin Moriah describes George C. Wolfe's creation as, 'an act of metadrama that became a catalyst for another conversation about racial diversity on Broadway' (Moriah, 2017, p. 178). Indeed, critics were impressed by the necessary task Wolfe took on and the impact of the show. Jesse Green points towards Wolfe's reparative efforts: 'Wolfe bombards a core of ideas about race and culture with a billion showbiz protons to produce both a gorgeous spectacle and a big, smoking crater where your former ideas of Broadway once stood.' (J. Green, 2016)

This chapter explores how Glover's choreographic tactic of creating movement that embodies the nostalgia of the dances from the 1920s also expresses contemporary assertiveness with his more urban-based moves; sheds light on the social and cultural complexity that operated in musical theatre in 1921; and stakes a claim for the African American foundations of musical theatre now. Further, the African American body on stage, as set forth by Wolfe and put in motion by Glover, emblematizes so much of the labour that went into the foundations of Broadway, labour which is largely unrecognized today. Glover's intensity and complexity of move- ment propels this show with a palpable 'no holds barred' ethos that claims a futurity for tap dance and the African American body in performance. As Thomas F. DeFrantz explains, 'movement provokes metacommentary and suggests narratives outside the physical frame of performance' (2002, p. 14). Glover's insistence on paying homage to the lineage of tap in *Shuffle Along* and his assertion to 'create sounds that allow one to think' (Catton, 2016) reanimates the African American presence on Broadway and is a critical call to challenge previous histories and systems of social beliefs that surround the emergence of modernity at the beginning of the twentieth century in the United States. Glover's dedication to the project is further seen in his willingness to go into the show himself, as news was escalating around lead performer Audra McDonald's pregnancy and upcoming leave.

Early Closure

From the beginning, what cannot be overlooked in a discussion of *Shuffle Along – Or The Making Of The Musical Sensation of 1921 And All That Followed* is that, unlike the original *Shuffle Along* of 1921 that enjoyed a 504-performance run and tours for nearly three years after, as well as numerous revivals, the 2016 *Shuffle Along* played only 100 performances and 33 previews. Much press circulated around Audra McDonald's preg- nancy causing the show's early closure. However, McDonald was always planning to leave the show for at least some time to reprise her 2014 Tony Award-winning role in *Lady Day At Emerson's Bar & Grill* in London. The news of her pregnancy nonetheless seemed to have stalled ticket sales, though an excellent replacement, Grammy award winner Rhiannon Giddons, was ready to step in. Catherine M. Young gives three plausible reasons for the show's closure:

> There are three important reasons a show as great as *Shuffle Along* is closing and they don't involve a pregnant star. The show is expensive to run, may be too 'inside' for the casual Broadway consumer, and it could not get out of the long shadow cast by *Hamilton*.
>
> (Young, 2016)

These pragmatic reasonings ring true and help to explain the broader socio-economic functioning of Broadway. Kristin Moriah further explains the complexity surrounding the closure: 'In *The Making Of*'s closing we are witness to some of the paradoxes behind the seeming ascendance of ethnic diversity on the popular stage.' (Moriah, 2017, p. 179) Moriah explains the continued challenges to navigating race and ethnicity in popular entertainment, observing, 'embodied performances of blackness and nuanced depictions of African American history are still at odds with audience expectations' (2017, p. 179). This lack of alignment, however, should not be a reason to stall the creation of works about the African American experience, as is explained by Sandra Seaton, whose great uncle was Flournoy E. Miller. Seaton describes in a 2016 article in *The Dramatist* that when artistic director Jack Viertel was thinking of reviving the original *Shuffle Along* in 2002 as part of the *Encores!* series, he communicated his worries of receiving 'political resistance, especially from the very population we'd be trying to honor', to playwright August Wilson (Seaton, 2016, p. 47). Wilson replied:

> Its presentation would be a historical reminder of that contribution, and its images and portrayal of blacks, though less than sterling, would not be a perpetuation of these images, but a historical reminder of a time when such portrayals were part of the popular culture. I think that is important.
>
> (Wilson in Seaton, 2016, p. 50)

Though the numerous and complex reasons behind the closure 'demonstrates the unsteady role that race and ethnicity continue to play in popular entertainment' (Moriah, 2017, p. 179), avoiding these encounters altogether further underserves those communities. Wolfe and Glover come together to trouble the complexity of this paradoxical framework with a necessary insistence that reanimates and recuperates African American foundational contributions to the musical theatre.

Dramaturgical Strategies

Shuffle Along (2016) revises the original 1921 African American musical, and in so doing speaks to the importance of the continued transformation, and necessary refining and retelling, of musical theatre history for future generations. As part of Wolfe's dramaturgical framework, *Shuffle Along* addresses and then dismantles the commonly accepted historical record many have come to believe – that the foundations of musical theatre were predominantly put in place by white artists such as Ira and George Gershwin, Jerome Kern, Oscar Hammerstein II, and Cole Porter, among others. Wolfe's previous works, such as *The Colored Museum* (1986) or the musical *Jelly's Last Jam* (1992), come from a foundational place aimed to 'unsettle the status quo and upend racial expectations' (Elam, 2014, p. 384). Wolfe's work in *Shuffle Along*, though packaged in perhaps a more heartening manner than the other shows above, is no less punctuated with affirmations of African American contributions to society and theatre, in his ongoing goal to 'carv[e] a new space for African American drama' (Elam, 2014, p. 384). As Jesse Green described earlier, Wolfe shatters previous assumptions about the chronology of US musical theatre history by presenting an alternate historiography which engages with the labour of African American creative practitioners. In this historical sojourn, Wolfe ties the show together using chronological ordinances, helped along by various projections of dates and places, juxtaposed with production numbers and plot points of the original 1921 show to clarify this forgotten history. This self-referentiality (or repossession of theatre by theatre) is key in helping to demonstrate the danger of ignoring this story, and missing the development of society and the role of performance within it.[2]

Wolfe's innovative weaving together of theatrical elements crosses documentary theatre with the contemporary sensibilities and technologies of current Broadway musical theatre. To start, he includes as an insert in the Playbill of the 2016 show a reproduction of the 1921 programme in sepia tones, which contains a half-dozen pictures of the original artists and ensemble, as well as period advertisements. The show alternates between scenes following the narrative of the original show (the story of the shenanigans behind a quasi-fixed mayoral race), and the creating and staging of that show.

Collaboration with Savion Glover

In the historical restructuring of *Shuffle Along*, Wolfe's collaboration with Glover, a Tony Award-winning choreographer for his work in *Bring in 'da Noise, Bring in 'da Funk* (1996), is central to the success of the show and Wolfe's overall mission to bring awareness to the African American ownership of US musical theatre. Glover is able to both navigate and bring together the temporal divide of the show with an intense physicality that speaks to the past, present, and future. Glover is deeply aware of the genealogy and historical rhythms of tap; however, his personal contribution to the form is his determined shift in the genre from an emphasis on entertainment towards a focus on sound and physical expression. The tension between these two dimensions of tap dance in *Shuffle Along* make Glover's work uniquely urgent and powerful. Brian Seibert in *What The Eye Hears: A History of Tap Dancing*, describes the many layers in Glover's work in the earlier *Noise/Funk*: 'Glover's choreography, in its wordless eloquence, conveyed the resilience of African Americans in a form at once symbolic and physical' (Seibert, 2015, p. 469). Glover's choreography has both an embodied sense of the past and a boldness to it that directly re-declares the African American ownership of tap in musical theatre.

Further in this historical vein, the collective emotional connections and explorations of the past Wolfe takes on in *Shuffle Along* set up a nostalgic impulse inherent in the show, one also embodied in the choreography. This embodied nostalgia, however, does not constitute a longing for the past or a looking back through rose-coloured spectacles, but troubles; what

Svetlana Boym calls (in *The Future of Nostalgia*, 2001) 'reflective nostalgia'. Reflective nostalgia suggests a meditation on and retracing of the past; one that opens up the possibility for considering alternate perspectives that may go on to influence future individual actions and reparations. Boym suggests reflective nostalgia 'cherishes shattered fragments of memory and temporalizes space', and that this action advances the possibility for multiple consciousness and levels of meaning (Boym, 2001, p. 49). As Thomas F. DeFrantz observes in a lecture on the work and mission of choreographer Jawole Willa Jo Zollar, 'our bodies are profound not just in the metaphors they inspire but in the memories they contain' (DeFrantz 1997, p. 25). By investigating these embodied memories in performance much can be understood about modernity, our present circumstances, and our relationship with history and culture.

Wolfe's *Shuffle Along* operates in this manner as the show looks to the past as a way of moving forward in regard to African American ownership and authorship of US musical theatre today. Moriah observes, 'In staging their awareness of the dynamics of the popular stage and the limitations of its tropes, black performers in *The Making Of* appeared not just as consumable products but as cultural agents' (2017, p. 181). Markedly, the dancers and choreography of the 2016 *Shuffle Along* bring these ideas forward for consideration. As Jayna Brown describes in *Babylon Girls: Black Women Performers and the Shaping of the Modern* (2008), the female chorus of the original *Shuffle Along* helped shape modernity. She observes, 'the meanings of the black woman's body in motion were central to the anxieties and hopes imbedded in white ideas of the modern city space as well as the politics of black cultural self-referentiality' (Brown, 2008, p. 2). Glover, through his complex choreographic signature, is pointedly staking a claim that black performers of the past, particularly the female chorus dancers, were agents of change both on stage and off. The exuberance, energy and dynamism of the original female chorus in *Shuffle Along*, to draw on the work of Daphne Brooks, 'crafted new forms of narrative agency and corporeal representation in theatricalized spaces' (Brooks, 2006, p. 11). Indeed, the 1921 *Shuffle Along* increased the visibility of female African American dancers and launched the career of various famous performers that emerged from the chorus, including Josephine Baker, Adelaide Hall, and Florence Mills. Brown further explains that the 'New Woman' of the 1920s 'embraced black expressive forms, adopting racialized gestural vocabularies to shape and redefine their own bodies as modern' (2008, p. 3). The immense success of the original *Shuffle Along* thrust these movement and aesthetic styles into mainstream culture to enormous effect and subsequent consumption. As Brenda Dixon Gottschild describes, 'these aesthetic principles became integral signifiers of modernism and were embraced by white Americans as well as Europeans' (Dixon Gottschild, 2000, p. 11). The assumption of African American styles emphatically linked, as Dixon Gottschild observes, 'the black swing era aesthetic and global trends in modernism movements of African American on stage' (2000, p. 5). The complexity within Glover's choreography in the 2016 *Shuffle Along* explicitly gestures to what a landmark production the original was, one that David Savran states 'made jazz and tap dancing obligatory on Broadway' (Savran, 2009, p. 76). Glover's choreography punctuates that point nearly a century later. He situates the female ensemble in the 2016 version with a dominance and dynamism reminiscent of the original chorus.

Choreographic Strategies and Dance Styles

The dance styles of the early twentieth century, when performed in Wolfe's *Shuffle Along*, rich in the flairs and fashions of the 1920s, create the possibility of nostalgic impulses in the audience – longings for a personal or public past, envisioning an alternate or preferred past, seeking a sense of home – that help them to connect to the reparative message of the production. This embodied nostalgia within the dancing bodies to a greater or lesser extent connects to the present moment by its strategic layering of tap, African American social dance styles, and importantly Savion's modern innovations, expertly executed by the energetic and extraordinarily capable cast. The juxtaposition of the new and the old opens up a space that demonstrates that Broadway musical theatre as we know it today owes very much to the inventions of African American artists in both music and dance. In an interview with Adam Green, Glover explains his process of melding the old with the new, 'It's adding the steps and style of the past to the rhythms and sounds of today. It's performing an old-school step with a new-school style – or maybe you take a step from today and execute it in a style from the past' (A. Green, 2016). Through this blending, Glover's choreography is both an homage to the past and a genuflection towards righting the historical record. This move is particularly poignant and steeped in social and political resonance given the cultural forces at work today in social equality movements like Black Lives Matter.

Background: Savion Glover

Glover's history in tap circles and dance communities is well known. He appeared on Broadway at 10 years old in *The Tap Dance Kid* (1985), and went on to *Black and Blue* (1989), for which he became the then youngest person ever to be nominated for a Tony Award. His first collaboration with director and writer George C. Wolfe was in *Jelly's Last Jam* (1992), where he performed with his teacher and tap icon Gregory Hines. Described by Joan Acocella of *The New Yorker* as 'the greatest tap virtuoso of our time, perhaps of all time', and given his training by the fathers and grandfathers of tap, Glover is in effect the bodily archive or physical repository of tap dance (Acocella, 2014). Glover's main mentors, along with Hines, include tap dance greats Buster Brown, Chuck Green, Jimmy Slyde and Lon Chaney. He devoured everything they (and others) had to offer, and developed a well-rounded understanding of the form. Dancer Lisa La Touche, working with Glover in *Shuffle Along* from the very beginning of the initial workshops for the show explains: 'anytime I've ever been in a studio with him, I just get this tiniest window of what this could have been like with any of those guys' (La Touche, 2017). The embodied history that travelled through the greats, from shuffles (the brushing back and forth of the sole of the foot to achieve two quick noises), where feet barely came off the floor, to Jimmy Slyde's slides across the stage, to the fully physicalized style of Hines where the percussiveness of the taps extended through his whole body, is present in Glover. Through his work with these early innovators Glover acquired a fine-tuned knowledge of the history of tap, which he was able to push and pull against en route to devising his own urban, percussive, grounded style of movement. His style emerged as very different from the upright-postured, early tap dance sounds, derived in parts from the loose swinging shuffles and soft-shoe methods. Seibert suggests that perhaps Glover's greatest contribution to the genre is that he 'made tap a young person's game' (Seibert, 2015, p. 463). Glover made it acceptable to internalize the form, to move away from the presentational style previously associated with tap and movie musicals into a mode of interpretation that shared many sensibilities with more modern aesthetics, such as hip hop and street dance. Young dancers were inspired by the more authoritative urban style of percussive and hard-hitting dance, performed to modern music.

Director George C. Wolfe describes the dualities and depth within Glover: 'Savion is a living repository of the history of rhythm [. . .] He got it from the guys who got it from the guys who got it from the guys. But he's also a bridge to the future.' (A. Green, 2016) Having Glover at the creative helm of the movement signature and choreographic structure of the 2016 musical serves to offer up an often overlooked epistemology of the foundations of musical theatre in the United States. Glover's choreography embodies this resurrection (and innovation) by his taking full advantage of the dynamics and depth of tap dancing as a repository of the original movement styles of the production, and melding them with urban sensibilities and design. Glover's choreography functions in this assembly to both shed light on the social and cultural complexity that operated in the performance of musical theatre in 1921, and to stake a claim for the choreographic contributions, historical and ongoing, of African American artists in musical theatre.

The collaboration between Glover, Wolfe, and the onstage contributions of some of the most talented performers on Broadway (Audra McDonald, Brian Stokes Mitchell, Billy Porter, Brandon Victor Dixon) makes *Shuffle Along* a tour de force that emphasizes the fundamental foundation African Americans laid, and the vital contributions they continue to make to musical theatre. The revised musical, 'one of the season's essential tickets', as described by *New York Times* critic Ben Brantley, signals a move to both remind and redefine the foundation of musical theatre, and champion the voices and bodies that made significant inroads at a time when musical theatre was in its nascent form (Brantley, 2016). The unfortunate early closure of the show is telling of various limitations of the musical form. Since the beginning of the genre, headliners and star performers seemed always to be part of producers' plans to guarantee box office returns. Such is the fickle nature of Broadway shows, as sometimes even winning a Tony or Pulitzer Prize will not guarantee a long run, as was the case with *Next To Normal* (2008).

The ephemeral nature of live performance is felt in the disappointment professed by heartbroken cast members and fan groups. In effect, this twist of fate has not allowed *Shuffle Along – Or The Making Of The Musical Sensation of 1921 And All That Follows* to be seen by a vast number of people, inevitably lessening the intended impact. The lack of a cast album and readily available libretto add to the difficulty of reviving the show. La Touche talks about the double meaning within the narrative of the original show being forgotten and the 2016 one coming to a close:

> We lived our version of it, some really dark corners that turned and some huge celebrations and the fact that our cast, our ensemble really stuck together. We became so close throughout the whole process, everyone looked out for one another and it really mattered. Obviously any gig that you have is super significant but you could tell there was a certain vibe that everyone had to be able to tell this story. It was more – we get to tell the story versus we get to be on Broadway.
>
> (La Touche, 2017)

La Touche describes how the dramaturg explained the history leading up to the original show, and how various assistants would put up newspapers on the rehearsal room walls each day, reporting news from the same day 96 years previously.

In *Highbrow/Lowdown: Theater, Jazz, and the Making of the New Middle Class*, David Savran specifies the impact of jazz music on musical theatre that happened with the original show: '*Shuffle Along* modernized musical comedy by introducing a sparkling mélange of ragtime, operetta, and jazz that did more than carry audiences away.' (Savran, 2009, p. 76) This crossover of music styles extended to the show's physical movement, as social dances and movement rhythms evolved alongside jazz music. European dances of the time such as the waltz or the Schottische were taken over by more popular and physically liberating dances of the times, such as the high-energy Charleston.

Wolfe is certainly attuned to the mark *Shuffle Along* made on Broadway in 1921 in terms of the changes in musical styles. He includes a clever moment in the show where Lottie Gee (Audra McDonald) is rehearsing a song to be put in the show – 'I'm Just Wild About Harry' (Harry being a third candidate that enters the mayoral race and comes to win the hearts of citizens, while the two crooked candidates fight among themselves). The song is presented for Lottie to sing as a waltz, one of the common musical structures used in European-styled musical comedy at the time. The song, which has gone on to be one of the most recognizable songs of *Shuffle Along* and often a standalone hit, is practically unrecognizable as a waltz, comical in its construction as a lilting 3/4 time composition. Lottie protests that no one is doing waltzes anymore and asks if some swing could possibly be injected into it. In this moment in the 2016 show there is both humour and artistry on a larger level regarding the style shift, that nods to the proliferation of jazz rhythms into musical comedy. 'I'm Just Wild About Harry' expands into a larger production number as Gertrude Saunders and numerous ensemble members join Lottie. The song is resplendent with the dynamism of jazz and rhythmic complexities, rising to be one of the highlights of the show. This convention in musical theatre of a song starting quite innocently between a singer and a pianist and quickly building to a full-on production number is part of the magic of musical theatre, and of course 'I'm Just Wild About Harry' serves the same purpose. Other examples from the first half of the twentieth century include *Girl Crazy* (1930), with music and lyrics by George and Ira Gershwin, particularly in 'I've Got Rhythm', and *Annie Get Your Gun*'s memorable 'There's No Business Like Show Business' with music and lyrics by Irving Berlin (1946). Dramaturgically, however, in the 2016 *Shuffle Along*, with 'I'm Just Wild About Harry' Wolfe is attempting to capture the transition in musical styles and showcase it for the audience in order to remind them of the aural depth of the shift, demonstrating how musical comedy sounded before and after the influence of African American jazz. The timing of this move coincided with the increased and rapidly growing mechanization of America since the late nineteenth century. The rhythm of America was changing, and nothing symbolized this more than jazz music. The shift in rhythms and move away from European sensibilities was new, yet felt natural in the progressive moment of the 1920s. The infiltration of jazz was unavoidable in many aspects of daily life, and when *Shuffle Along* came along there was an abundance of sounds and physicalities that Wolfe and Glover successfully recreate and recall in their *Shuffle Along,* telegraphed from the start in the lengthy subtitle – *Or The Making Of The Musical Sensation of 1921 And All That Followed.*

Keeping in mind that, as Savran notes, the original *Shuffle Along* was a mix of many strands of music, comedy routines and even costumes, it was still a sort of patchwork of sounds and movements that had worked before in other venues (Savran, 2009, p. 74). From a dance perspective, this meant using forms that were working in the African American performance venues of the moment, from dance halls to smaller cabarets. Tap, shimmies, and animal dances such as the Turkey Trot were part of the swirl of styles that got inserted into the original *Shuffle Along* as it went through road tryouts.[3] Glover's choreography today has similarities: it encompasses the many different dimensions from the past as well as contemporary, of-the-moment dances, just as in the original *Shuffle Along.*

Tap as a Conversation

One of the most striking moments in the 2016 musical comes when there is a stand-off between those performers who went on to the musical *The Chocolate Dandies* (1924) and those who went on to *Rang Tang* (1927). Wolfe has Glover embody this heated conflict, using the ensemble to perform a sort of competition between the two casts of the shows. By creating an intense physical argument or competition between performers, Glover does two things. Firstly, he both celebrates and underlines the importance of the conversational style that always and already existed in tap dance. Much like improvisation in jazz music, there exists in tap dance a fundamental passing back and forth of rhythms, or call and response, as a mode of showmanship and physical communication. In so doing, Glover makes sure that this basic characteristic of tap dance is represented. Secondly, in this conversation there is a trading and negotiating back and forth of styles, beginning with more traditional styles increasing to more contemporary tap modulations showing the progressive nature of tap dancing, while also locating it in the origins of the form as a competitive dance practice.

This communicative style can be considered thematic of Glover's work, as seen in *Noise/Funk*. Glover creates conversation through movement. This back and forth dance-off, happening midway through the second act of the 2016 *Shuffle Along*, becomes a stepping-off point towards more contemporary choreography in the show. Later in the second act, Glover has the ensemble dressed in long pants and flat shoes performing behind and around a scrim, functioning as a sort of framing device to the growing complications between the artists. The ensemble, no longer in the 1920s show's makeshift costumes, or in the everyday wear of the 1921 framing narrative, execute more percussive and rhythmic moves that have a force and dynamism; this brings the African American tenure of the form distinctly into the present moment. Stomps are louder, arms ricochet forward and back in reaction to moves that bound or slide further from the body using greater risk and complications. The dance becomes more authoritative, as it is executed in a position lower to the ground, with knees deeply bent and shoulders hunched.

Different Styles of Tap

As mentioned, Glover's work in *Shuffle Along* is a compilation of styles and methods, each with their own historical resonance. In order to understand this history in musical theatre, one must continuously acknowledge the complicated roots of tap dance defined by DeFrantz as: 'a hybrid form that drew on, at least, African and Irish traditions of percussive musicality' (2002, p. x). Constance Valis Hill further explains that any tidy or brief explanation of the history of tap:

> [...] ignores tap's more complex intercultural fusions, which occurred through the interactions of Irish indentured servants and enslaved West Africans in the Caribbean during the 1600s, African American folk and Irish American laborers in the southern United States during the 1700s, and African American freemen and Irish American performers in northern urban cities in the 1800s.

(Hill, 2010, p. 2)

Keeping this Afro-Irish fusion, or melding of foundational styles, in mind helps to understand the back and forth of movement between ethnicities and how the notion of exchange, or a conversation or competition, is always at the forefront of the form. Hill reminds us that the challenge nature of tap is 'a battle for virtuosity and authority, [and] puts into focus issues of race and ethnicity; it inevitably takes on the history of race, racism, and race relations in America' (2010, p. 3). *Shuffle Along* (2016) does not have the space in the production to unravel the complicated historical dimensions of tap, and that is not the task of the show; however, any movement analysis must recognize the complexity embedded in the art form, particularly when looking at the tap challenge section.

The different styles of tap dance are commonly divided into two broad categories – 'Broadway Style' and 'Hoofing' – and what performers learn first varies. The 'Broadway Style' is more lifted, with greater emphasis placed on arm gestures (redolent of Fred Astaire). The 'Hoofing' style is much lower, and the centre of gravity is decidedly towards the floor, with the arms as a manifestation of the movement, not placed in accordance with a specific syllabus or standardized method. Glover has essentially embodied this more exploratory, rhythmically focused, hard-hitting style his entire career, though his abilities in all designations of tap are astonishing. Glover's melding of these two styles is the unique approach he brings to *Shuffle Along*. Fundamentally, the two styles can often be separated into the tap dance performed by female dancers wearing shoes with high heels or men in more supple jazz oxfords, to both men and women wearing more flat, hard, square heeled shoes, often built up in the sole to be quite heavy, the weight helping to punctuate heel drops and stamps. The ensemble, particularly noticeable in the women, switches from the former shoe to the latter as the show goes on. There is a moment shown on stage in *Shuffle Along*, a conversation, as the break-up of the four creators is looming. One reports that 'Flo Ziegfeld' hired the chorus girls to teach his dancers to stomp, shimmy and shake.[4] What might perhaps seem flattering at first became the beginning of the cultural appropriation of tap dance by white dancers, who went on to teach the style to their own students, eventually passing down the white styles (or interpretation of African American styles) through the ranks of instructors teaching a much more refined version many decades later.

Though Glover recognizes this differentiation, he explains this inevitable evolution of tap in performance: 'Tap on Broadway varies through time. There's the Tommy Tune or Susan Stroman approach versus the Henry LeTang, Cholly Atkins, Honi Coles style [...] Then something else becomes popular.' (Theys, 2015).

The physicality provided by Glover encompasses the desperations and high stakes of the trials and tribulations the cast went through en route to the historic Broadway premiere. In the production numbers from the original musical, the dancers embody an 'old-fashionedness' in their earnestness and youthful execution. This movement dynamic (visible in the overall lightness, abandon and presentational style), used to evoke the qualities of the original show, stands in contrast to the more powerful dancing in the second act when the cast of *Shuffle Along* is split up and enters into the previously described dance-off outside the story of the original musical, but within Wolfe's narrative. The physicalized turn towards the past has a reflective element to it, in the nostalgic manner suggested by Boym. There is a contemplative look at conditions of the past and meditations on their importance in relation to the present. This can be seen in the contrast between the dance in the 'original' show embedded in Wolfe's production and that in the framing narrative. While the chorus of the 2016 *Shuffle Along* is all African American, like the original 1921 cast, their collective presence hints at the continued difficulties on Broadway today for non-white dancers. Though a musical like *Hamilton* is celebrated for its mixed race casting, there is still much to do beyond just casting to repair the historical record, including using more African American composers, choreographers, and directors.

Conclusion

Wolfe's reincarnation of *Shuffle Along* is a necessary and reparative reframing of the historical momentum in musical theatre instigated by African Americans. The sensational and determined *Shuffle Along* (2016) blows the dust off the archival files for scholars and practitioners alike, and opens up the space to not only applaud the tremendous effort of those involved in *Shuffle Along* (both in the 1921 original and 2016 revisioning) but to reinstate the historical importance and foundational contributions that African Americans made and continue to make towards the development of US musical theatre. The hope is the show may one day have a healthy life in the touring circuit to bring its message to audiences outside New York City. Just as the original *Shuffle Along* tour in the 1920s helped in part to desegregate theatre around the United States, Wolfe and Glover's 2016 *Shuffle Along* will hopefully help to restore the status of the original and solidify a more honest and inclusive history. La Touche (2017) explains Wolfe's mission to keep the past alive: 'George always said please remember why we are doing this, we are doing it for them.'

Notes

1. Patting is the use of handclaps and body percussion to imitate sounds of drums. Patting was originated by African Americans out of necessity when drumming was banned in cities and on plantations. The Stearns (1994) describe how patting started 'as any kind of clapping with any dance to encourage another dancer, [and] became a special routine of slapping the hands, knees, thighs, and body in rhythmic display'. It was often called 'Patting Juba' as William Henry Lane (nicknamed 'Juba') brought it into a solo performance. Patting also 'became part of the more pretentious style of the Charleston: crossing and uncrossing the hands on the knees as they fan back and forth' (Stearns and Stearns, 1994, p. 29). The Harmony Kings were a vocal quartet that grew out of a gospel group. Their professional status was solidified by their involvement in the original *Shuffle Along* (see http://classicurbanharmony.net/2016/05/10/review-of-shuffle-along-and-the-saga-of-the-four-harmony-kings-group-harmony-pioneers, accessed 10 December 2017).
2. Paula Vogel's 2016 play, *Indecent*, that resurrects the story of the cast and performances of Sholem Asch's *God of Vengeance* (1907), does similar restorative work in regard to telling the story of censorship surrounding the play upon its arrival in the United States. Wolfe, like Vogel, sheds light on the injustices that operated in US theatre, engaging the audience on both an intellectual and visceral level, incorporating music and movement in the retelling and reminding of historical incidents.
3. Marshall Stearns in *Jazz Dance: The Story of American Vernacular Dance*, arguably the most authoritative book on the evolution and development of jazz dance, describes the Turkey Trot as a 'fast, marching one-step, arms pumping at the side with occasional arm flapping emulating a crazed turkey' (Stearns and Stearns, 1994, p. 96).

4. Marshall Stearns describes how Florenz Ziegfeld purchased routines. Dancer Ethel Williams describes, 'I went down to the New York Theatre and showed the cast how to dance it [. . .] they were having trouble. None of us was hired for the show.' (Stearns and Stearns, 1994, p. 130)

References

Acocella, J. (2014) Soaring Savion Glover in 'OM'. 8 July 2014, *The New Yorker*. Available at: www.newyorker.com/culture/culture-desk/soaring-savion-glover-in-om. Accessed 28 September 2017.

Boym, S. (2001) *The Future of Nostalgia*. New York: Basic Books.

Brantley, B. (2016) *Shuffle Along* Returns to Broadway's Embrace. *New York Times* 28 April 2016. Available at: www.nytimes.com/2016/04/29/theater/review-shuffle-along-returns-to-broadways-embrace.html. Accessed 15 May 2016.

Brooks, D. (2006) *Bodies in Dissent: Spectacular Performances of Race and Freedom, 1850–1910*. Durham, NC: Duke University Press.

Brown, J. (2008) *Babylon Girls: Black Women Performers and the Shaping of the Modern*. Durham, NC: Duke University Press.

Catton, P. (2016) Savion Glover on Choreographing *Shuffle Along*. *Wall Street Journal*, 13 April. Available at: www.wsj.com/articles/savion-glover-choreographs-shuffle-along-1460561090. Accessed 27 May 2018.

DeFrantz, T. (1997) Booty Control. In DeFrantz, T. (2002) (ed.), *Dancing Many Drums* (pp. 24–25). Madison, WI: University of Wisconsin Press, 2002.

DeFrantz, T. (2002) (ed.) *Dancing Many Drums*. Madison, WI: University of Wisconsin Press.

Dixon Gottschild, B. (2000) *Waltzing in the Dark: African American Vaudeville and Race Politics in the Swing Era*. New York: St. Martin's Press.

Elam, H.J., Jr. (2014) Post-World War II African American Theatre. In J.H. Richards & H.S. Nathans (eds.), *The Oxford Handbook of American Drama* (p. 384). Oxford Handbooks Online. Accessed 2 October 2017.

Green, A. (2016) Tap-Dancing Legend Savion Glover Reanimates the Game-Changing Broadway Musical. *Shuffle Along. Vogue*, 207(5). Available at: https://www.vogue.com/article/tap-dance-legend-savion-glover-broadway-musical-shuffle-along. Accessed 3 July 2017.

Green, J. (2016) Theater Review: *Shuffle Along* Is a Gorgeously Staged, Life-Changing Show. *Vulture*. 28 April 2016. Available at: https://www.vulture.com/2016/04/theater-review-shuffle-along.html. Accessed 15 May 2016.

Hill, C.V. (2010) *Tap Dancing America: A Cultural History*. New York: Oxford University Press.

La Touche, L. (2017) Interview with the author, 19 September 2017.

Moriah, K. (2017) Shuffle and Repeat: The Making of *Shuffle Along*. *American Quarterly* 69(1), 177–186.

Savran, D. (2009) *Highbrow/Lowdown: Theater, Jazz, and the Making of the New Middle Class*. Ann Arbor, MI: The University of Michigan Press.

Seaton, S. (2016) *Shuffle Along* and Ethnic Humor: 'The Proper Push.' *The Dramatist*, May 2016, 45–50.

Seibert, B. (2015) *What the Eye Hears: A History of Tap Dancing*. New York: Farrar, Straus and Giroux Books.

Stearns, M. & Stearns, J. (1994) *Jazz Dance: The Story of American Vernacular Dance*. New York: Da Capo Press.

Theys, E.M. (2015) Ten Minutes With Savion Glover. *Dance Magazine*, 89(7), 18. Available at: www.dancemagazine.com/10-minutes-with-savion-glover-2306965504.amp.html. Accessed 3 July 2017.

Woll, A.L. (1989) *Black Musical Theatre: From Coontown to Dreamgirls*. Baton Rouge, LA: Louisiana State University Press.

Young, C.M. (2016) Don't Blame a Pregnant Star for *Shuffle Along* Closing. Available at: http://howlround.com/don-t-blame-pregnancy-for-shuffle-along-closing. Accessed 11 September 2017.

Part III

Musical Structures: Identity and Social Change

9

Musematic Relationships in Jeanine Tesori's Score for *Fun Home*

Rebecca Applin Warner

Introduction

In 2015, Jeanine Tesori and her writing partner for *Fun Home*, Lisa Kron, were the first all-female writing partnership to win a Tony Award. Their success did not lead to immediate changes on Broadway; indeed Mark Shenton, writer for *The Stage*, noted that in the 2016–2017 season only two musicals had writing contributions from women (Shenton, 2017). Problematically, Tesori's significant output on Broadway has received little in the way of serious critical musicological responses. Her work is extremely eclectic, both in terms of the types of projects that she undertakes and her compositional style. She has demonstrated a flair for commercial popularity in the score of the adaptation of the DreamWorks 2001 animated film *Shrek the Musical* (2008) with lyricist/librettist David Lindsay-Abaire. The score for *Shrek* features a multiplicity of musical sound worlds in a collage of pastiche material amid a primarily pop-driven language. At the other end of the spectrum, her score for *Caroline or Change* (2003) with lyricist/librettist Tony Kushner demonstrates a more experimental through-sung score that has a continually evolving fragmented style. Tesori's music in *Caroline or Change* encompasses many different sound worlds to create a complex score which verges at times on the avant-garde. The richness of musical language that is found in Tesori's work demonstrates the sophistication of craft which places a dramaturgical approach at the heart of the compositional process; the musical style of each of Tesori's musicals is a sound world which is the most effective for the storytelling of that particular piece.

Indeed, the dramaturgical function of Tesori's score for *Fun Home* is highlighted by the *New York Times*: 'The music is woven so intricately into Ms. Kron's time-juggling script that you'll find yourself hard pressed to recall what exactly was said and what was sung.' (Brantley, 2015) Amid the range of Tesori's musical works, she has not shied away from challenging subject matters such as those found in *Caroline or Change*, which explores the story of an African American maid to a Jewish family in Lake Charles, 1963 (and the removal of a Confederate statue) and in *Fun Home* (Kron and Tesori, 2013), which was 'dubbed the first-ever mainstream musical centering on a young lesbian' (Smart, 2015, p. 48) and is the focus of this chapter.

Fun Home is an adaptation of Alison Bechdel's autobiographical graphic novel of the same name (2006) and is an exploration of Alison's identity viewed through the standpoints of her relationship with her gay father, her dysfunctional family life, and her own sexuality, as James Lovelock addresses at length in Chapter 11 of this collection. The structuring of *Fun Home* revolves around a narrating device in terms of adult Alison guiding the progression of events according to her memories and thought processes, while she sketches and creates captions for her memories. However, she is not a narrator in the sense of having a direct line of address with the audience. She is living the memories in the moment, as Kron points out:

> Alison isn't telling these things to an audience. She doesn't know about the audience. She's not a narrator. She's a character doggedly pursuing a goal as characters do, combing through her past on a hunt to piece together a truer version of her father's life than the one she's hung on to since he died.
>
> (Kron in Kron and Tesori, 2015, p. 8).

Alison's memories involve two younger versions of herself: Small Alison (9 years old) and Medium Alison (19 years old), each making discoveries about themselves (herself) and their (her) family in their own present. While much of the piece is a memory play, and therefore an examining of Alison's past experiences is crucial, Kron and Tesori are insistent on the driving factor of the musical being about looking forwards. The oscillation between Alison's past memories and her present, and the coming together of these time frames in order to move forward, form the structural heart of the musical. Alison sets out her own key question at the beginning of *Fun Home*: in 'It All Comes Back' she repeats the question 'Am I just like you?' (Kron and Tesori, 2015, p. 11). Tesori confirms that this is:

> The essential question, which I think is true for a lot of sons and daughters of people who commit suicide, is: is that my fate? Is that my destiny? Am I like them? To me, that's what became the essential question.
>
> (Tesori in Myers, 2015)

This chapter aims to investigate the ways in which this question is explored in the score of the musical. It does so through analysing small musical units and the relationships that they establish between Alison and her father Bruce; between Alison and her former selves; and between the family as a whole. In the analysis to follow we will explore how Tesori has written a musical relationship between Alison and her family that supports Alison's quest for an understanding of her own identity, and her lived experience as a lesbian within her family unit. We will also explore how Tesori has built within the score a sense of forward motion reflecting the idea of Alison's future discovery.

Musematic Analysis: Unpicking Fragments

To analyse the songs in detail, cellular analysis allows us to explore the workings of the score at a close level, examining the building blocks that Tesori uses to convey Alison's key relationships. Analysis on the micro level is particularly relevant in this piece given the moment-by-moment nature of the concept of the score. *Fun Home* is a musical which is constructed of fragments of memory, culminating in what Alison calls 'A picture of my father made of little marks' (Kron and Tesori, 2015, p. 77). The score also contains many such fragments, making a close cellular analysis at the micro level a relevant method of enquiry. Philip Tagg's method of musematic analysis holds much potential for musical theatre and has not previously been used in this way. Tagg created his method in the 1970s for the purposes of analysing popular songs. His stance is based on a semiotic system, viewing songs as a method of communication: Tagg's examination of ABBA's 'Fernando' begins by stating that his analysis will explore the factors that people tend to notice most readily about music. The first stage of Tagg's method of musematic analysis is to take into consideration a comprehensive checklist of musical parameters by observing matters such as tempo, harmonic language, instrumentation, and use of vocabulary (see Tagg, 1982, p. 47). Tagg acknowledges that to make observations about all of the parameters on the checklist is not a method in itself, but the step is necessary to ensure that certain parameters of music are not omitted from consideration. The 'checklist of parameters of musical expression' (Tagg, 1982, p. 47) is the first step of Tagg's musematic model, with the subsequent stages entailing the identification of 'musemes' and the relationships between them, particularly through methods of comparison and substitution.

Tagg's method has particular potential for musical theatre analysis because it breaks down sung material into its building blocks, revealing how the song can drive certain narratives and readings. While this has most commonly been applied to individual songs, applying the method over the course of an entire musical's score demonstrates relationships between musemes over a longer trajectory, and thereby reveals large-scale architecture as well as micro-level detail.

In this chapter I will focus solely on the identification stages of Tagg's method, in particular paying attention to the fundamental part of the model which comprises identification and analysis of 'musemes'. This was a term appropriated from Charles Seeger, who stated in 1960 the potential of a three-tone unit, or 'museme', which for him formed a 'complete, independent unit of music-logical form or mood in both direction and extension' (in Tagg, 1979, p. 71). Musemes are smaller than the musical phrase; independent musemes can be joined together to form a museme 'string' or placed simultaneously (or vertically) to form a museme 'stack'. Similarities can be seen between the use of musemes and the way that leitmotifs function. There is a difference in terms of potential size – musemes are always small units of material, whereas a leitmotif may encompass a whole musical phrase – but the idea of units of material gaining associations of meaning which are then developed and manipulated throughout a work is very similar between the techniques. However, certainly in the case of *Fun Home*, and perhaps more widely for musemes, their meaning is not precisely definable. Rather the shared palette of musematic relationships brings about connections and resonances between characters and themes which create a sense of shared experience. In his analysis of the theme song for the 1970s television programme *Kojak*, the work through which Tagg first proposed his musematic method, the analyst subdivides musemes into three different categories: '1) melodic, 2) accompanying, 3) contrasting' (Tagg, 1979, p. 147). The analysis to follow will be similarly subdivided, exploring melodic, accompanimental and contrasting musemes in *Fun Home*. Musemes will be considered in relation to the 'essential question' of Alison's relationship with her father and her own identity and lesbian experience, both in relation to, and independent from, her family.

Exploring Melodic Musemes in the Vocal Line of *Fun Home*

Melodic musemes primarily entail musemes which occur in the vocal line of the score. The exploration of the way that musemes are used gives indications as to musical relationships between characters and whether these function to highlight key factors about their dramatic relationships. We will begin with the musemes that make up the statement of Alison's 'essential question' discussed above, as this is the primary establishment of the dramatic themes which are to be addressed in the musical to follow. The statement is found in 'It All Comes Back' in two musical phrases, for Bruce alone at bars 87–92 (Tesori and Kron, 2014, p. 8), and then at the climax of the song, the duet between Alison and Bruce at bars 115–120 (p. 12). Despite the importance of the relationships throughout the musical between Alison and her two younger selves, the duet of the essential question being between Alison and Bruce at this early juncture establishes the father–daughter relationship as the primary concern of the question, and indeed of the musical. The musemes which make up these two phrases are shared between father and daughter, and for the most part are in unison, making the melodic musemes shared which in turn compounds the shared lyric; Bruce is searching for truth at this point as much as is Alison, and it is important that the phrase originates with Bruce in bars 89–94. However, standing outside of the two-phrase question is Alison's essential question of whether she is like her father at bar 114 (p. 11). This is a solo for Alison, and it is from the museme here that the musemes of the rest of the essential question can be seen to follow. This *Just Like You* museme which forms the root of the others is Alison's alone, establishing her as the protagonist, despite Bruce's shared quest for truth. The melodic *Just Like You* museme is a three-note figure: a semitone descent followed by a rise of a minor third. In the phrase which follows, Alison elaborates on her aims. The first melodic museme of this phrase is a repetition of the *Just Like You* museme, though adapted; it is now prefaced by a three-note ascending scale (*Anticipatory* museme), and when she sings she wants to 'know what's true' (p. 12) the *Anticipatory* museme and the *Just Like You* museme are joined together.

In the museme which follows this sense of upbeat of the *Anticipatory* museme is shortened to become a single-note anacrusis[1] (*Anticipatory 2*). The quaver semitone descent from *Just Like You* is adapted into a triplet, continuing down a further tone and thus making the ascending step into a perfect fourth rather than a minor third as it was in the original *Just Like You* museme (*Just Like You 2*). *Anticipatory 3* (on the question 'what') is a derivation of the new anacrusis figure, initially repeating the leap of a perfect fourth between B ♭ and E ♭ and then closing the gap between the leaps into a minor third (*Anticipatory 4* on the question 'why') and finally a tone (*Anticipatory 5* on the final question 'when'). The three-note rise of the *Anticipatory* museme, seen merely as an upbeat in variants 2–5, is augmented in bars 119–120 to become an extended ascent (*Anticipatory 6* – this time with a tone pattern of semitone-tone as opposed to tone-tone as seen in the *Anticipatory* museme). The *Anticipatory 7* museme for Alison is the inversion of the three-note ascent of the original *Anticipatory* but this time with a descending dotted figure ('gives way to'). *Anticipatory 8* repeats the three pitches of *Anticipatory 6* but augmented further still to give an elongated rise which forms a melisma[2] on the word 'then', highlighting this word in the text as if to linger on the past. Tesori states that

Alison 'goes backwards to go forwards' (Tesori in Myers, 2015) and the use of the *Anticipatory* museme derivations in bars 119–122 demonstrates this through mirroring the musical setting of the key words **now** (her present) and **then** (her past). Musematically, *Anticipatory* is used for both words but through progressive augmentation, the melodic ascent is gradually given more weight. Interestingly, the two-part harmony between Alison and Bruce through this phrase demonstrates that while Alison's line progressively moves forwards, Bruce does not move forward and is static on his top Es for 'until now', and is similarly sedentary on F for 'then'. The harmony between father and daughter creates a dissonance of a tone here, which then resolves through to Alison being a perfect fourth above Bruce, musically symbolizing and foreshadowing Alison's potential breaking free from her father's patterns. Florian Weinzierl (2016) has noted the dissonance of this momentand highlights its significance:

> It is thus Alison who strives for harmony and reconciliation with her father and ends up being the one having to adapt. The significance of her adapting to her father on the word 'then,' which denotes the past, points to the central conflict that Alison is going through, namely coming to terms with her past and trying to change it or her position towards it.

> (p. 14)

'Then' is the end of the two melodic phrases of Alison's key question, and therefore the whole question is made up of a museme string of *Anticipatory* and its variants and *Just Like You* and its variant for the first phrase. These phrases are not repeated as often in the musical as perhaps might be expected given their important dramatic association, but they are used again in isolation at the beginning of 'Helen's Etude', as if to evoke the next memory.

One striking museme which is recurrent throughout the score is first heard in 'Welcome to Our House on Maple Avenue'. Helen begins the song with the museme *He Wants*, a descending minor third with the pronoun as an anacrusis leading to the downbeat stress being placed on the second word. This word is further emphasized by its pause, created by the dotted quaver rhythm. The second line begins with the same museme, establishing it as a prominent unit in the song. This is confirmed by the perpetuating of the *He Wants* museme which is developed in bars 13–18 (Tesori and Kron, 2014, p. 17). In bars 13 and 15, the interval is reduced to a descending tone, with the first beat quaver rest maintained but having lost the dotted quaver on 'wants' (*He Wants 2*). The iterations of the museme fall closer together here until, in bars 17 and 18 (p. 18), three statements of it are placed together in a museme string; this time with the falling interval (originally a minor third in *He Wants* and then a tone in *He Wants 2*) having increased to a perfect fourth. The museme string develops the idea of the anacrusis leading to a stressed note by displacing the unit across the bar, creating a syncopated effect. This leads to the second iteration of the museme shifting the stress onto the pronoun. This is an important dramaturgical detail given that the song demonstrates the household revolving around Bruce's desires, and this stress, the accent as well as the rhythmic displacement, demonstrates that those desires belong only to Bruce, implying that the desires of others in the household are of lesser importance. Within the space of one verse structure of the song, the *He Wants* museme has been used seven times, in three different variations of interval. It is not the interval which makes it recognizable as the same museme, but the two-note descent, the opening quaver rest as part of the museme and of course its repeated association with the same lyric.

The importance of the *He Wants* museme for Alison is demonstrated in two excerpts of later material: Bruce's encounter with Roy and in 'Party Dress'. Both of these sections raise questions for Alison relating to her father's sexuality, and to her own. In Bruce's encounter with Roy, the museme takes on a resonance of sexual desire. Bruce's awareness of his own desires is demonstrated through the change in lyric to '*I* want' – here he sings of his own internal desires, rather than his wants for the perfect home as previously sung by his family. In 'Party Dress', while Small Alison argues with Bruce about not wanting to wear a dress, Medium Alison takes over the 'I want' museme, at a moment in her own trajectory when she is shortly to meet Joan and experience her own sexual realization ('Changing My Major to Joan'). A link is created here, brought about through the use of the one museme; a shared language between father and daughter, and their respective realizations about their sexuality.

Another shared museme between parent and child is the wordless figure first introduced in 'Helen's Etude'. The idea of a wordless refrain (here in its initial version sung to 'la's) sits alongside Bruce's encounter with Roy, simultaneously occurring in separate parts of the house but occupying the same stage space. This introduces the *La* museme as holding connotations of Helen forcibly trying to block out what is going on in her surroundings as she continues to play the piano while Bruce seduces Roy. The singing of la is akin to someone putting their fingers in their ears and randomly singing la so as to deliberately not hear what is going on, or being said. The museme is developed by Small Alison in 'Party Dress' after her altercation with her father regarding her attire for the party. It is then developed further in 'Raincoat of Love' where Small Alison sings the wordless phrase (this time the museme is sung to bah) to begin the whole song: in itself a larger structure of escapism which she uses to block out her parents' vicious argument.

Related to the *La* museme is the *Maybe Not Right Now* melodic unit. Again, Helen first introduces this while Bruce is with Roy. The museme is originated by Helen, and towards the end of the musical it is firmly established as a musical unit associated particularly with her in its adapted incarnation in 'Days and Days' (*Maybe Not Right Now 2*). The shape of the museme has changed by the time it is heard in 'Days and Days' but the cell is recognizable by the contour of its last four notes.

There is a sense with the wordless museme (*La*), as with the *He Wants* museme and the *Maybe Not Right Now* museme that these are musical metaphors of learned behaviours for Alison. Each one of them is first established by one of the parents in the chronology of the score, and they are then picked up and developed by one of the Alisons. In this way the shared melodic musemes function as an allegory for Alison questioning whether she too is like them: in that she has 'inherited' their musematic material, the question is implied as to whether she has inherited their personality traits and identity. Alison has not had a role model in respect of openly living authentically as a lesbian, and her inherited musematic language raises the question as to whether she too will be trapped by her parents' lack of acknowledgement and willingness to confront and accept Bruce's homosexuality, and whether she too will repeat that pattern with her own sexual experience.

Accompanying Musemes and Indications of Subconscious Desire

Accompanying musemes are important in the score to *Fun Home*. One such recurrent accompanying museme opens the musical in 'It All Comes Back', composed of a figure of three semiquavers marking out a G major triad (the *Triadic* museme). The museme is repeated a tone above, marking out an A minor triad, and a third time to return to the G major triad, creating a museme string. The beginnings of a harmonic alternation between sonorities a tone apart is thereby established in the repetition between the G major and the A minor sonorities, confirmed by the continuous alternation of the figure in bars 3 and 4. In this first occurrence, the museme's iteration is only brief, but the figure recurs at vital moments throughout the musical. In its association with the opening of the musical in which the audience is introduced to adult Alison in the 'present', the figure assumes connotations of her thought process, her sketching, or her conjuring the memories which are to become the substance of the musical. The connotations are not precise in nature, but the figure is nevertheless established as important to the question which Alison attempts to resolve throughout the show. The museme recurs at 'Just had a Good Talk with Dad', 'Read a Book' and 'Let Me Introduce You to My Gay Dad'. Each one of these moments involves the unit being iterated amid underscore, and always in association with a key part of Bruce's behaviour: in the first of these in his positive support of Alison, in the second in his scathing outbursts at Helen, and in the last as Medium Alison introduces her girlfriend Joan to Bruce. Each of these moments is an important memory for Alison as regards her relationship with Bruce and her working through the various parts of his personality. Finally it is heard as underscore at 'This is What I Have of You' when Alison brings together her various memories to try to make sense of her father. Preceding this moment, and Bruce's suicide in 'Edges of the World', Alison has questioned her father's suicidal motives and her own part in that event:

> What did it feel like to step in front of a truck Dad? [...] Was it because of Me? I'm afraid it wasn't. That's the crazy thing Dad, I'm afraid it wasn't.
>
> (Kron and Tesori, 2015, p. 71)

Alison is concerned that her coming out as a lesbian to her parents was what caused her father's suicide, and the placement of the accompanying *Triadic* museme would seem to make it the most aligned with that question.

The *Triadic* museme raises two further important aspects of the accompanimental language: the use of arpeggio figuration and the sonority of the alternation between seconds. The continuous string of the *Triadic* museme in bars 3 and 4, itself a harmonic alternation between the G major and A minor triads, is accompanied in the bass by a different kind of alternation of a second, between the notes D and E (*Alternation* museme). This is an example of a museme stack, whereby the *Triadic* museme is placed in a string in the upper line, and the *Alternation* museme is in the lower line. The interval of a second, and the alternation between seconds is used throughout the score of *Fun Home*, in both accompaniment and in melody. Sustained chords are also used as a feature, often accompanying recitative-like vocals, and also often alternating between sonorities a second apart. This is seen from the accompaniment to the very first vocal line in the musical, as the bass moves by a rising second, maintaining a sustained B(sus2) chord, but first placing it over D sharp and then over E. The spoken introduction to 'Thanks for the Care Package' uses a similar sustained alternation between two chords a tone apart as Medium Alison writes a letter to her parents. *Triadic* is placed three times in a string, at a slower tempo following this, as underscore while Joan starts to get closer to Medium Alison; the sustained chords rise here, with the figure then returning at the end of the scene. 'A Flair for the Dramatic' begins with the sustained chord idea, with a more rapid alternation in the bass, to underscore Alison's question as to whether her Dad went cruising in the particular memory the audience has just witnessed. 'Shortly After We Were Married' also begins with the alternating sustained chords, underscoring Helen's memory of her early marriage with Bruce. The alternations between seconds becomes particularly prevalent in 'It was Great to Have You Home' as both the piano and the cello oscillate between pitches as the underscore to Alison directly addressing her father, 'What did it feel like to step in front of a truck Dad?' (2015, p. 71), while he is simultaneously frantically addressing her as 'Al' (p. 70) in letter form: father and daughter simultaneously addressing each other without the other hearing, represented through the continuous oscillation between two polarities of pitch.

Arpeggio figuration as an accompaniment is particularly introduced in 'Helen's Etude' in the exercise-like Alberti pattern[3] (*Alberti* museme) that she plays diegetically,[4] and which becomes the accompaniment to the section discussed above as Bruce seduces Roy. This is repeated as underscore in 'Party Dress' and accompanies the *La* and the *Maybe Not Right Now* melodic musemes discussed above, thereby creating a museme stack of both accompanimental and melodic musemes. The Alberti figuration is by nature constructed of an alternation between two notes, with one of the pair often moving in pitch while the other remains more static as a pedal note. This is another example of the use of alternation in the detail of the make-up of the score. The Alberti figure is distinctive in its association with Helen and her determined lack of confronting Bruce's sexuality and the problems of their marriage. However, there are many other musical units which permeate the idea of alternation and figuration throughout the whole score. For example, 'Not Too Bad' begins with a slower alternation of arpeggios between harmonies a tone apart – C major and B♭ major – before using the *Triadic* museme and then returning again to an underscore of the C and B♭ major sonorities; 'Welcome to Our House on Maple Avenue' uses another form of Alberti movement, perhaps appropriately given that the substance of the song emanates from Helen, the pianist of the family. Alison's verse sections in 'Telephone Wire' are accompanied by a two-note alternation which takes on a departure from the arpeggiated material associated with Helen. It is at this point that adult Alison merges in theatrical space with her own memories, going in the car with Bruce instead of Medium Alison. Here, Alison literally pushes her former self out of the way and takes on more agency in terms of confronting her memories as opposed to reliving them, and this departure can be heard in the change of accompanimental style at this juncture.

Contrasting Musemes

Tagg lists contrasting musemes as part of his categories of identification, and while to do so in full across the score would be too substantial to undertake here, it is interesting to note which songs in *Fun Home* do not make overt use of the shared musemes which have been discussed.

'Come to the Fun Home' is one such number in that it stands apart from much of the score in terms of both style and intention: here Small Alison and her brothers create their own playful promotional video for the Bechdel Funeral Home, and the change in musical style indicates its change of musical landscape for this dramatic function. Two songs which significantly do not draw on shared musemes are 'Changing My Major' and 'Ring of Keys'. Both of these songs are personal moments of past memory for Alison which focus on two stages of her realizing that she is a lesbian. 'Changing My Major' is sung by Medium Alison following her sexual encounter with Joan as a college student, while 'Ring of Keys' is Small Alison's realization of the affinity she feels with the delivery woman who arrives at the funeral parlour. In 'Ring of Keys' Small Alison is unable to finish her sentences, as if she is trying to process her thoughts and work out what they mean. 'Changing My Major' conversely goes to the other extreme, with Medium Alison working through the repetition of musical patterning in her vocal line in order to reach a point of completion in her understanding of her sexual feelings. In neither of these songs does she share musematic material with either of her parents: importantly there is no allusion to any of the musemes which occur during Bruce's sexual expressions. Musematically, this points towards the finale that while Alison's character has shared musematic material with her parents, by the ending in 'Flying Away' all three Alisons have their own musemes which are not derived from her parents.

A Shared Musical Language

Fun Home's score weaves together both melodic and accompanying musemes to create a patchwork of material at the cellular level. What is important here is that the musemes create a shared musical language between the family, thereby symbolizing the musical's core as a piece about working through the interrelationships between its characters. While the focus of the musical is particularly on the relationship between Alison and Bruce, many of the musemes also originate from Helen, making her role in the way the score functions crucial. It was noted earlier that musemes create a shared thematic language without being specifically definable. An example of this is seen with the *He Wants* museme being first established in terms of Bruce's wants of controlling the home environment and a certain sense of belligerence in going after his heart's desire, a meaning which then develops connotations to be associated with his sexual encounters, and then being transferred to Alison's sexual awakening. This museme has a general connotation of 'desire' but with various meanings and associations in different contexts.

The shared musematic language can be used not only to highlight connections between the family, but also to demonstrate a divergence in shared experience through absence of shared material. This divergence can be seen in *Fun Home* in the musemes of Alison's personal experiences, which do not consist of shared musematic material from her parents. The three Alisons also do not share a great deal of musematic language with each other. As has been seen, the key songs for each of them do not use shared material. This means that 'Flying Away', the final number of the musical, is the one time where Small, Medium and Adult Alison sing as a trio without any other cast members: in her mind, Alison has metaphorically broken free from her parents by the end of the piece. Tesori does not, however, give the Alisons a moment of unison, or of homophonic sung texture to show a unity between them. Instead, the one word that they share is fly, and within the setting of this word the only museme they share is that of a rising second. To begin with, Adult Alison sings 'flying away' to a descending pattern, and it is Medium Alison who turns this into a rising scalic figure. Small Alison then also sings the museme as a rising second, before Adult Alison then sings a rising perfect fourth. Adult Alison finally sings the rising second 'Fly' (Tesori and Kron, 2014, p. 111), thereby completing the shared museme between the three Alisons. While the *Fly* museme is essentially new material, it bears resemblance to Alison's rising 'then' in her duet with Bruce at the final climax of the song in 'It All Comes Back'. As was seen, this is an important setting out of the character's agenda of exploration, and it is fitting that her resolution should in some way bear relation to that museme, albeit significantly altered. It brings about a sense of resolution as Alison does break free from the patterns of her parents' behavioural influence.

Musematic analysis is an effective framework for investigating a musical theatre score, enabling a small-scale study of musical detail and the narrative connotations which musemes accumulate over the course of a musical.

It can bring about an enhanced understanding of a character's identity through the way they express themselves in music on a micro level, and how that identity is portrayed in relation to other characters within the piece. A shared musematic language between characters is particularly appropriate in *Fun Home* because of the essential question of whether Alison is like her father and whether her destiny is also shared with him. In this way, the technique of musematic analysis highlights the detail of the score which portrays the essential question of Alison exploring her identity. Tesori has expressed her viewpoint on the answer to whether Alison is like her father as 'complicated because the answer is "Yes and no"... You're exactly like them and you're exactly not like them, which is true of any parent and child' (Tesori in Myers, 2015). The importance of the alternation between the interval of a second in the musemes of *Fun Home* would seem to represent this viewpoint. The score is underpinned by continual oscillation: between harmonic sonorities as well as between specific pitches. This oscillation gives a feel of uncertainty, of working out a solution, and of alternating between the 'yes and no' that Tesori highlights. As can be seen through analysis of the musical's key musemes, while Alison breaks free from her parents' destiny, demonstrated through her move away from their shared musematic language, *Fun Home* is not a musical which gives categorical answers to the complexities of familial relationships. Alison's progression away from the familial musemes, however, does demonstrate a score which symbolically portrays her move away from her father's lack of acceptance of his sexuality. The show concludes with a message of positive liberation for Alison, a crucial component for the significance of an important Broadway musical which centres on sexual identity.

Notes

1. An 'anacrusis' is an upbeat.
2. A 'melisma' is when a single syllable of text is set to several notes.
3. A pattern commonly found in music of the Classical period which marks out a triadic chord, often moving from root to fifth, to third, to fifth.
4. Meaning Helen is consciously aware of playing the piano within the narrative of the piece.

References

Brantley, B. (2015) Review: 'Fun Home' at the Circle in the Square Theater. *New York Times*. Available at: www.nytimes.com/2015/04/20/theater/review-fun-home-at-the-circle-in-the-square-theater.html?partner=bloomberg. Accessed 1 December 2017.

Kron, L. (2014) *Fun Home*. London: Samuel French.

Kron, L. & Tesori, J. (2015) *Fun Home*. New York: Samuel French.

Myers, V. (2015) Composer Jeanine Tesori on Her Artistic Process and Rewarding Female Ambition. *Indiwire*. Available at: https://www.indiewire.com/2015/03/composer-jeanine-tesori-on-her-artistic-process-and-rewarding-female-ambition-204160/. Accessed 17 August 2017.

Shenton, M. (2017) Where are the Women Writing Musicals? *The Stage*. Available at: https://www.thestage.co.uk/opinion/2017/mark-shenton-women-writing-musicals. Accessed 1 December 2017.

Smart, J. (2015) Meet the Maker: Jeanine Tesori and Lisa Kron, 'Fun Home'. *Back Stage, National Edition*, 30 April, p. 48.

Tagg, P. (1979) *Kojak: 50 Seconds of Television Music. Towards the Analysis of Affect in Popular Music*. New York: The Mass Media Music Scholars' Press Inc.

Tagg, P. (1982) Analysing Popular Music: Theory, Method and Practice. *Popular Music* 2(January), 37–67.

Tagg, P. (2000) *Fernando the Flute*, 3rd edition. New York: The Mass Media Music Scholars' Press Inc.

Tesori, J. & Kron, L. (2014) *Fun Home Vocal Selections*. London: Samuel French.

Weinzierl, F. (2016) Making a Fun Home: The Performance of Queer Families in Contemporary Musical Theater. *Current Objectives of Postgraduate Study*, 17(1–22). Available at: https://copas.uni-regensburg.de/article/view/255/335. Accessed 17 August 2017.

10

'Dedicated to the Proposition...' Raising Cultural Consciousness in the Musical *Hair* (1967)

Sarah Browne

In memory of Galt MacDermot

The period of 1954 to 1968 saw the struggle for African American civil rights re-emerge into the public arena and become one of the most significant, pressing social issues the US had faced. The 1960s marked a period in American history where marginal voices in America were straining to be heard; such voices were 'counter' to the hegemony of the 'American Dream' (which had been reiterated and promoted through the onstage practices of musical theatre). Groups excluded from previous visions of the American Dream (on the grounds of race, gender and sexuality) sought to reinvent America by 'stressing the utopian aspects' of inclusivity (Sayres in Campbell and Kean, 2012, p. 38): a better world in which marginalized voices were not excluded from or subdued by the discourse, but enriched the country through diversity.

The famous 1963 speech of Martin Luther King during the 'March on Washington for Jobs and Freedom' utilizes language which stresses the utopian aspects of the American Dream. Standing in front of the Lincoln Memorial, before a quarter of a million protestors,[1] King made reference to the Declaration of Independence, the Constitution and Lincoln's Emancipation Proclamation. But Dr King used language that specifically appealed to all classes, dominant and marginal; white, middle-class citizens who had benefited from a society obsessed with materialism as well as black citizens who had yet to reap the benefits. He drew upon the ideals of the counterculture which spoke of the disenchantment that America's dream imagery had been 'hijacked by the corporate organisation man' (Campbell and Kean, 2012, p. 36) but also cleverly managed to appeal to the same corporate class by using language that spoke of 'cashing checks [sic]' and 'signing a promissory note', while warning that the nation must not return to 'business as usual' (King, 1963, pp. 1–2). Asserting that he refuses to believe 'the bank of justice is bankrupt' (p. 2), King employed both the language and the spectre of Lincoln to recall the ideals of the founding forefathers: 'Five score years ago a great American in whose symbolic shadow we stand today signed the Emancipation Proclamation' (p. 1). King uses language that is grounded in tradition, history and ideology, while simultaneously infusing it with central ideas of rebirth and renewal. The most famous section of the speech reiterates the phrase 'I have a dream' and it is this repeated stance that hints at wish fulfilment in a way which 'sought to integrate the redemption of the oppressor with the aspirations of the oppressed' (Campbell and Kean, 2012, p. 99). Central to King's message was the notion that by allowing African American people to have a voice, to have access to equal rights, America could become a better place. Through reinforcing the mythology central to the American Dream, King's speech proposes that by acknowledging its diverse cultural identity, America could transform into the land that it always promised to be; it could reinvent and renew.

King's speech is symptomatic of a period when black civil rights activists were attempting to 'assert pride and claim identity' (Schlesinger, 1998, p. 79). Despite the resistance of black performers and creators, musical theatre and other popular forms of entertainment had historically undermined African Americans through the use of parody and misrepresentation, resulting in entrenched stereotypes which saturated popular culture throughout the twentieth century. On initial examination, the musical *Hair* (which premiered at the Public Theater on 17 October 1967) presents representations of African American cultural identity which appear to be merely stereotypes, created and shaped by a white creative team, reinforcing the dominant discourse of the male, white heterosexual. As Hilton Als asserts in his review of the 2009 Broadway revival, 'there is not one believable black character in *Hair*. In fact, its strangled, hackneyed depiction of black masculinity is painful to watch' (Als, 2009). Of course, as a black man, Als' voice is essential in constructing discourse surrounding any staging of *Hair* and it is quite possible that the inclusion of black characters in the Tribe functions to merely 'validate the white hipness of the show' (Als, 2009). However, reframing our reading of this musical might actually open up a space whereby we can discuss such issues and the complexities which arise in doing so. Considering *Hair*'s representations of African American identity in greater depth provides opportunities to reveal the intricacies of the time in which the piece was written, and our understanding of the nature of identity in the postmodern age. In broader terms, the musical is representative of the larger civil rights struggle taking place in American society and echoes the view that cultural identity is subject to transformation; while the characters onstage are presented often in fixed, essentialized terms, the context of the scenes in which they appear show characters who are subject to the 'play' of history, culture and power. It is these moments that require further interrogation.

In Chapter 1 of this collection, Donatella Galella compels 'those with racial privilege to do anti-racist work', and in shifting my reading of *Hair* to focus on the performance of blackness I hope to develop a counter-discourse to the work that already exists on this musical; work that tends to overlook and disregard certain scenes which feature members of the 'Tribe' speaking powerfully of the ways in which America can be better. Barbara Lee Horn's 1991 publication, *The Age of Hair*, offers some useful context on the creative process but fails to situate these observations within the era of civil rights, only briefly mentioning 'America's racial inequality' and Vietnam as an example of racial exploitation (p. 76). Similarly, Elizabeth Wollman's *The Theater Will Rock* (2006) considers *Hair* as a rock musical, perhaps in recognition of its subtitle rather than as an exploration of the multiple styles and genres of music actually used in the score. Eric Grode's publication somewhat redresses the balance by affording Hud the same depth of character analysis as, for example, Sheila. Grode makes careful mention of the theme of 'race' running through the musical, briefly connecting this observation to the 'burgeoning civil rights movement' (Grode, 2010, p. 10). However, Wollman's later article assessing *Hair*'s female characters focuses largely on the Sheila/Berger/Claude 'love triangle' which results in the observation that the musical is 'conservative' in its treatment of women (Wollman, 2014, p. 5). Had this interrogation been broadened to include other members of the Tribe, it may have revealed moments where history, culture and power collide to produce powerful commentaries on racial and gender inequality in the US. This is perhaps most clearly elucidated in Act Two, where a black, female member of the Tribe performs the role of Abraham Lincoln in the song 'Abie Baby'. Here, the black female voice is celebrated, particularly evident in the 2009 Broadway Revival, where it signifies an act of rebellion against the 'legit' Broadway vocal style of the other Tribe members and where, interestingly, the musical perfect cadence which falls on the phrase 'happy birthday, Abie baby' is delayed, allowing for a full exploration of the vocalist's tessitura and presenting a musical 'moment of collective catharsis [which is] extremely important in reinforcing a sense of cultural solidarity' (Wilson, 1999, p. 169).

To overlook certain members of the Tribe is to fail to celebrate the multiplicity which lies at the heart of *Hair*. This chapter will attempt to reframe a reading of the musical by exploring the Act One song 'Colored Spade' to demonstrate how African American characters in *Hair* transform their identity through rewriting and retelling their own history in their own terms, which subsequently allows for an alternative imagining of their role in American society. The musical itself presents a seminal moment in musical theatre history; the musicological, structural and dramatic aspects of *Hair* indicate a shift in the approach to storytelling in musical theatre, its experimentation with form and narrative perhaps signal an end to the Golden Age of musical theatre and hint at the multiple forms still to be explored. Through examining and interrogating how marginal identities are represented on stage (specifically through an exploration of the character Hud), I will consider how *Hair* challenged and liberated the stereotypes that had been promoted and reiterated via the traditions of the American musical theatre stage. It is only by adopting this way of reading musicals that we begin to recognize how these traditions promulgated what are essentially racist representations of African Americans; situating those considered to be 'at the margins' firmly at the centre of our focus allows us to reveal these inherently racist structures and directly challenge such traditions. As such, this reading will elucidate how *Hair* reflects American popular culture of the 1960s by capturing the beliefs and aspirations of the countercultural movement of the decade, but it does so by situating the musical firmly in the era of civil rights and illustrates how *Hair* can be read as both shaping, and being a product of, the cultural moment. In Act One of the musical, many of the scenes featuring African American characters rely on stereotypical representations. However, upon closer analysis, these representations do not serve to denigrate African Americans but function as moments where cultural identity is re-appropriated. The analysis of the song 'Colored Spade' highlights how the character of Hud defines the social structure but, through doing so, re-appropriates blackness.

Hud and Hendrix: The Power of Music and Visual Imagery

The dialogue cue for 'Colored Spade' in Act One is Woof's assertion that 'we are all one', but what follows suggests the opposite is in fact true. The character, Hud, appears onstage hanging upside down from a pole, carried by two white boys. This firmly establishes an order in which the white middle-class male is dominant and presents an image of the African American as slave. Furthermore, it portrays the black male in animalistic terms; a slaughtered beast, the hunted prize. The resemblance between Hud's costume (in both the original and 2009 revival production), and the style favoured by the popular musician Jimi Hendrix, is striking. The overgrown afro hairstyle with a headband, coupled with the bell-bottomed trousers, flowing shirt and necklaces of beads is reminiscent of the image that Hendrix carefully crafted following his emergence on the transatlantic music scene and echoed on a number of his album covers and in publicity shots. In her study of Hendrix and racial politics in the 1960s, Lauren Onkey (2002) observes that some critics of Hendrix noted how the musician adopted 'white' fashion but also outlines the 'revolutionary potential of [his] style for blacks';

> But a grinning, crazy-haired Hendrix in hussar's jacket suggested something else entirely – a redskin brave showing off the spoils of a paleface scalp, perhaps, or a negro 'buffalo soldier' fighting on the side of the anti-slavery Yankee forces in the US Civil War.

> (Spencer in Onkey, 2002, p. 196)

The choice of words used to describe Hendrix's appearance is particularly interesting and also highlights the popular fascination with Native American Indian traditions (denoted in the use of the term 'tribe' in *Hair*). Furthermore, this describes Hendrix in terms related to two groups of dispossessed people in American society.

As for his music, Onkey argues that his stage performances were not recognized as a 'staple in black popular musical performance' and his 'flamboyance on stage was not understood as signifying "black"' (2002, p. 198). Hendrix used his electric guitar as a symbol of rebellion; plucking the strings with his teeth and using distortion to mimic the sounds of gunshots and the screams of war, suggest signs of wild rebellion. To many critics it seemed that Hendrix was merely satisfying white stereotypes of the black male; erotic, dangerous, violent and highly sexual. Labelled as a 'psychedelic Uncle Tom',[2] Hendrix appeared to do little to advance race relations beside present 'a beautiful Spade routine' (Christgau in Onkey, 2002, p. 199), an accusation frequently levelled at Hendrix following the Monterey Pop Festival of June, 1967.[3] This complex representation of Hud in the opening scenes prompts the audience to conflate several cultural references to male African Americans. While presenting Hud in racially stereotyped terms (through his first appearance hanging from a pole), the audience are reminded of the supposed wild, rebellious nature of dispossessed groups in American society. This is juxtaposed against the staged, constructed rebellion of rock music, favoured by Hendrix, particularly in his live performances. By making reference to both, the audience are presented with a complex set of signs that perhaps speak loudly of the potential dangers the civil rights movement posed to the dominant, white mainstream culture. The similarities between the fictional character of Hud and Jimi Hendrix are laid bare in both appearance and in the title of the song.

When read in conjunction with the visual imagery, analysis of the score offers further insight into the function of this particular song. 'Colored Spade' begins with a syncopated bass line and when Hud begins to sing, his melody is one that is firmly rooted in intervals of a third. In the Western classical tradition the interval of the third indicates major or minor tonal harmony, and in blues music the third appears flattened in all versions of the scale; hexatonic,[4] heptatonic and octatonic. The restricted nature of this melody is illuminating for two reasons. Firstly, the inclusion of the flattened seventh in the melodic line suggests that the song is constructed in a blues style. In European derived musics, the flattened seventh occurs naturally with the dominant chord. Here in 'Colored Spade' the same note is sounded against the tonic chord, a technique reminiscent of blues music which is further reinforced by the repetitive use of both the tonic and dominant in the bass line. The omission of the flattened third of the scale, but the inclusion of the flattened seventh, suggests that this could possibly be a version of the blues octatonic scale which is a chromatic variation of the Western major scale. The third and seventh degrees of this scale alternate between their normal and flattened versions, creating a nuanced blues tonality.

Bar 3 of 'Colored Spade' (MacDermot et al, 1967, p.22)

Further parallels can be drawn here with the music of Hendrix. The 'transformative hybridity' (Onkey, 2002, p. 206) apparent in his music mainly stems from the result of mixing blues music with rock and roll. But black musicians of the mid-to-late 1960s were searching for a more 'authentic' black aesthetic, shunning the potentially integrative power of Hendrix's music and instead using funk music that carried with it a message of black power. Originating in the mid-1960s, and rooted in a blend of jazz, soul and rhythm and blues, funk music is characterized by its strong rhythmic emphasis created through the use of electric bass and drums to produce a sound less focused on melody and harmony. Funk music frequently focuses on improvising over a single, sustained chord rather than following the established chord progressions of its predecessors. The opening bars of 'Colored Spade' appear to attempt to bring all these elements together; the element of rock and roll, coupled with the suggestion of blues music reinforce the integrative image of Hendrix already presented through costume. This, juxtaposed with the message of the lyrics and the funk bass line, suggests that the song seems to incorporate the entire message of the civil rights movement throughout the 1960s: the shift from integration to highlighting and reinforcing difference.

Secondly, the simple nature of the restricted melody coupled with a rhythmically complex bass line appears to highlight a key feature of African (and later, African American) music. Simon Frith suggests that the appeal of African American music lies in the 'rhythm focused experience' of the music, which allows for the body to be 'engaged with this music in a way that it is not engaged with European musics' (1996, p. 141). Earliest reports in the English language dating back to 1620 indicate that every event in the West African community is marked by 'public dances, which are accompanied with songs and music suited to the occasion' (Equiano in Southern, 1971, p. 5). This tradition was carried into the colonies in the eighteenth and nineteenth centuries and, as Olly Wilson states, is part of the 'heterogeneous sound ideal' which still pervades African American music of the twentieth century; the desire to 'incorporate physical body motion as an integral part of the music making process' (Wilson, 1999, p. 159). The harmonic and rhythmic features of 'Colored Spade' therefore suggest the participatory nature of African American music making.

'Colored Spade' ends on an imperfect cadence which allows the flattened seventh to resolve and present itself as the major third of the dominant chord.

Bars 34 and 35 of 'Colored Spade' (MacDermot at al, 1967, p.24)

Although in essence, the use of the imperfect cadence suggests that the song appears 'unfinished', the resolution of the flattened seventh would suggest that the blues style this represents has been subdued in order to reach what Susan McClary describes as 'narrative closure'. The use of this term in McClary's work refers specifically to the use of keys and tonal systems that 'stand in the way of unitary identity' (McClary, 1993, p. 330). The tonal system of 'Colored Spade' throughout has suggested both the blues scale and the Western scale of G major. The vocal line has heavily utilized the flattened seventh (F natural) and only states F sharp when the lyrics 'United States of Love' appear (perhaps most clearly seen in bars 17 to 19).

Bars 17 and 18 of 'Colored Spade' (MacDermot at al, 1967, p.23)

The use of the flattened seventh throughout the song has created tension between the two tonal systems that at some point must be resolved in order to achieve unity. This resolution would suggest that the Other (in this case, the African American and by association, the blues tonal system) has been subdued in the interests of unitary identity, and by the final bar all suggestions of the blues tonality have been eradicated. However, it cannot be denied that the use of an imperfect cadence suggests that this song is, to the ear, unfinished and that there is much more still to be expressed about the position of the African American both within the Tribe and in the larger society.

Reclaiming Racial Epithets

What is perhaps most interesting about this particular song is the interplay between the lyrics and music. Mike Haralambos, in his survey of black American song, suggests that blues lyrics concentrate on the experience of failure by stating 'this is the way it is, and this is how I am suffering' (Haralambos in Frith, 2007, p. 213). The lyrics of 'Colored Spade' essentially form a typical musical theatre 'list song' which has specific functions, also discussed by Broderick Chow in Chapter 2. This list consists of a barrage of derogatory terms used to locate the African American through the understanding of the white European class (in this case, the creative team[5]). These terms not only refer to the somewhat limited employment opportunities available to African Americans but also literary characters who had been victims of parody (Uncle Tom, Aunt Jemima, Little Black Sambo[6]). The use of such terms seems to fulfil two very distinct purposes. The first appears to present the constructed, attractive mythology that white Americans have assigned not only to black Americans, but to all Other cultures that exist outside of the white, male heterosexual discourse. This is appropriately summarized in Charles Shaar Murray's study of Jimi Hendrix: 'black people represent the personification of the untrammelled id – intrinsically wild, sensual, dangerous, "untamed" in every sense of the word' (1989, p. 78), and is perhaps most easily recognized in the use of the terms 'Voodoo, zombie, Ubangi-lipped' (bars 13, 14). These lyrics promote a sense of threat, particularly given the inclusion of Voodoo, a religion which has been subject to a number of negative connotations and misconceptions. The fact that these lyrics are placed in between descriptions of the job roles African Americans have been consigned to suggests that they should be read as words and practices that are equally benign:

Elevator operator, table cleaner at Horn and Hardart, Slave [...].

(MacDermot, Rado and Ragni, 1967, p. 23)

In his survey of *Hair*, Scott Miller proposes that when these racist epithets are heard in quick succession they become 'ridiculous' and 'lose their power' (2003, p. 112). From a white perspective, this may be one of the ways in which this performance could be read, but this was certainly not the case for black performers in the original production. In a 2003 interview,[7] MacDermot himself states that the writers of the musical wanted to consciously address civil rights. He adds that although the words of 'Colored Spade' have no power on their own, the original Hud (Lamont

Washington) experienced a great deal of difficulty in learning and performing the lyrics, finding them 'distasteful'. At the time of the original production, with the fight for civil rights at the forefront of American consciousness, it is easy to understand Washington's initial reaction to these lyrics. To reinforce and reiterate the stereotypes assigned to black people would appear to give credence to these epithets. E. Patrick Johnson in his book *Appropriating Blackness* (2003) states that 'the tropes of blackness that whites circulated in the past – Mammy, Sambo [...] have historically insured physical violence, poverty, institutional racism and second-class citizenry for blacks' (p. 4) so it is little wonder that Washington would be reticent to recite them again. As Galella astutely remarks in her opening chapter to this publication, racism is not merely the utterance of any racial epithet but is also when those who benefit from racial privilege keep such power for themselves.

Paul Gilroy (1991), in 'It Ain't Where You're From, It's Where You're At', proposes that music provides a means by which black culture can develop its struggles through the communication of information, and this hints at the second purpose for such distinct lyrics: they can express the reality of what Johnson (2003) describes as the 'living of blackness'. In debating the use of language and the politics of authenticity, he proposes that language is one of the ways in which the 'living of blackness' is communicated:

> [...] blackness does not only reside in the theatrical fantasy of the white imaginary that is then projected onto black bodies, nor is it always consciously acted out: rather, it is also in the inexpressible yet undeniable racial experience of black people – the ways in which the 'living of blackness' becomes a material way of knowing.
>
> (2003, p. 8)

He notes the manner in which contemporary black and white youths appropriate the language of each other which prompts authenticity to be called into question based on the relationship between skin colour and the performance of 'culturally inscribed language' (p. 6), so it is interesting to consider how this dynamic shifts when the language is then re-appropriated. While the climate of the 1960s may deem this language sensitive, in subsequent productions this scene may be read differently. There is no denying that these epithets exclude whites, and in that respect alone there is power in the use of such words. The contemporary (acceptable) use of a number of terms deemed to be extremely offensive illustrates the cultural process which has taken place whereby a group has reclaimed a term that had previously been used to describe that same group in a disparaging manner. It could be argued that the intra-group use of such a term denotes a sense of community. The use of the term among whites is still considered taboo and, therefore, the re-appropriation of this term is considered a form of socio-political empowerment.

It is worth noting, however, that lyrics alone may not shape the ideals and attitudes of the listener. Frith suggests that song lyrics frequently go unnoticed or are misunderstood and asserts that interpretation of song words is best approached by considering them in relation to their expression: 'words in performance' (1996, p. 166). It is through adopting this approach that the second function of the song 'Colored Spade' becomes clear. The character of Hud and the music and lyrics he is assigned allow for audience identification. His solo functions as a means through which African Americans could reassert their own identity, albeit in relation to others, and as a way in which African Americans could reinforce their collective identity through acknowledgement of their shared historical struggle. A 1970 interview with the actor playing the role of Hud in the Chicago production confirms that cast members felt *Hair* gave them the 'chance to express anger at white exploitation, slavery, white capitalism, the draft. The chance to be satirical about things black people have known for a long time' (McCloden in Miller, 2003, p. 112). Hud's song expresses cultural difference, presenting images of how white men have defined and confined black men. The scene begins with the image of the African American as slave. He (Hud) is dressed in the same manner as an African American popular icon. From the opening of this scene, we are presented with images of how African Americans have been enslaved, confined and defined by white Americans. The performance allows for simultaneous readings; the first is one that is, of course, degrading and racist. But the performance of the song could also be read as empowering for the cast member; by repeating and adopting the numerous derogatory terms listed in the lyrics, Hud has made these words his own, rendering them ineffective and removing the possibility of them being employed in an offensive way.

Remembering and Re-Remembering the Struggle

As with many of the protest movements of the 1960s, the African American civil rights movement had used music and song as forms of communication, as 'a tactic of social contestation in the struggle for desegregation' (Martin, 2004, p. 3). As discourse in the struggle for civil rights moved from assimilation to an enhanced sense of black cultural identity, so too did the type of song used by black power movements to heighten awareness of the political issues of the climate. Furthermore, as frustrations at the pace of change grew and the Black Power era began, the type of music performed by those connected to the SNCC (Student Nonviolent Coordinating Committee) shifted to Afro-centricity, and African musicians exiled in the USA (Miriam Makeba, Hugh Masekela and Jonas Gwangwa) now became the 'sound' of the civil rights movement; 'the early civil rights ideals of peace and black-white co-operation seemed to have collapsed, and that collapse seemed [...] to be symbolised by the new music, the wild and aggressive funk' (Denselow, 1989, p. 54).

'Colored Spade' uses the style of 'wild and aggressive funk' and addresses the political issues in such a way that it allows both the performer and the listener to make sense of the song through a subjective and collective identity. The song's 'release' (or chorus) reveals the true nature of this quasi-protest number; the slogan. It is here that the song functions most comfortably as a protest song, with its assertion that Hud is President of the United States 'of Love'. Again, Hud has re-appropriated a stereotype for transformative purposes; he is reclaiming the use of the stereotype of the 'Black Buck'; violent and displaying sexual prowess, particularly towards white women. In addition, the use of the word 'President' indicates a moment of liminality; the status and previous identity of the black character has now been stripped away and the possibilities for a reinvented future are laid bare: 'by posing the world as it is against the world as the racially subordinated would like it to be, [. . .] musical culture supplies a great deal of the courage required to go on living in the present' (Gilroy, 1991, p. 10).

Symbolically, at this point in the 2009 Broadway revival, Hud (here played by Darius Nichols) raises his right fist, performing the Black Power salute; the music and lyrics remain unchanged from its original incarnation, as does the intention of the song: to reinforce a black collective identity based on the shared reminiscence of an historical struggle. The song hints at a challenge to the white dominant establishment; the African American has reimagined his future; he has moved from a separation to a liminal phase and now hints at re-assimilation, but on his terms. In this same revival, Hud is no longer carried onstage hanging from a pole, and is already an established member of 'the Tribe'. His opening request to the audience to 'step to the back of the bus' with him is one that recalls the earlier struggles of civil rights campaigners, most notably Rosa Parks and her resistance of bus segregation. This shift serves to reinforce the function of 'Colored Spade' as a protest song.

In several productions of this song, the accompanying choreography contains echoes of the Jim Crow dance, clearly signifying minstrel performance practice. This dance, originated in 1832 by Thomas Dartmouth Rice, was purportedly based on his observations of an old black slave (Strausbaugh, 2006, p. 58). Bent legs and hips are evident, in addition to a form of the soft-shoe shuffle and the most famous element of the dance: the slow heel-and-toe spin. The construction of a black identity through movement appears to serve a purpose similar to that of the music and lyrics of this song, one that recalls moments of black inferiority in American history. In discussing the combination of music and dance in the musical *Jelly's Last Jam*, Kathryn Edney proposes that this confronts 'the place of African Americans both within the history of the United States and on the musical theater stage' (Edney, 2013, p. 113). The use of the slow heel-and-toe spin bears a direct relation to the minstrel parodies of Dartmouth Rice and Zip Coon, and here this parody is re-appropriated to elucidate 'those contradictions of history whereby African Americans are at once the source of "American" culture and erased from the history of that culture' (Edney, 2013, p. 115). This re-appropriation allows black performers to powerfully reclaim and reassert their own history. Much of the choreography in the original Broadway production stemmed from group exercises conducted with the cast[8] and the original choreographer, Julie Arenal, would 'isolate individual moves from people and build a vocabulary'. Original cast member Marjorie Lipari confirms that the movement was 'organic. It came out of our bodies' (Grode, 2010, p. 53). African American cultural dance functions in the same way as oral traditions, passed from generation to generation and developed over time, so it can be argued that this performance is an embodiment of history and culture. However, Broadway productions are carefully choreographed and while some of the movements may have been embedded in the body and the movement vocabulary of the black cast members, it is quite possible that the choreographer chose to embellish and exaggerate such movements. Arenal's building of a vocabulary that so many cast members refer to may indicate an example of white people's appropriation of black traditions. Similar movement appears in the staging of 'Four Score/Abie Baby' in Act Two and the link to black slavery is more explicit in this later number.

In their personal accounts of performing in the original cast of the Broadway production of *Hair*, both Lorrie Davis and Jonathon Johnson note the racial separation present in the cast, reinforced by the nature of the material. Following the untimely death of one of the black cast members, Kramer (a white member of 'the Tribe') recalls the matinee performance on the day of the funeral: 'It's a strange thing, black people could play white roles, but white people couldn't play black roles. I sang "Colored Spade". Whoever thought whites would have to do black parts?' (Kramer in Davis, 1973, p. 181). Davis, a black member of 'the Tribe', provides an alternative view, noting that 'only bit parts were being racially interchanged' (p. 237) and lists instances where racial injustice appeared to be present in all aspects of the production. She refers to occasions when black civil rights protests entered public consciousness, stating 'I tried to get what little black message there was across with the part of Hud' (Davis, 1973, p. 241). Such statements point to the performative elements in the score of *Hair* and indicate that the black tribe members used these opportunities to reinforce a collective black identity and highlight the civil rights they were fighting for. It is evident from Davis's remark that she clearly felt this was a struggle.

The early placement of 'Colored Spade' within the musical often results in the importance of the song being overlooked. In her 1991 publication, Barbara Lee Horn includes a few sentences describing the song and outlines its function as a song that 'introduces Hud' (Horn, 1991, p. 68). While the song does indeed function in this manner, it actually serves to introduce the nature of being African American in the politically charged era of the 1960s. As a unit, the song encapsulates the three phases of van Gennep's 'Rites of passage' (1960): separation, liminality (or transition), and re-assimilation or incorporation. The music and lyrics are Hud's expression of separation; both work together to define the unique experiences of black people in American society. By using music rooted in the traditions of African Americans, and lyrics that articulate their historical experiences in society, Hud is able to clearly separate the lived experience of black men from white men. The chorus functions as a protest song and is performed in this manner; the lyrics emphasize the liminal period, suggesting that African Americans can redefine their place in society, defy the laws and customs that bind American society and become President (albeit in this instance, of the United States of Love). As the song closes, we are offered a glimpse of the re-assimilation stage. The tonality of the final bars appears tenuous and unfinished but with the added threat implied by the final phrase[9] the status of Hud is now inverted. Through re-appropriation of the negative language and images assigned to African Americans, Hud has transformed the song into one of hope and empowerment.

Reinventing the Future

Two calls for action emerge from this reading of *Hair*: the first is one which implores us to revisit established works in the Broadway canon and revise the position from which we read those works. Doing so may prompt us to ask difficult and extremely complex questions whereby the answers may undoubtedly prove uncomfortable for any white scholar. The second call to action is one which invites scholars of musical theatre to develop and adopt analytical approaches which stem from other disciplines. The analysis presented here has largely been grounded in methods employed in popular music studies and has allowed for a consideration of the place of African American music in the history of that genre and, more specifically, its contribution to musical theatre. Adopting such an approach in an analysis of *Hair* has presented opportunities to place this musical in its specific historical moment, identifying how social and political events inform cultural production, and how those events were played out on the Broadway stage. Some 50 years after its release, *Hair* remains relevant. In an attempt to explain the social and political events of 2018, scholars are revisiting 1968 to explore the relationship between such events and the cultural product. Undertaking such work provides the opportunity to continue to highlight the social and artistic structures which have dictated the ways in which we understand identity and its associated performance.

While seeking to promote its universal message of peace, love and harmony, it can be argued that *Hair* often negates the multicultural voices heard throughout American history, presenting instead somewhat stereotypical representations of, in particular, African Americans. I argue that *Hair* fundamentally celebrates a multiplicity which could have provided the blueprint for a fractured American society. The musical uses stereotypes to communicate the nature of black culture in American society, but while appearing to subscribe to the tradition of presenting stereotypes of African Americans it instead uses these methods to highlight the separation inherent in American society and to prompt the audience to think critically about the issues being presented on stage. As Anju V.R. argues, in reference to the Black Arts Movement: 'taking one existing meaning and (re)appropriating it for new meanings [...] is an effective counter strategy to contest the racialised regimes of representation' (V.R., 2018, p. 32).

These scenes in *Hair* illuminate how stereotypical representations of the African American have been used and subsequently performed in order to re-appropriate black identity, offering ways in which marginalized voices in America may 'know the present and invent the future' (hooks, 1996, p. 213). Although these scenes present an ambiguous subject, the subjects are far from invisible, and yet earlier analyses of *Hair* have indeed rendered them as such by focusing instead on the principal white, male roles. I have attempted to reframe our approach to this musical by placing and celebrating the multiplicity and diversity of the Tribe at the centre of my analysis. In doing so, I have illustrated how African American characters in *Hair* experiment with the ways in which they are culturally defined and how the moments of liminality provide opportunities for both the audience and performers to consider what the resulting re-assimilation phase may be: to dream of a better world in which 'all men' (and women), regardless of race or culture, 'are created equal'.

Notes

1. This figure included at least 75,000 white people in addition to the white families watching on television in their homes.
2. The Uncle Tom caricature portrays black men as faithful, happy, generous, selfless and submissive servants. They 'endear themselves to white audiences and emerge as a hero of sorts' (Bogle, 1994, p. 6).
3. In addition to Robert Christgau's review, Onkey also cites the reviews of Mablen Jones and Craig Werner.
4. The hextatonic scale is built on the minor pentatonic scale. In blues performance, both the major and minor pentatonic scales are frequently used and the result bears resemblance to a number of modes, particularly mixolydian and dorian. The modal system of scales existed prior to the Western harmonic system and was used as the harmonic basis for folk melodies and music of Non-Western tradition.
5. James Rado and Gerome Ragni brought the lyrics of 13 songs (of which one was 'Colored Spade') to the composer, Galt MacDermot. The duo had written these lyrics as a result of research conducted by talking to characters on the streets and reading press articles. (Rado, 2009)
6. 'Little Black Sambo' is a character created by British novelist Helen Bannerman and refers to perhaps the most controversial portrayal of the caricature and stereotype of the 'picaninny'; portrayed as lazy, shiftless and child-like.
7. The interview was recorded in New York in 2003 and features raw footage used for the documentary *Broadway: The American Musical.*
8. Davis (1973), Grode (2010), Johnson (2004).
9. Hud's final threatening phrase makes mention of the 'boogie man' (MacDermot, Rado and Ragni, 1967, p. 24). The spelling of the word 'boogie' is of particular interest; all historical implications of 'bogeyman' have been erased and instead, the reference is firmly grounded in the importance of music and movement.

References

Als, H. (2009) Not So Free Love: Breaking Out and Up in 'Hair' and 'Reasons to be Pretty'. Available at: www.newyorker.com/magazine/2009/04/13/not-so-free-love. Accessed 19 April 2018.
Bogle, D. (1994) *Toms, Coons, Mulattoes, Mammies and Bucks: An Interpretive History of Blacks in American Films.* New York: Continuum.

Campbell, N. & Kean, A. (2012) *American Cultural Studies*. Oxon: Routledge.
Davis, L. (1973) *Letting down My Hair; Two Years with the Love Rock Tribe – From Dawning to Downing of Aquarius*. New York: Fields Books.
Denselow, R. (1989) *When the Music's Over. The Story of Political Pop*. London: Faber and Faber.
Edney, K. (2013) Tapping the Ivories: Jazz and Tap Dance in *Jelly's Last Jam*. In Symonds, D. & Taylor, M. (eds.), *Gestures of Music Theater. The Performativity of Song and Dance* (pp. 113–127). New York: Oxford University Press.
Frith, S. (1996) *Performing Rites*. New York: Oxford University Press.
Frith, S. (2007) *Taking Popular Music Seriously*. Hampshire: Ashgate Publishing Ltd.
Gilroy, P. (1991) It Ain't Where You're From, It's Where You're At. The Dialectics of Diasporic Identification. *Third Text*, 5(13), 3–16.
Grode, E. (2010) *Hair. The Story of the Show that Defined a Generation*. London: Goodman.
Hooks, B. (1996) *Reel to Real. Race, Sex and Class at the Movies*. New York: Routledge.
Horn, B.L. (1991) *The Age of Hair. Evolution and Impact of Broadway's First Rock Musical*. New York: Greenwood Press.
Johnson, E.P. (2003) *Appropriating Blackness. Performance and the Politics of Authenticity*. Durham, NC: Duke University Press.
Johnson, J. (2004) *Good Hair Days. A Personal Journey with the American Tribal Love-Rock Musical Hair*. Lincoln: iUniverse.
King, M.L. (1963) *I Have a Dream. Speech at the March on Washington*. Available at: www.archives.gov/press/exhibits/dream-speech.pdf. Accessed 5 June 2014.
MacDermot, G. (2003) Interviewed by Michael Kantor.
MacDermot, G., Rado, J. & Ragni, G. (1967) *Hair: Piano-Conductor's Score*. New York: Tams-Witmark.
Martin, B.D. (2004) *The Theater Is in the Street*. Massachusetts: University of Massachusetts Press.
McClary, S. (1993) Narrative Agendas in "Absolute" Music. In Solie, R. (ed.) *Musicology and Difference* (pp. 326–344). Berkeley, CA: University of California Press.
Miller, S. (2003) *Let the Sun Shine In. The Genius of Hair*. New Haven, CT: Heinemann.
Murray, C.S. (1989) *Crosstown Traffic*. London: Faber and Faber.
Onkey, L. (2002) Voodoo Child: Jimi Hendrix and the Politics of Race in the Sixties. In Braunstein, P. & Doyle, M.W. (eds.) *Imagine Nation. The American Counterculture of the 1960s and '70s* (pp. 189–214). New York: Routledge.

Rado, J. (2009) *Hair the Musical.* Available at: http://hairthemusical.com/history. html. Accessed 15 August 2017.

Schlesinger, A.M. (1998) *The Disuniting of America. Reflections on a Multicultural Society.* New York: Norton.

Southern, E. (1971) *The Music of Black Americans*, 3rd edition. New York: W.W. Norton.

Strausbaugh, J. (2006) *Black like You. Blackface, Whiteface, Insult and Imitation in American Popular Culture.* New York: Penguin Group.

V.R., A. (2018) Black Is [Really] Beautiful: Role of Black Arts Movement in African American Literature. *Singularities*, 5(1), 32–36.

Van Gennep, A. (1960) *The Rites of Passage.* Chicago, IL: University of Chicago Press.

Wilson, O. (1999) The Heterogeneous Sound Ideal in African American Music. In Dagel-Caponi, G. (ed.) *Signifyin(G), Sanctifyin' and Slam Dunking: A Reader in African American Expressive Culture* (pp. 157–171). Amherst, MA: University of Massachusetts Press.

Wollman, E. (2006) *The Theater Will Rock: A History of the Rock Musical, from Hair to Hedwig.* Ann Arbor, MI: University of Michigan Press.

Wollman, E. (2014) 'Busted for Her Beauty: Hair's Female Characters', *American Music Review*, XLIII(2), 1–7.

11

'What about Love?': Claiming and Reclaiming LGBTQ+ Spaces in Twenty-First Century Musical Theatre

James Lovelock

'Broadway: Not Just For Gays Anymore', the opening number to the 65th Tony Awards in 2011 at the Beacon Theatre, presented an affectionate parody of the long-established trope that musical theatre is a homosexual art form. David Javerbaum and Adam Schlesinger's musical number used cast members from Tony-nominated musicals to ostensibly bolster the heterosexual credentials of the musical, while the music resembled 'The Company Way' from *How To Succeed In Business Without Really Trying* (1961) and the vintage choreography paid homage to Busby Berkeley with its use of box steps, kick lines and canon. The ambiguity of these heterosexual/homosexual overtones was embodied in Neil Patrick Harris, a gay actor then best known to the general public for his role as womanizing Barney Stinson in *How I Met Your Mother* (2005–2014). The performance simultaneously proclaimed inclusivity for a heterosexual (male) audience while continuing to display the level of 'camp' traditionally associated with musical theatre.

The success of the number relied on the myth about musical theatre and homosexuality continuing to have currency for both the TV audience and, as Grace Barnes notes, as an 'in-joke' for theatre professionals sat in the auditorium (Barnes, 2015, p. 109). The stereotype clearly reaches further into popular culture than this, as exemplified in a 2003 episode of *The Simpsons* where Grady, a gay character, tells Homer that 'almost anyone who's ever written, starred in, or even *seen* a play is gay'

187

(Kirkland, 2003). As David Halperin writes, 'a stereotype doesn't have to be generally valid in order to contain some truth' (2012, p. 91), and there is evidence in the work of D.A. Miller (1998) and John Clum (1999) that gay men in the 1950s and 1960s had a special relationship with musicals.

The early twenty-first century has seen an increase in explicit representations of queer characters in musical theatre. Until recently, the majority of queer characters portrayed in musicals were gay men who largely adhere to three narrative tropes that might be labelled as the 'drag queen', the 'drama queen' and the 'dancing queen'. Clum's suggestion that 'Broadway's version of a gay musical is always problematic, foregrounding a comforting, stereotypical version of gayness for the bus-and-tunnel crowd' (1999, p. 10) resonates with the use of these tropes, which often minimize the 'queerness' of the characters involved.

The Drag Queen

Musical theatre has a long history of characters in drag, although such characters were largely used for comic value until the 1970s. Since then, drag has often been used as a mask for queer characters. In the case of characters such as the Emcee in *Cabaret* (1966) and Frank-N-Furter in *The Rocky Horror Show* (1973), it serves to maximize their sexual ambiguity by allowing the maximum possible gender combinations in sexual partnerships. Contrastingly, Albin's female persona of Zaza in *La Cage Aux Folles* (1983) allows him to access aspects of his personality that his own persona does not achieve. John Clum notes that Albin's use of drag allows the audience to identify Albin and Georges as 'a classic butch-femme couple' and criticizes the 'conservative' values of the musical, noting that the love duet 'Song on the Sand' could be applicable to any middle-aged couple regardless of gender (Clum, 1999, p. 14). Later musicals such as *The Producers* (2001) and *Billy Elliot* (2005) do not always differentiate clearly between the character and their drag persona, resulting in an uncomfortable conflation between drag and homosexuality, although *Priscilla, Queen of the Desert* (2006) explores the differences between the gender and sexual identities of the three drag queens more effectively, in particular through its treatment of Bernadette as a transgender character.

The Drama Queen

In 2013, James Rawson noted in his film blog for *The Guardian* that 56.5 per cent of gay, bisexual and transsexual characters whose portrayals were nominated for Academy Awards died by the end of their respective films, compared to 16.5 per cent of heterosexual characters. In fact, Rawson notes that only four of the 23 gay, bisexual and transsexual characters get a happy ending across his 19-year survey (Rawson, 2013). The tendency to kill off or otherwise punish gay characters is also prominent in musical theatre history, resulting in a 'drama queen' trope that results in many gay protagonists failing to find a happy ending.

One of the earliest examples of the 'drama queen' trope comes in *A Chorus Line*, where Paul, a Puerto Rican ex-drag queen, falls and injures himself during a tap sequence. This ensures that Paul does not make the final selection of eight dancers for the chorus line (and neither does Greg, the other openly queer character) and thus frustrates his possible happy ending in a violent manner. Paul's life story was apparently based on Nicholas Dante, who co-wrote the book (Viagas et al., 2006, pp. 101–102), and it is possible that there is a sense of cathartic relief in this depiction. Indeed, given the backdrop of the AIDS crisis and the subsequent backlash against queer sexualities, it is unsurprising that many queer characters of the 1980s and 1990s met an untimely end in musical theatre. The depiction of Marvin's partner Whizzer's death in *Falsettoland* (1990) was written in the midst of the crisis and its immediate aftermath, and songs such as 'Something Bad is Happening' and 'Unlikely Lovers' are given an added poignancy as both the queer characters and the writer come to terms with this threat to their identity. 'Unlikely Lovers' is particularly unusual in that it is a quartet written for two same-sex couples – the couple sing a bickering love duet as Marvin refuses to leave Whizzer's side, before they are joined by Cordelia and Charlotte ('the lesbians from next door') in a rich harmonic reprise of the chorus complete with trumpet descant. The recurring phrase 'let's be scared together' (Finn and Lapine, 1995, pp. 140, 142) anchors the number in the specific moment of the AIDS crisis while also touching the universal and timeless emotion of the fear of death.

Through the 1990s and 2000s, the 'drama queen' trope often focuses on the twin pressures of individual self-loathing and gay hedonism. Jason in *Bare: A Pop Opera* (2000) overdoses on drugs after splitting with his boyfriend Peter, and Mile End Lee in *Closer To Heaven* (2001) suffers a similar fate. The majority of 'drama queen' characters are written by gay and bisexual writers and the impulse to tell some of the difficult and tragic stories of queer life post-Stonewall is understandable, particularly given the emotional potential of musical theatre as a genre. Nevertheless, the focus on writing tragedy contributes to a wider tendency to deny positive outcomes for gay characters across a variety of narrative forms.

The Dancing Queen

The return of the musical comedy at the beginning of the twenty-first century saw the satirical tone of shows such as *South Park*, *The Simpsons* and *Monty Python's Flying Circus* transferred to musical theatre. While the parodies are largely affectionate – *Spamalot*'s Sir Lancelot remarks, on getting married to Prince Herbert, 'just think, Herbert, in a thousand years this will still be controversial' (Idle and Du Prez, 2005) – the numbers tend to re-emphasize the stereotype of the 'dancing queen', a threefold conflation between camp, homosexuality and musical theatre, without promoting any alternative representations of queer characters. *Avenue Q* (2003) is an exception to the above rule in that it allows the character of Rod a believable journey despite the fact that he begins as a stereotypical closeted Republican. Rod has to come to terms with the fact that he is in love with his housemate Nicky, who does not feel the same way as him. In fact, Kate Monster's realization that if 'someone doesn't love you back/it isn't such a crime' (Marx et al., 2010, p. 93) could equally apply to Rod, and this parallel is explored further through Rod and Kate's duet 'Fantasies Come True'. While *Avenue Q* does contain a satirical number in 'If You Were Gay', it is led by Rod's heterosexual housemate Nicky and seeks to develop their relationship rather than satirizing homosexuality per se – possibly because of the involvement of Jeff Marx and Jeff Whitty, who both identify as queer. *Avenue Q* succeeds in creating themes that are universal and applying them to straight and queer characters alike – this is apparent in 'The Internet is For Porn', where all the male characters are treated in the same way through the universal theme of masturbation.

The idea of universal themes leads towards the thorny topic of assimilation, and the question of whether rejecting the concept of the 'gay musical' dilutes the representation of queer identity. In fact, the opposite is true – by exploring the fundamental differences between queer and straight experiences, musicals can produce a wider range of queer characters that carry an authenticity that is often missing from characters that follow established tropes. David Halperin's suggestion that 'making the Broadway musical more explicitly gay-themed […] does not succeed in making the musical itself more satisfactory as a vehicle of gay desire' (2012, p. 106) seems to underestimate the political power of LGBTQ+ representation on stage, particularly in terms of encouraging younger LGBTQ+ audiences to connect with the form. It is possible that, through denying the importance of LGBTQ+ characters in the musical, Clum and Halperin are unwittingly buying into the heterosexist standpoint of critics such as Mark Steyn, who in a chapter entitled 'The Fags' asks: 'if the entire genre has a gay sensibility, who needs a show specifically addressing the subject? (1998, p. 201)

'Not Just for Gays Anymore?' – Musical Theatre as a 'Safe' Queer Space

Steyn's argument can be seen as the culmination of the age-old trope of musical theatre as a safe 'queer space'. Scholars point to the contribution of gay writers such as Novello, Coward, Hart, Kander, Ebb, Loewe and Sondheim. They cite the proliferation of gay men in the audience and onstage, and they note the affection that gay men show diva performers such as Judy Garland or Bernadette Peters (see Clum, 1999, pp. 133–196). Yet these observations mask the fact that the 'queer space' has rarely extended explicitly into the fictional worlds on stage. The importance of 'queering' and 'divadom' in the history of LGBTQ+ identities should not be underestimated, but, 50 years after the legalization of homosexuality in the United Kingdom, it is apposite to ask whether the supposed 'queerness' of the musical theatre genre has been utilized as an excuse to maintain an impoverished queer heritage within a genre that is uniquely positioned to externalize the idiosyncrasies of what it means to be queer. In particular, the focus on the relationship between musical theatre and homosexual men has obscured the lack of representation of lesbian, bisexual and transgender characters in musicals until recently.

Contemporary Queer Spaces

The past few years on Broadway and in the West End have seen LGBTQ+ writers begin to explore 'queer spaces' of their own. Since 2014, Broadway has seen revivals of *The Color Purple* (2015, via the 2013 Menier Chocolate Factory production in London) and *Falsettos* (2016), alongside new musicals such as *Fun Home* (2013 then 2015 on Broadway), *If/Then* (2013) and *Come From Away* (2015). Alongside *The Color Purple*, London has seen its first productions of *Yank!* (2017 via the Hope Mill Theatre in Manchester), *Soho Cinders* (2012), *Everybody's Talking About Jamie* (2017) and *Fun Home* (2018). The range of LGBTQ+ characters represented in these productions demonstrates the importance of the lived experience of LGBTQ+ people both in source material and as book writers, lyricists and composers. This chapter analyses four musicals that foreground LGBTQ+ writers – *The Color Purple*, *Yank!*, *Fun Home* and *Everybody's Talking About Jamie* – to understand how exploring 'queer spaces' in history and in the present can contribute to LGBTQ+ representation in musical theatre.

'I'm Beautiful … and I'm Here' – *The Color Purple* as a Womanist Utopia

In her 1983 prose collection *In Search of Our Mothers' Gardens*, Alice Walker proposes the term 'womanist' as 'a black feminist or feminist of color' and 'a woman who loves other women, sexually and/or non-sexually' (Walker, 1983, p. xi). In *The Color Purple* (1982), Celie is a black, lesbian woman who is abused by her stepfather and her husband, but who finds her identity through her relationship with various women within her community. Walker's focus on Celie is thus an act of resistance against the compulsory white heterosexuality that polices the American novel (Bealer, 2009, p. 38) as well as an exploration of the 'womanist' principles explored in her later collection. E. Patrick Johnson's development of 'quare studies', as derived from the 'African American vernacular for queer [that]... always denotes excess incapable of being contained within conventional categories of *being*' (Johnson, 2001, p. 2), is based on Walker's etymology, and both 'quare' and 'womanist' principles are integral to an understanding of *The Color Purple* as a Broadway musical. Yet the musical is rarely read intersectionally by musical theatre scholars – and thus both 'womanist' and 'quare' readings are often lost.

The Color Purple (2005) challenges the white, heterosexist and patriarchal privileges enjoyed by mainstream musical theatre writing through its depiction of Celie and Shug as black, female and queer characters written by a writing team with combined lived experience across all these identities. Johnson notes that 'most often, white theorists fail to acknowledge and address racial privilege' (2001, p. 5), and since this chapter is written from a white, gay male perspective, it is important to interrogate the intersectional qualities of Celie and Shug's relationship. In particular, there is a different emphasis in the way that Alice Walker explores the social disadvantages of Celie's position as a black woman in society but allows Celie and Shug to operate outside of traditional social attitudes towards same-sex relationships within black communities. Barbara Smith argues that black heterosexual women tend to marginalize black lesbian women as 'heterosexual privilege is usually the only privilege that Black women have [...] maintaining "straightness" is our last resort' (Smith et al., 1982, p. 171); none of Squeak, Nettie or Sofia reacts in this manner towards Celie and Shug's relationship. Alice Walker's explicit descriptions of Shug and Celie's sexual relationship in the novel also defies Evelynn M. Hammonds' description of a 'politics of silence' surrounding black women and their sexuality (1983, p. 94) as Celie and Shug openly embody 'womanist' and 'quare' principles in their narrative.

Celie's attraction to Shug is first introduced in the sixth chapter of *The Color Purple* when Celie is given a picture of Shug Avery by her stepmother (who does not appear in the musical). Celie instantly recognizes Shug as 'the most beautiful woman I have ever seen': 'I ast her to give me the picture. An all night long I stare at it. An now when I dream, I dream of Shug Avery.' (Walker, 1982, p. 13) In the musical, Celie is aware of Shug – 'She Mister ol' girlfriend' (Funderburg, 2006, p. 139) – but she does not establish an attraction to her until Shug's first appearance on stage. Before her meeting with Shug, Celie performs a number of short solos about different women (Nettie at the beginning of 'Our Prayer' and in 'Lily of the Field', and Sofia in 'Dear God, Sofia'). In the 2014 revival, these passages are accompanied by marimba, piano and woodwind, with an occasional use of muted trumpet. Contrastingly in 'Dear God, Shug', there is a prominent off-beat click that represents Celie's excitement, and the paired clarinets are supported by the marimba before the jazz saxophone and trumpet enter the orchestration. As Celie sings 'Not like Nettie, not like Sofia, not like no-one else' (Funderburg, 2006, p. 138), her solo is accompanied by electric guitar, bass and drum kit for the first time as her sexuality is awakened by Shug.

Shug's own attraction to Celie is made explicit in 'Too Beautiful For Words' as she encourages Celie to look in the mirror to discover her beauty. Shug's conclusion that the 'grace' that Celie brings into the world is 'too beautiful for words' (Funderburg, 2006, p. 142) is quite different to the parallel scene in Walker's original novel, where Shug uses the mirror to teach Celie how to masturbate: 'I look at her and touch it with my finger. A little shiver go through me. Nothing much. But just enough to tell me this the right button to mash. Maybe.' (Walker, 1982, p. 49) In the musical, 'Push Da Button' is transformed from an intimate scene between Shug and Celie into a jukejoint number in which Shug addresses all of the black men and women present. Patricia Hill Collins suggests the intersection between black and lesbian identities often reinforces the white stereotype of black female sexuality as 'deviant' through 'the co-joining of Black heterosexual women's sexual deviancy as lying in their excess sexual appetite with the perceived deviancy of Black lesbians as lying in their rejection of what makes women feminine, namely, heterosexual contact with men' (Collins, 2002, p. 146), and there is a sense in which Shug's highly sexualized public performance acts to obscure her private same-sex relationship with Celie. Indeed, Shug's bisexuality is seldom mentioned during critical analysis, and there is the danger that the musical is unwittingly engaging in Hammonds' 'politics of silence' through altering the context of 'Push Da Button'.

Nevertheless, the convention of the love duet in 'What About Love?' clearly establishes a queer relationship between Shug and Celie. Allee Willis, one of the songwriters, has offered the duet as evidence that the musical does not water down the relationship – 'I hope anybody who sees it understands it's real love' (Stockwell, 2005). The number combines a coming-out moment for both Celie and Shug with a more conventional pop music duet, thus both resisting and repurposing the heterosexual mode of the love duet. Celie begins by confessing that she is 'lifted up to the clouds' by Shug's kiss (Funderburg, 2006, p. 149), reaffirming that her lesbian identity is established through the kiss that seals the romantic attraction between the women immediately before the duet. Shug, too, confirms that her feelings for Celie have taken her by surprise as love was the one thing that she 'knew all about' (Funderburg, 2006, p. 149), suggesting that Celie is the first to awaken Shug's bisexuality.

Musically, the duet is in the vein of 1980s soul duets such as 'Endless Love' in its homogeneous thirds in the verses and choruses and vocal counterpoint in the bridge sections. Similarly, the use of piano and strings places the number as a conventional love duet – but with two female voices rather than the more traditional male/female arrangement. The evocation of the love duet through the use of musical genre makes it difficult to read the number as anything other than a lesbian duet, particularly considering the simplicity and directness of the lyrics. Thus while many of the explicit scenes from the novel are erased in the musical adaptation of *The Color Purple*, the writers adapt existing conventions in order to support the original queer narrative.

Celie's identity as a lesbian woman is as central to her character as her position as an oppressed black woman within her society, and categorizing *The Color Purple* as a 'black musical', a 'feminist musical' or even a 'lesbian musical' fails to understand the importance of all of these intersections as part of Walker's 'womanist' narrative. Apryl Denny offers the persuasive observation that *The Color Purple* 'offers not a depiction of how the world is but of how it might be if society were to repudiate hierarchy and embrace Womanism' (Denny, 2009, p. 284). Celie's rejection of Shug's promiscuity in 'I'm Here' does not nullify her lesbian identity, but it does release Celie from the patriarchal society of compulsory heterosexuality in which she was contained in the first act of the musical – above all, Celie is 'thankful for loving who I really am' (Funderburg, 2006, p. 173).

'It Isn't Right or Wrong, Just Something True' – *Yank*! as a Reclamation of LGBTQ+ Spaces in Golden Age Musical Theatre

While *The Color Purple* creates a queer space through a utopian vision of the historical period in which it is set, David and Joseph Zellnik's *Yank!* aims to 'stitch queer stories back into the larger narrative of the "Greatest Generation"' (Zellnik and Zellnik, 2017), through a reimagining of the Golden Age musical. *Yank!* is inspired by the oral histories in Allan Bérubé's *Coming Out Under Fire* (1990), which notes that during the 1930s and 1940s, young people who had homosexual desires had little in the way of help in recognizing their identity:'They were likely to lead isolated lives, not knowing anyone else like themselves, with no one to talk to about their feelings and often unsure what they were' (Bérubé, 2010, p. 6). Bérubé suggests that the mobilization for the Second World War allowed young men and women to mix with different groups of people and to recognize others that felt the same as them, both in military camps and at gay bars and nightclubs that began to flourish around the cities in which the military was stationed. These new 'queer spaces' are fully explored by the gay and lesbian characters in *Yank!*, allowing a very different perspective on the period dominated by the so-called Golden Age musicals.

The Zellnik brothers cite Oscar Hammerstein II as a major influence on the show, and theatre critic Dominic Maxwell describes *Yank!* as 'the kind of show Rodgers and Hammerstein might have written if they had chosen as their hero a gay 18 year old in combat and in love' (Maxwell, 2017). Nevertheless, there is some truth in John Clum's depiction of Hammerstein as 'the musical's bard of heterosexual normality' (1999, p. 92), and it is possible that focusing on Hammerstein's legacy of the integrated book musical obscures part of the queer history that *Yank!* utilizes in reclaiming a LGBTQ+ space in traditional musical theatre. The show itself begins in 1943 and the musical language seems as akin to Rodgers and Hart as Rodgers and Hammerstein, broadening the musical pastiche to incorporate the queer sensibilities in Hart's lyrics.

Yank! is bookended by the song 'Rememb'ring You', which is the inscription in the fictional journal of Private 'Stu' Stewart that frames the narrative. The number is performed by Mitch Adams, Stu's sweetheart in the musical, and is tinged with regret at a lovers' parting: 'No matter what I do/I keep rememb'ring you' (Zellnik, 2017, p. 4). The staging of 'Rememb'ring You' encourages the audience to read the song as 'queer', as Mitch is singing directly to the modern-day young man that has discovered Stu's diary (the same actor that plays Stu in the rest of the show), and this aligns the number with the lyrics of Hart, Cole Porter, Ivor Novello and Noël Coward. In particular, the sentiments reflect the unrequited love of Hart's 'It Never Entered My Mind' ('Once I laughed when I heard you say/that I'd be playing solitaire'), and 'I'm Talkin' To My Pal', which was cut from the 1942 production of *Pal Joey* ('I can't be sure of girls/I'm not at home with men/I'm ending up with me again'). This link is even more explicit in the shower scene in the title number of *Yank!*, where Stu discusses how he hates being around men – 'maybe that means I'm even more normal than them, and not how I sometimes feel: like a fella somehow born in the wrong kind of body' (Zellnik, 2017, p. 11).

The musical language of 'Rememb'ring You' acts as a portal into a queer heritage inhabited by the great queer lyricists of the 1930s and 1940s, and it is possible to read *Yank!* as a continuation of Rodgers and Hart's sensibility within the framework of Hammerstein's book musicals. In particular, Stu's acceptance of his own homosexuality breaks with the Rodgers and Hammerstein tradition, as Stu is not given his own musical number until midway through the second act. In Act One, Stu is often given the final verse in ensemble numbers as he comes to terms with his feelings for Mitch as 'the most beautiful man I've ever seen' in 'Polishing Shoes' (Zellnik, 2017, p. 19) and the fact that he does not feel 'all the good and normal things that other fellas do' in 'Betty' (Zellnik, 2017, p. 33). Ultimately it is up to Artie, a homosexual photographer for

Yank magazine, to take Stu under his wing through teaching him about the 'queer spaces' available to conscripted GIs. Artie's character is immediately defined in his cheeky verse to 'Click': 'How do you find your match? How do you pick?/Follow your heart and follow your–' (Zellnik, 2017, p. 42).

The number subverts the typical MGM film tap numbers of the early 1940s through using tap to symbolize the methods of attracting male attention in gay bars. The audience never sees Stu and Artie in these locations outside of the 'Click' dream sequence, but their promiscuity becomes a bone of contention when Stu returns to the squad after a period as a Yank reporter. Artie's second number, 'Light On Your Feet', utilizes a similar dance idiom to teach Stu and Mitch how to avoid indictment. Artie's carefree attitude contrasts with Louise, the lesbian officer, who advises Stu and Artie that they need to 'always strive to be a credit' (Zellnik, 2017, p. 50) in order to involve detection.

During the unfolding of Stu's journey, the public 'queer spaces' conjured by Artie in his 'dream sequences' are contrasted with the private 'queer spaces' within the confines of Stu's conscription. Stu and Mitch's relationship thrives in the private spaces of showers, bunk beds and (literally) closets – the only available closed spaces within their homosocial environment. Their sexual relationship is contrasted with the intimate relationships of their fellow squad members, who have their own 'buddies' that they protect and occasionally share a dance with. Eventually Mitch proposes a utopian vision for 'A Couple of Regular Guys' after the war has ended: living in the house he has already put a payment down on, 'the perfect size/For a couple of regular guys' (Zellnik, 2017, p. 67).

This number is more in the Rodgers and Hammerstein tradition of 'dream songs' – there are clear similarities with 'If I Loved You' from *Carousel*, 'I Have Dreamed' from *The King and I* and 'Sixteen going on Seventeen' from *The Sound of Music*. It is unsurprising that Stu's reprise of the song at the end of the musical is interrupted by Mitch puncturing the homonormative vision that he has set up. Yet Stu has already expressed his acceptance of his sexuality in 'Just True'; he explains that 'what we have is special/what we are is not': they are two of hundreds of thousands (Zellnik, 2017, pp. 85–86). Ultimately Mitch marries his childhood sweetheart Becky, but Stu has completed his journey of coming out: 'You already found me, Mitch. And Artie found me. And I found me' (Zellnik, 2017, p. 104).

Despite the bookending of the musical with the modern-day young man listening to 'Rememb'ring You', many critics chose to focus on the heterosexual elements of the story. Alfred Hickling in *The Guardian* remarked that 'the chief honours go to the lone female, Sarah-Louise Young, who portrays every mom, sweetheart and radio idol that helped to get these brave, frightened men through the war' (Hickling, 2017), while Alun Hood compared the 'depiction of men under unimaginable pressure finding solace in unattainable and impossibly glamorous women' with *Kiss of The Spider Woman* (Hood, 2017). These critical responses might be compared to the two renditions of 'Rememb'ring You' in *Yank!*. The 'original' version is heard in the middle of Act One, performed by Dinah for the forces on the radio. Dinah is described in the script as 'a girl-next-door type with a kittenish sound' (Zellnik, 2017, p. 52), and the swung rhythm locates the song as part of the repertoire designed to keep up the morale of the troops. However, the audience has already heard Mitch singing the song directly to the young man, and thus Dinah's version feels insincere and inauthentic against the queer specificity of the opening number. It is possible that this reading itself comes from the recognition of a queer space that is inaccessible to some critics of the musical.

'Ring of Keys' – The Unfinished Work of Coming Out in *Fun Home*

Although *Fun Home* is not the first Broadway musical with a lesbian protagonist, it is currently the only Broadway musical that features a lesbian character where the original source material, the book and the lyrics are all written by lesbian women. The musical is based on Alison Bechdel's autobiographical graphic novel of the same, and is adapted by book writer and lyricist Lisa Kron. Furthermore, the musical is unique in that it portrays a gay male character (Alison's father Bruce) from a lesbian perspective – both in the writing of the show and from the perspective of the fictional Alison in the show. Alison's verbal 'caption' at the end of 'Welcome To Our House on Maple Avenue' neatly summarizes the theme at the heart of the musical, as Alison notes that both she and her dad were 'gay', but 'he killed himself, and I became a lesbian cartoonist' (Kron and Tesori, 2015, p. 17). At its heart, *Fun Home* explores the relationship between a daughter and her father, as Rebecca Applin Warner's chapter in this volume addresses. As Applin Warner notes, Alison's central question is 'am I just like you?' (Kron and Tesori, 2015, p. 11) and this question is explored through both the text and the music within the musical.

Fun Home follows the thematic structure of the graphic novel, focusing on three key periods in Alison and Bruce's relationship – Alison's childhood, Alison coming out while at college, and Alison reaching the same age as Bruce was when he committed suicide. Each period involves Alison and Bruce negotiating their respective 'coming out' in different ways, highlighting that the process is continuous rather than a singular occurrence and reminding the audience that the characters are still negotiating the heterosexual matrix despite the inherent 'queer space' of their relationship.

By the time that Alison has explicitly 'outed' herself and her father to the audience, we have already experienced Bruce's alienation from his family in 'Welcome To Our House On Maple Avenue'. As the family tidy up the house for Bruce's visitor from the local historical society, Bruce is upstairs putting the finishing touches to his make-up. Bruce utilizes one of the key lyrical motifs of the musical – 'not so bad if I say so myself' – as he admires himself in the mirror, but when he joins the family his music is in a one-bar canon with the rest of the family, showing Bruce to be out of step with the familial group. In the original graphic novel, Bechdel suggests that Bruce 'used his skillful artifice not to make things, but to make things to be what they were' (2007, p. 16). This can be seen in Bruce's first 'coming out' scene, where he seduces his ex-student Roy. Bruce repeats the 'not so bad, if I say so myself' motif and repurposes the 'he wants' motif from 'Maple Avenue' into his 'I want' motif. Alison comments that Bruce's relationship with Roy is like a '1950s lesbian pulp novel' in its 'tawdry love' (Kron and Tesori, 2015, p. 30), and Bruce's use of alcohol in the seduction points towards a darker side of his 'coming out' being for an exclusive audience of young male ex-students.

Contrastingly, Medium Alison's self-loathing is largely contained in a short scene outside the Gay Union at college, where she asks God not to make her a 'lesbian' or a 'homosexual'. Indeed, by her next scene, Alison has come out both to herself and to her friend Joan and is preparing to come out to her parents. At this stage, Alison has yet to sing anything other than the 'not so bad if I say so myself' motif, which she uses to describe her drawing process. A short scene between Alison as a child and her father indicates that Bruce is at least partially responsible for this reticence – Alison is refusing to wear a dress to a party (preferring 'a boy shirt and pants'), but Bruce manipulates her into conforming by suggesting that 'people will talk about you behind your back' (Kron and Tesori, 2015, p. 37). This scene leads back to Medium Alison coming out to her parents by letter, again repurposing one of Bruce's motifs: 'I want, I want, I am … a lesbian'. Nevertheless, Alison is still worried about fitting in with the 'real lesbians', stating that she is 'asexual' until Joan's kiss convinces her that she is attracted to women.

'Changing My Major To Joan' is the first solo in the musical as Medium Alison comes to terms with her first sexual experience. The number combines Lisa Kron's stream-of-consciousness lyrics with Jeanine Tesori's tonally and metrically shifting accompaniment to portray the unfamiliar giddiness that Alison is experiencing. Tesori avoids the tonic of A♭ throughout the opening section as Kron's lyrics cycle between the phrases 'last night', 'Joan' and 'Oh my god'. As Alison begins to pour out the details of her first passionate encounter where she was 'too enthusiastic', the music still avoids a clear statement of the tonic chord, which is only heard in its first inversion. At the end of the section, Tesori suggests that she is working towards a II-V-I perfect cadence, but unexpectedly arrives on an implied E7 chord as the dominant of A major, literally 'changing' the 'major'. The first clear statement of a tonic chord in root position comes on the phrase 'sex with Joan', and the first perfect cadence comes on 'kissing Joan', suggesting that Alison is beginning to formulate her identity more securely. Alison's lyrics begin to unfold through repetition as her confidence increases in this section – she first sings of changing her major to 'Joan', then to 'sex with Joan', and finally to 'sex with Joan with a minor in kissing Joan' (Kron and Tesori, 2015, p. 40).

This technique of extending lyrically and musically continues in Alison's second verse, which lasts for 16 bars rather than the original 14-bar section as Alison reminds herself that there is no need for 'dignity' in this situation. The bridge section returns to the more tentative mood of the opening section – the music gradually becomes more tonally ambiguous before returning to a clear perfect cadence into the new key of B♭ major for the final chorus. The coda section recalls the phrasing of the introduction, but this time Alison clearly knows where she is heading musically and lyrically – back to Joan and a final cadence in B♭ major.

The placement of 'Changing My Major' as Alison's first solo song is important since it emphasizes the chronology of Alison's thought process. Older Alison chooses to remember her 'coming out' at college as a three-stage process, where she comes out to herself (and subsequently Joan), and then comes out to her parents by letter, and finally 'consummates' the process through her encounter with Joan. Her memories of her coming out are interrupted by childhood memories of her father – 'Changing My Major' is followed by a sequence in which Bruce criticizes Alison for her 'half-baked' attempt at drawing a map. In 'Maps', Older Alison discovers that she can draw a circle around the key events of Bruce's life, with the audience increasingly aware that Alison herself is still trapped within that circle. While Medium Alison is still unaware of her father's sexuality, Older Alison remembers a number of occasions during her childhood in which Bruce covered for his own indiscretions with young men. This triggers an earlier 'coming out' memory, when Small Alison first recognises something of her identity in an 'old-school butch' delivery woman (Kron and Tesori, 2015, p. 56).

'Ring of Keys' is musically much simpler than 'Changing My Major To Joan' – it is in a lilting 6/8 and remains in the key of E major throughout. The number contains a similar tension between the tentative verses and the confident choruses, this time through Kron's use of ellipses in her verse lyrics to show Small Alison reaching for a truth that she cannot yet articulate. 'Ring of Keys' also utilizes an unfolding list in the chorus to show how the delivery woman's 'butch' appearance makes an impression on Alison through her 'lace-up boots' and her 'ring of keys' – a rebuttal to her father's insistence on the feminine dress code of party dresses and hair barrettes. The song culminates in Small Alison's recognition that 'I know you', which she restates three times. It is clear that Small Alison has undergone a 'coming out' process of her own – not necessarily recognizing her sexual orientation, but understanding that she does not conform to the gender identities offered by her family.

The final section of *Fun Home* contrasts Alison's coming out with Bruce's inability to come to terms with his own sexuality. It is Helen that tells Alison about Bruce's infidelity with young men, and it is clear that Helen is struggling to accept Alison's sexuality as she refers to Joan as Alison's 'friend'. Contrastingly, Bruce seems to utilize Alison's revelation to become more open with his daughter, but it is clear that he is unable to see outside his own 'circle' in order to connect with Alison. 'Telephone Wire' is a representation of Alison and Bruce's last car journey where the two characters are in completely different tonal and rhythmic areas. Bruce consistently pulls Alison's urgent 4/4 A major into a nostalgic 3/4 G major as he remembers his own formative experiences, while Alison tries to 'say something/talk to him'. Alison modulates into B♭ major but is unable to persuade her father to 'see' her before the car journey ends.

'Telephone Wire' moves straight into 'Edges of the World', where Older Alison imagines her father's suicide through Bruce's performance. 'Edges of the World' acts as Bruce's counterpart to 'Changing My Major To Joan' as Bruce recognizes his own identity. Bruce's narcissistic personality means that this recognition is projected inward instead of outward, and whereas Alison's identity is realised in Joan, Bruce sees himself in the broken-down house that he is restoring. Bruce's 'I could still break a heart or two' motif is restated at the climax of the song, and the emotional truth of Bruce's self-obsession is ever-present in the chorus as he asks, 'why am I standing here?' (Kron and Tesori, 2015, p. 72). Older Alison is finally able to make peace with her memories of Bruce through recognizing the importance of the opening frame of the musical, where Bruce is playing 'airplane' with Small Alison. Alison states that 'every so often there was a rare moment of perfect balance when I soared above him' (Kron and Tesori, 2015, p. 77), and thus establishes an answer of some kind to the original question: 'Am I just like you?'

'Out of the Darkness, into the Spotlight' – LGBTQ+ Characters and Inclusivity in *Everybody's Talking about Jamie*

The representation of contemporary LGBTQ+ identities is a major challenge for musical theatre writers. Often contemporary musicals are based on much older source material that does not present LGBTQ+ characters in an inclusive manner, if indeed they are presented at all. Thus the 2015 musical adaptation of *Bend It Like Beckham* incorporates homophobic jokes about 'lesbian footballers' from its 2002 source material, and this cannot be rectified by its recasting of Jesminder's friend Tony as a gay man. Similarly, the 2016 adaptation of the 1993 film *Groundhog Day* maintains the casual misogyny and homophobia that characterizes the original source material despite the addition of a minor gay character. As with *Yank!* and *Fun Home*, the most successful LGBTQ+ characters in recent musical theatre have come from real life – such as Kevin Tuerff and Kevin Jung in *Come From Away* (2017), a musical based on the day that 38 planes were forced to land in Newfoundland during the September 11 attacks in 2001.

Dan Gillespie Sells and Tom MacRae's *Everybody's Talking About Jamie* (2017) is inspired by the 2011 BBC3 documentary *Jamie: Drag Queen at 16* (Popplewell, 2011). Jamie New is a 16-year-old boy that plans to attend his high school prom in a dress, and eventually aspires to perform as a drag queen for his career. Jamie is supported by his mum and her best friend Ray, but is frequently thwarted by the heteronormativity of his environment. Gillespie Sells and MacRae relocate the story from Durham to Sheffield, setting the story against a multicultural backdrop in a traditionally working-class city. Jamie's story thus takes place within an environment that is simultaneously inclusive and hostile – a city that has largely accepted multiculturalism but still conforms to traditional values of gender roles.

Everybody's Talking About Jamie offers a twist on the traditional coming-out story. Jamie is already open about his homosexuality with his family and classmates, but he has not yet revealed his desire to be a drag queen to anyone other than his mother and Ray. Jamie's clarity about his drag identity is in marked contrast to other 'drag queen' characters in musical theatre – he tells his friend Pritti that 'I want to be a boy. Who sometimes wants to be a girl' (MacRae and Gillespie Sells, 2017, p. 30). For Jamie, drag is fun rather than sexual, and the musical's narrative demonstrates how Jamie's drag identity allows him space to fully accept his own identity.

Tom MacRae's book presents a nuanced overview of the homophobic conditions faced by many LGBTQ+ teenagers growing up. Jamie's dad refers to his son's drag performances as 'disgusting', and it transpires that he used this word when he first discovered Jamie dressing up in his mum's clothes. The ramifications of this phrase are explored in Jamie's song 'The Wall In My Head', where Jamie describes how his dad's words keep 'building' inside him. The word 'disgusting' is also used by Dean's dad when he complains about Jamie's plan to attend his school prom in a dress. Dean represents an openly antagonistic presence at school, referring to Jamie as a 'queer' in front of the rest of the class. Dean's homophobia is implicitly reinforced by Miss Hedge, Jamie's teacher, who pretends not to hear Dean's use of pejorative language and sees Jamie's nonconformity as a way of him making himself the 'centre of attention'. Miss Hedge is explicitly connected to Dean in 'Work of Art', where they taunt Jamie as he walks through the school with his misapplied make-up, and later takes Dean's side in forbidding Jamie to go to the school prom in a dress. Miss Hedge is representative of the heteronormative culture in many schools – her motto to 'keep it real' is well-meaning but her failure to recognize the multiplicities of identity in her class is symptomatic of the problematic school experiences that many LGBTQ+ people face in the UK.

It is Jamie's use of drag that allows him to access a number of 'queer spaces' in order to navigate the heteronormative structures surrounding him. Jamie receives a pair of Jimmy Choo shoes from his mother for his birthday, and these allow him to embody his own 'queerness' – after trying them on in front of Pritti, Jamie finds that he is able to respond to Dean's bullying for the first time:

Yeah Dean, I'm gay. I *am* gay – so if *I* call me gay then being called gay isn't an insult. Cos I am bent, and I am queer, and I am a faggot batty bum boy.

(MacRae and Gillespie Sells, 2017, p. 32)

Jamie's decision to find a dress for his prom leads him to meet Hugo and his drag alter ego Loco Chanelle, along with her drag entourage, who persuade Jamie to go 'Over The Top' by performing in drag at the local Working Men's Club in front of his excited schoolmates. 'Over The Top' can be seen as the antidote to 'The Wall In My Head' as Jamie invents the drag persona Mimi Mee as an embodiment of his new identity, allowing him to temporarily combat the prejudices of Dean and Miss Hedge. However, Jamie is shattered by his dad's rejection, especially since Margaret has covered for her ex-husband through buying birthday cards and presents on his behalf. This allows MacRae to take the traditional drag narrative one step further as Jamie finally re-embraces his own identity as 'a boy who sometimes wants to be a girl' in preference to the persona of Mimi Mee:

> You said to keep it real Miss, and I have. Prom – it's a fairytale. But this – me like this – is real.

> (MacRae and Gillespie Sells, 2017, p. 127)

Everybody's Talking About Jamie is able to negotiate twenty-first-century drag identities through drawing on the real-life experiences of Jamie Campbell. The musical also touches on non-conformist parenting, with Margaret's best friend Ray acting as an unofficial father figure to Jamie in the absence of his dad. Finally, the insistence of Jamie's schoolmates that he is allowed into the Prom suggests a shift in values within the younger generation – this moment is based on the real-life events of *Jamie: Drag Queen at 16* and draws attention to the changing generational attitudes towards gender and sexuality.

'Who's Got Extra Love?' – Further Explorations of the Queer Space in Musical Theatre

The four musicals analysed above are a representative sample of musicals with LGBTQ+ characters written by LGBTQ+ writers that have been produced since 2014. It is notable that two of these musicals deal specifically with gender ambiguity (*Fun Home* and *Everybody's Talking About Jamie*) and that *The Color Purple* includes a bisexual female character originally written by a bisexual woman. These new identities require musical theatre scholarship to move away from the binary of discussing 'sexuality – both hetero- and homo-' (Taylor and Symonds, 2014, p. 169) and to begin to consider bisexual, asexual, transgender and genderfluid identities.

It is unfortunate that this chapter does not include any examples of transgender characters written by transgender writers; this is largely because musical theatre is yet to fully embrace transgender characters (although the recent film version of *The Rocky Horror Show* (2016) starring Laverne Cox brings up some interesting issues). Nevertheless, there are a number of other musicals that might benefit from further study in their use of queer spaces – the fantasy homonormative world of *Zanna Don't!* (2003), the use of alternate realities in representing the bisexual character of Lucas in *If/Then* (2013) and the exploration of online spaces in *Soho Cinders* (2012). The recent revivals of *La Cage Aux Folles* and *Falsettos* suggest that there may be other musicals with LGBTQ+ characters to be recovered and reframed in future productions. There are many queer spaces still to be explored – and LGBTQ+ musical theatre writers, creatives and scholars must be at the forefront of this exploration.

References

Barnes, G. (2015) *Her Turn On Stage: The Role of Women in Musical Theatre*. North Carolina: McFarland.

Bealer, T. (2009) Making Hurston's Heroine Her Own: Love and Womanist Resistance in *The Color Purple*. In LaGrone, K. (ed.), *Alice Walker's The Color Purple* (pp. 23–32). Amsterdam: Rodopi.

Bechdel, A. (2007) *Fun Home: A Family Tragicomic*. Boston: Houghton Mifflin Harcourt.

Bérubé, A. (2010) *Coming Out under Fire: The History of Gay Men and Women in World War II*. Chapel Hill: University of North Carolina Press.

Clum, J.M. (1999) *Something for the Boys: Musical Theater and Gay Culture*. New York: St. Martin's Press.

Collins, P.H. (2002) *Black Feminist Thought: Knowledge, Consciousness, and the Politics of Empowerment*. New York: Routledge.

Denny, A. (2009) Alice Walker's Womanist Reading of Samuel Richardson's *Pamela* in *The Color Purple*. In LaGrone, K. (ed.), *Alice Walker's The Color Purple* (pp. 251–286). Amsterdam: Rodopi.

Finn, W. & Lapine, J. (1995) *Falsettos*. London: Samuel French, Inc.

Funderburg, L. (2006) *The Color Purple: A Memory Book of the Broadway Musical*. New York: Carroll and Graf.

Halperin, D.M. (2012) *How to Be Gay*. Cambridge, Mass.: Harvard University Press.

Hickling, A. (2017) Yank! Review – Gay Love Story is an Ode to Courage Under Fire. *The Guardian*. Available at: www.theguardian.com/stage/2017/mar/17/yank-review-hope-mill-manchester-joseph-david-zellnik-gay-servicemen. Accessed 29 January 2018.

Hood, A. (2017) Review: Yank! (Charing Cross Theatre). *Whatsonstage.com*. Available at: www.whatsonstage.com/london-theatre/reviews/yank-charing-cross-joseph-david-zellnik_44081.html

Idle, E. & Du Prez, J. (2005) *Monty Python's Spamalot: The Original Broadway Recording* [CD], Decca Broadway.

Johnson, E.P. (2001) 'Quare' Studies, or (Almost) Everything I Know about Queer Studies I Learned from My Grandmother. *Text and Performance Quarterly*, 21(1), 1–25.

Kirkland, M. (2003) *The Simpsons: Three Gays of the Condo* [DVD], Twentieth Century Fox Home Entertainment.

Kron, L. & Tesori, J. (2015) *Fun Home*. New York: Samuel French.

MacRae, T. & Gillespie Sells, D. (2017) *Everybody's Talking About Jamie*. New York: Samuel French.

Marx, J., Lopez, R. & Whitty, J. (2010) *Avenue Q: The Musical – The Complete Book and Lyrics of the Broadway Musical*. New York: Applause Theatre Books.

Maxwell, D. (2017) Theatre review: *Yank!* at Charing Cross Theatre, WC2. *The Times*. Available at: https://www.thetimes.co.uk/article/theatre-review-yank-at-charing-cross-theatre-wc2-hnk506hlc. Accessed 29 January 2018.

Miller, D.A. (1998) *Place for Us: Essay on the Broadway Musical*. Cambridge, Mass.: Harvard University Press.

Popplewell, J. (2011) *Jamie: Drag Queen at 16*, BBC3, 60 mins. https://learningonscreen.ac.uk/ondemand/index.php/prog/01DCABD4. Accessed 29 January 2018.

Rawson, J. (2013) Why Are Gay Characters at the Top of Hollywood's Kill List? *The Guardian*, 11 June. Available at: www.theguardian.com/film/filmblog/2013/jun/11/gay-characters-hollywood-films. Accessed 29 January 2018.

Smith, B., Hull, G.T. & Scott, P.B. (eds.) (1982) *All the Women are White, All the Blacks Are Men, But Some of Us Are Brave: Black Women's Studies*. New York: Feminist Press.

Steyn, M. (1998) *Broadway Babies Say Goodnight: Musicals Then and Now*. London: Faber & Faber.

Stockwell, A. (2005) Allee up! Long before she cowrote the stage musical of The Color Purple, Allee Willis was writing hit songs and making outrageous art. Meet the wildest artist of them all. *The Free Library*, 6 December. Available at: https://www.thefreelibrary.com/Alleeup!-a0139601065. Accessed 29 January 2018.

Taylor, M. & Symonds, D. (2014) *Studying Musical Theatre: Theory and Practice*. New York: Palgrave Macmillan.

Viagas, R., Lee, B. & Walsh, T. (2006) *On the Line: The Creation of A Chorus Line*. Pompton Plains, N.J.: Limelight Editions.

Walker, A. (1982) *The Color Purple*. Orlando: Harcourt.

Walker, A. (1983) *In Search of Our Mothers' Gardens*. New York: Harvest.

Zellnik, D. (2017) *Yank!: A WWII Love Story*. Unpublished.

Zellnik, D. & Zellnik, J. (2017) Telling the stories of gay soldiers during the war is a 'vital act' say YANK writers. *The Gay Times*, 29 June. Available at: www.gaytimes.co.uk/life/78025/telling-the-stories-of-gay-soldiers-during-the-war-is-a-vital-act-say-yank-writers. Accessed 29 January 2018.

12

'Bonding Over Phobia': Restaging a Revolution at the Expense of Black Revolt[1]

Wind Dell Woods

Intro: Exposing Exposition and (Up)Setting the (St)Age

In 2017, I attended a conference at Princeton University which was assembled to recognize and mourn the all-too present and untimely deaths of black people at the hands of State, and State-sanctioned, forces. During a needed break from the weighty topic, I wandered outside where I noticed a small group of conference attendees gathered around two young black boys who were in the middle of a lively and impressive rendition of the song 'Alexander Hamilton' from Lin-Manuel Miranda's musical *Hamilton*. This was a *peculiar* setting – amid investigations of black death and structural violence – to encounter the figure of Alexander Hamilton, to hear the young duo singing the lyrics of the opening number.

On the other hand, perhaps, Hamilton's presence, as conjured through the young black bodies of these performers, wasn't all that peculiar. After all, Miranda has turned the man who was about to be removed from the back of the 10-dollar note into nothing short of a pop icon with his hit musical. The nation appears to have fallen in love with (and been hypnotized by) this retelling of the country's first Secretary of the Treasury 'turned' immigrant Hip Hop hero, so much so, that a self-diagnostic term has been created to describe the fans' engrossment: 'Hamiltonitis'.[2] This excitement (or affliction) seemed to be illustrated in the applause from the conference onlookers as one of the boys turned to the other and asked in the call and response of the title song what his name was, to which the other, as well as several members of the crowd, sang the name, Alexander Hamilton, in reply. As I wandered off to find the next conference panel, I couldn't help but wonder what was the connection between what 'we' had just seen in the performance and the problematics being investigated at the conference. This chapter seeks to interrogate the socio-political space between a project like *Hamilton* and the ethico-political task of meditating on black suffering and the ways it is tethered to structures of violence, both historically and in our current times.

Despite *Hamilton*'s immense success and recognition, historian Annette Gordon-Reed points out that 'one of the most interesting things about the *Hamilton* phenomenon is just how little serious criticism the play has received' (2016). Gordon-Reed's observation is an ideal starting point for investigating *Hamilton* and the critical discourse (or lack thereof) that surrounds it. Compared to the musical's immense praise, serious and sustained critical analysis has, so far, been scarce.[3] *Hamilton*, however, does have an ever-growing number of critics who have worked to problematize the role of race and ethnicity in relation to the musical's larger political framework. The historian Lyra Monteiro argues, for example, that simply plugging in 'people of color' does nothing but continue a tradition of glorifying 'the deeds of "great white men"' (Monteiro, 2016, p. 90), while at the same time erasing the contribution of black and brown people who were *actually* around during that era (Onion, 2016). Similarly, the poet and essayist Ishmael Reed critiques the deployment of black actors in the musical, while taking to task the lack of attention paid to slavery's role in America's founding. Reed is critical of Miranda's representation of Alexander Hamilton, claiming that in Miranda's hands Hamilton has been 'scrubbed with a kind of historical Ajax' (Reed, 2015).

James McMaster's criticism follows a similar theme in his article, 'Why *Hamilton* Is Not the Revolution You Think It Is'. Here, McMaster evaluates the role and representation of women in the musical, as well the musical's reliance on the bootstrap narrative and the myth of meritocracy. The logic of these American myths, McMaster argues, 'neglects and obscures the material obstacles and violences (structural racism, predatory capitalism, long-burned bridges to citizenship) imposed on racialized immigrants within the United States in order to celebrate the (false) promise of the American dream and the nation-state' (McMaster, 2016). A similar criticism is brought forth by theatre scholar Donatella Galella in a sober review in which she applauds *Hamilton* for its artistic brilliance, yet laments the fact that the musical adheres to a conservative political orientation. The myth of meritocracy, Galella argues, serves to 'rationalize the oppression of immigrants, people-of-color, poor and working-class people, and women' (Galella, 2015).[4]

Monteiro, Reed, McMaster and Galella, as well as a growing handful of others, have offered important critical contributions, earning them the title 'Hamilton-haters' by many who feel the need to protect the play from criticism. David Marcus, for example, in his article 'Hamilton Haters Are Why We Can't Have Nice Things', takes to task 'social justice warriors' (a term he uses pejoratively to target Monteiro and others) for always finding the problematics of everything, as well as 'holding art to unattainable standards of race consciousness' (Marcus, 2016). The article demonstrates an inability to think of racism as a structural reality, and not a private or personal experience, which leads to a gross oversimplification of Monterio's critical intervention: Monterio's argument about black historical erasure in *Hamilton* is dismissed by Marcus, 'given that almost everyone on stage is either black or a person of color' (Marcus, 2016). The implication being that socio-political 'erasure' or 'whitewashing' cannot transpire if people of colour are holding the paintbrushes. Or, put differently, a political project that works against the interests of black people cannot be headed (at least on a representational level) by people with black and brown faces.

Unfortunately, this trend of turning a (colour)blind eye to racial difference, as well as the tendency to substitute sentimental assertions for criticism, is the norm rather than the exception in the discourse surrounding *Hamilton*. That is why I find the analytical interventions I mention above so important. Along these lines and critical tracks, however, there must *also* be a deeper interrogation, not merely of what the play does *with* the past, but what it does *for* the present. The phenomenon of *Hamilton* cannot be analysed effectively without a grave meditation on three conditions which animate our current times: first, the ongoing brutality and murder inflicted on black bodies at the hands, batons, and guns of police officers and their deputized 'Junior Partners' (Wilderson, 2003); second, a dismissal of, and deafness towards, black suffering which has been amplified by what some deem to be a 'post-racial society' in the wake of the Obama era; and third, a reemergence, in response to these conditions, of Black radical thought/movements that are incompatible and incommensurable with (neo)liberal progressive multicultural orientations and agendas.[5]

Considering these three conditions, which are constitutive of the historical moment that *Hamilton* emerges out of, allows us to get to the root of the central problem of the musical, as well as trace how it derives the political and ideological assumptions that are the cause of its 'revolutionary' limitations. The problem is that at the foundation of *Hamilton*'s political and ideological structure is a false analogy that the musical (and the discourse that surrounds it) cannot reconcile. This logical fallacy occurs when the musical, and its critical commentators, conflate 'immigrantness' with 'slaveness'. This conflation serves as the ideological glue that holds the musical together, providing the base ingredient not only for the coherence of the project, but also for its praise and reception. To be clear, I am not saying that *Hamilton* is 'unworthy' of praise, and I am *not* interested in evaluating its quality as a work of art. What I *am* saying is that there might be something else *in the air*.[6]

In this chapter, I am guided by the following questions: first, what is it about the historical moment that *Hamilton* emerges out of that makes black and Latino bodies able to, as Ron Chernow suggests, 'capture the fire and passion of the American revolution' in ways that no *other* bodies can (cited in Rosen, 2015)? Second, in what ways does this American musical employ (in the full sense of the word) black bodies to, as Toni Morrison observed in her book *Playing in the Dark* (Morrison, 1992), 'ignite critical moments of discovery or change or emphasis in literature not written by them' (p. viii), while concurrently enabling a type of forgetting or blindness towards the peculiarity of blackness on and off the stage? And finally, thinking with the lyrics of Hip Hop artist Lauryn Hill: 'I wrote this opus, to reverse the hypnosis' (1998), what type of motion or movement might 'reverse' *Hamilton*'s theatrical hypnosis and open space for more revolutionary possibilities?

What I offer, then, is a meta-analysis that seeks to interrogate the presence and problematics of the 'immigrant(ness)' and 'slave(ness)' conflation.

To do so, I make two analytical cuts into *Hamilton*'s discursive terrain: the first examines the rhetoric surrounding the musical's use of multiracial/multiethnic casting, and brings to light a type of blindness that occurs in regards to black bodies; the second investigates the ways that Miranda's dramaturgy must leave the violence of racial slavery and its afterlife *unthought* (Hartman and Wilderson, 2003) in order to keep intact (and add coherence to) a romanticized notion of American (neo)liberal multicultural progress centred on the figure of the non-black immigrant.

CUT 1: Colourb(l)inding: Now You See It, Now You Don't

One of the most praised features of *Hamilton* is its use of, what many commentators term, 'colourblind casting'. While it is undeniable that 'actors of colour' are playing white historical figures, colourblind casting is a misnomer. *Hamilton*'s casting, as only a select few have identified, may be *nontraditional*; however, its 'colourblindness' is a more complicated story.[7] Although much of the discourse uses the terms 'colourblind' and 'nontraditional' casting interchangeably, separating them opens space for a sharper analysis. Shakespearian Ayanna Thompson teases out the difference between the two terms: nontraditional casting is an 'umbrella term for different types of casting', whereas in 'colorblind casting' the audiences are 'not supposed to notice the race of the actor or the character, and are just supposed to be blind to it on stage' (Neary, 2008). Nontraditional casting has been described elsewhere as 'the casting of ethnic, female, or disabled actors in roles where race, ethnicity, gender, or physical capability are not necessary to the characters' or the play's development' (Davis and Newman, 1988, cited in Wilkins Catanese, 2014, p. 12).[8] All colourblind casting, then, is nontraditional, but not all nontraditional casting is colourblind. The function of colourblind casting, and this is key, is that the director, actor, and audience are supposed to remain *blind* to the race and/or ethnicity of the actors on stage.

It is not difficult to see the inherent problem in the concept of colourblindness. Being blind to race would naturally lead to a 'blindness' to the violence and inequalities resulting from structural racism. This is as true off-stage as it is onstage. Black performance scholar Lisa M. Anderson asserts that 'the effort toward colorblindness has not reduced or eliminated racism; rather, it has reinforced whiteness as neutral, "raceless", and "colorless"' (in Thompson, 2006, p. 101). Contrary to claims that 'we' have 'moved beyond' race or are 'post-racial', black people's lives and deaths continue to be profoundly affected by race; race continues to mean (and make meaning) even when one physically or theoretically looks away. Moreover, on and off the stage, Anderson argues, blackness not only 'signifies race; [it] also carries with it three centuries of sedimented meaning' (in Thompson, 2006, p. 92). To request a colourblind orientation to a black body is to ask the audience to forget by remaining blind to the 'sedimented meaning' of racial blackness; what poet and theorist David Marriott terms 'the occult presence of racial slavery' (Marriott, 2007, p. xxi). The desire to move beyond (let us say it outright) blackness is nothing other than a desire to have the 'afterlife of slavery', as Saidiya Hartman (2007) terms it, no longer a haunting reality in our modern times (p. 6). It is a willingness to be blind to the institutional and structural mechanisms, from chattel slavery to (extra)legal murders, that continue to violently subjugate black bodies.

What is curious about the ubiquitous (mis)use of the term 'colour-blind casting' in the discourse surrounding *Hamilton* is that at the same time it applauds the musical for its *blind* casting; it recognizes 'the power', 'revolutionary approach', and 'excitement' that arises from *seeing* black and brown actors as the Founding Fathers. Claims like 'what makes "Hamilton" *especially relevant* is that it *purposefully uses color-blind casting* to [...] *subvert* the familiar story of the Founding Fathers' (Godinez, 2016; emphasis added) speak directly to the purposefulness of the racial casting, as well as indicate the racial awareness needed for its efficacy. When much of the discourse demonstrates an awareness of not only race, but of the ways racially marked bodies shape the musical, what accounts for the persistent use of the phrase 'colourblind casting'? Is the discursive terrain simply unable to agree on what it means to be *blind* to race? What else might be afoot in these claims to a type of (colour)blind racial seeing?

These questions become even more puzzling when one realizes that Miranda and his creative team have, from the beginning, expressed the conceptual and race-conscious nature of the casting. In a 2015 interview with the *Hollywood Reporter*, Miranda affirms the 'intentional' casting approach when he states: 'In *Hamilton*, we're telling the stories of old, dead white men but we're *using actors of color*, and that makes the story more immediate and more accessible to a contemporary audience' (DiGiacomo, 2015; emphasis added). Miranda's belief that casting 'actors of colour' influences his-story by making it more 'immediate' and 'accessible' demonstrates that the casting choices are not only conscious, but conceptual as well. Miranda also admits that race informed his creative process, even during the early writing stages. In several interviews, Miranda divulges that he 'imagined' primarily black rappers in the roles, so much so that it shaped the content, rhyme scheme, and style of the rap lyrics in the musical.[9] Race, one would have to assume, again entered the picture when deciding which 'actor of colour' would play which Founding Father.

To be fair to critics and commentators, *Hamilton*'s artistic team is not always consistent about the type of casting the musical employs, possibly adding to the confusion. In *Hamilton: The Revolution*, Jeremy McCarter and Miranda relay a story about how the musical's historical consultant, Ron Chernow, came to the realization that the play would 'need' to employ 'race-blind' casting.[10] They recount that Chernow, '[n]ot being a rap listener [...] hadn't given much thought to the fact that the *people best able to perform the songs* that Lin [Miranda] had been writing might look nothing like their historical counterparts' (Miranda and McCarter, 2016, p. 33; emphasis mine). Here, Chernow's revelation appears to be at odds with the tenets of conscious casting espoused by Miranda. Where Miranda has asserted that the casting choices were intentional, seeking to, as he explains, make the cast 'look the way America looks now',[11] Chernow seems to deploy a type of liberal humanist colourblind rhetoric by suggesting the casting was based on which actors were 'best able to perform' the roles. In other words, Chernow's statement moves away from a race-conscious claim, one that will 'eliminate [the] distance' (Miranda in Weinert-Kendt, 2015) between the [white] past and the [multiracial] present, to a claim that the artistic team *had* to cast blacks and Latinos because of their ability to perform rap. The fact that there are accomplished white, Native American, and Asian (not to mention female and disabled) rappers seems to elude Chernow, as does the fact that his comments here are incongruous with statements he has offered elsewhere.

In a *New York Times* interview, for example, Chernow discusses the profound effect of seeing black and brown actors playing the Founding Fathers when he states, 'after a minute or two I started to listen and *forgot* the color or ethnicity of these astonishingly talented young performers. Within five minutes, I became a militant on the subject of color-blind casting' (in Rosen, 2015; emphasis mine). If what Chernow claims to have experienced is, indeed, a 'colourblind' experience, and if 'color-blindness ultimately signifies assimilation', as Lisa Anderson argues (in Thompson, 2006, p. 91), did Chernow forget that the 'astonishingly talented young performers' were actors of colour by reimagining them as white, like himself, like the Founding Fathers?[12] Did the actors' incredible performance allow them to be (re)assimilated into the frame of whiteness, to racially disappear? If their performance was less than astonishing, would they have remained actors of colour in, what Sylvia Wynter terms, Chernow's 'inner eyes' (Wynter, 2007, p. 146)?

These questions also trouble Miranda's own ideas, leading to contradictory statements about the casting. In an interview, for example, Miranda is asked about the effect of black and brown actors playing white slave owners. His answer oscillates between a colour-conscious and a colourblind casting approach when he states that the casting was a 'constant conversation' between him and the director, describing their aim: 'This is a story about *America then*, told by America now, and we want to *eliminate any distance* – our story should look the way our country looks.' He concludes that the team found the '*best* people' to 'embody' the roles (in Weinert-Kendt, 2015; emphasis mine). Miranda does not clarify if 'best' refers to symbolic resonance and dramaturgical function or to the talents and skills of the actors. This raises the question: is Miranda being *conscious* of the role race plays in his re-writing – rather, re-pigmenting – of America's Founding Fathers, but *blind* to the racial peculiarities of such casting within the musical itself? Does Miranda (and his artistic team) assume that *all* people of colour will have the same symbolic function or *affect* if cast in any of the roles? Asked differently, is a racially black Thomas Jefferson analogous to an Asian or Latino Thomas Jefferson? If so, what must be overlooked for this equivalence to be made (professed) and staged (performed)?

As an artist of colour, Miranda aligns himself with the doctrines of multiculturalism. He recognizes the importance of 'diversity' in the world of theatre and film. He recognizes that his casting uses ethnic difference to make a statement; however, his unwillingness to, as he states, 'differentiate between black and Latino actors',[13] at least when it comes to casting, is a restriction to his racial politics. Miranda cannot reconcile his multiculturalist orientation (that wants to fetishize difference) with his traditional liberal values (that seek to remain blind to difference). To settle these conflicting ideologies, Miranda replaces racial alterity (the positionality of black people) with ethnic pluralism (the relationality of the ethnic minority), an ideological move that overlooks the way global anti-blackness positions black people and non-black people (of colour) in the world in vastly different ways. Such an analytical oversight is best described by Jared Sexton's term, 'people-of-color-blindness', which he defines as 'a form of colorblindness inherent to the concept of "people of color"'. This blindness arises when a discourse 'bears a common refusal to admit to significant differences of structural position born of discrepant histories between blacks and their political allies, actual or potential' (Sexton, 2010, pp. 47–48).

Much of Miranda's ideas on racism, when he does offer them, are afflicted with 'people-of-color-blindness'. An example can be found in a curious comment Miranda makes about the function of *Hamilton*'s casting. Miranda argues that the casting of people of colour is 'a way of pulling you into the story and allowing you to leave whatever *cultural baggage* you have about the founding fathers at the door' (Piepenburg, 2016; emphasis added). What is this 'cultural baggage' that 'you' are invited to leave at the door, and do all people (of colour) share the same cultural baggage regarding the Founding Fathers, or the 'founding' of America, for that matter? Even more disconcerting than the potential answers to these questions are the ways in which the musical and the critical discourse labour to keep this 'baggage' packed, tightly fastened, and tucked away, out of sight. Whether this concealment occurs at a conscious or pre-conscious register, the rhetoric they deploy can be analysed at the level of its assumptive logic.

Hamilton as a musical relies on (neo)liberal multiculturalist ideology. In the musical (and the collective unconscious that it stages), the presence of the black body can emerge as spectacle, but the spectral politics of blackness must be suppressed. If not, what the musical labours to perform and proclaim through its casting, namely that all people of colour suffer equally under the structures and technologies of anti-blackness, would be revealed as a ruse. Moreover, the musical is haunted by a conflation of specific structural positions that is produced by the racial casting. As such, it cannot reconcile the contradiction that the immigrant may have 'baggage' regarding their relationship to the Founding Fathers, but the black captive is positioned in structural antagonism to America's founding. The former's ethnic diversity is incorporated into the story of American 'progress', while the latter's racial alterity, and the violence that creates it, is the nightmare that adds coherence to the American Dream.

The problem, then, is not solely the supposed colourblind casting of the musical, but rather, the 'people-of-color-blindness' that animates the politics such casting professes and performs. The mainstream commentary on the casting epitomizes what playwright Katori Hall warns against when she states, 'let us not *forget* that *brown* bodies are still being used to further mythologize and perpetuate the narratives of dead white men' (in Viagas, 2015; emphasis added). Note that Hall references only 'brown' bodies and their specific function in the political project. Here, she sets upon a problematic within the discourse's use of the term 'people of colour' within the context of American history. Because of chattel slavery, bodies marked as black differ from other ethnically marked bodies in their ability to 'further' and 'perpetuate' the myth of the white founders. This structural reality is ignored when *Hamilton*'s racial casting executes a visual and ideological ruse: on the performative level it fetishizes racial difference (now you see), while on the ethico-political level it subverts a critique of structural anti-blackness (now you don't). It is this sleight of hand that makes resurrecting the myths and narratives of dead white settlers on/through black and brown bodies appear to be a laudable revolutionary act.

In this *con*-text (pun intended), the phrase 'people of colour', rather than being a term of radical political solidarity, becomes a term that obscures the ethical demands made from black people's specific structural position. This problematic occurs throughout the discourse, but most noticeably when the term 'people of colour' is employed to discuss contemporary racial inequalities and historical violence under and after racialized slavery. To suggest that casting 'actors of colour' as the Founding Fathers re-inserts 'them' into American history assumes that *all* people of colour have been positioned into that history in the same way as European immigrants and their descendants have been. Such an inability to think with(in) these discrepant histories allows for undeveloped statements disguised as critical analysis to saturate the discourse; statements such as, '*Hamilton* is right in tune with today's debates about immigration and Black Lives Matter' (Schuessler, 2016). This quote forgets to remember that the structural realities a movement like Black Lives Matter seeks to address may not be congruent with 'debates about immigration'. Further, the statement refuses to meditate on the reality that an 'immigrant' (white or 'of colour') can arrive to these shores, 'settle', and be deputized by the State to control, police, oversee, and kill black people. To put it plainly, it is the discourse's inability (or refusal) to *not* think like a settler, or, perhaps better put, to want to 'multiculturalize' settler colonialism, that haunts *Hamilton* as a political project and that plagues its constellation of criticism.

CUT 2: Bringing His-Story into the Light or 'Playing in the Dark'[14]

Where the critical discourse surrounding *Hamilton's* deployment of racialized bodies is restricted (whether blindly or consciously) due to its 'people-of-color-blindness', Miranda's dramaturgy suffers from a similar shortsightedness when he conflates 'slaveness' with 'immigrantness'. In the musical, this conflation works to reference the suffering of the black captives only to dramatically re-employ it in an alternative narrative project. More specifically, black suffering under chattel slavery raises an ethical question, the weight of which must be quickly transferred away from a captive's narrative, towards one of white (settler) redemption, and one onto which neo-immigrants can graph themselves. Like Ron Chernow's assertion that *Hamilton's* 'color-blind casting' has the effect of making one forget the 'color or ethnicity' of the actors (in Rosen, 2015), the musical requires that the violence of racial slavery be disregarded as soon as it serves its dramaturgical function. What facilitates this relocating of the musical's ethical dilemma is a 'ruse of analogy' (Wilderson, 2010, p. 37) that structurally and symbolically conflates the peculiar position of the black captive population with that of immigrant populations. The conflation is employed throughout the musical, but it is no more apparent than in the opening lines of the musical which provide exposition for Alexander Hamilton as illegitimate, the son of a Scottish father who abandoned him, and a 'whore' who died, leaving him orphaned. After establishing Hamilton's impoverished upbringing, the character of Aaron Burr poses the question: how does a man from a '*forgotten* spot' grow up to be one of the Founding Fathers? (Miranda, 2015; italics mine)

Before one has time to contemplate the question or reach an answer, the character of John Laurens offers that Hamilton's success is brought about, solely, by his exceptional work ethic, intelligence, and motivation. This may all be well and 'true'; it certainly is in accordance with the myth of the rugged individual, one of the prototypical figures of the bootstrap narrative. But one is left wondering who are these 'others' who were unable to work hard, outsmart, and self-start? What the character of Laurens, at least in Miranda's hands, fails to recognize, is that Hamilton's success was because he could utilize 'the magic of skin color' (Spillers, 2003, p. 212). His whiteness endowed him with a body able to be viewed and valued as *his* body. This self-possession was not a byproduct of hard work, but a birthright. Nevis, where his-story begins, that unremembered Caribbean island, animated by the capturing, trafficking, and fatal labouring of millions of black bodies, serves as an ideal starting point from which Hamilton can 'rise up'; however, the implicit analogy drawn between one's 'humble' beginnings and one's enslavement is a ruse, one that requires a violent forgetting of those who suffer(ed) 'under and after slavery' (Wagner, 2009, p. 243).

Other critics have pointed out the ways *Hamilton* downplays, or whitewashes, the history of slavery and its role in the founding of America. To such criticism, Miranda's response has been twofold: on one hand, he argues that he does deal with the subject; that in fact a reference to slavery is in the show's third line (Weinert-Kendt, 2015). On the other hand, Miranda confesses that it was hard to write about the subject (or question) of slavery because successive generations have put off dealing with it; 'there's only so much time you can spend' on slavery 'when there's no end result to it' (Weinert-Kendt, 2015). What is interesting about his second response is that it reveals how *Hamilton*'s artistic team relied on the liberal humanist assumption that America is, indeed, an 'open-ended and universally available narrative' and that *Hamilton* can bring this 'to life on stage' (Gopnik, 2016). Miranda supports (and supposes) the idea that (re) imagining America as a nation of immigrants has the capacity to incorporate enslaved and indigenous populations, rather than reinforce and restage 'the protocols of violence that undergird the twin pillars of U.S. social formation: racial slavery and genocidal conquest' (Sexton, 2008, p. 4). What Miranda's 'no end result' to slavery statement reveals (even as it attempts to conceal), is the fact that the position of the black captive troubles the notion of American progressivism so much that to reestablish narrative coherence, the violence of slavery must remain 'unthought' (Hartman and Wilderson, 2003), or, at least, psychically and thematically, 'kicked down the field', as Miranda would have it (Weinert-Kendt, 2015).

Dramaturgically, then, Miranda is accurate in his statement that there is 'only so much time you can spend' on slavery within the context of the musical as a form. His statement reveals a curious anxiety as well. Miranda is cautious (we might say fearful) of having the musical consumed by the subject of slavery. To avoid slavery (and its *afterlife*) overwhelming *Hamilton* (both the musical and the man), Miranda must relocate his-story where narrative can (actually) take shape, which is *not* within the space/time of the black captive.

In his *New Yorker* article, Adam Gopnik critiques the musical's treatment of slavery through the character of Thomas Jefferson. Gopnik contends that the musical's 'version of Jeffersonian liberalism involved, obviously, mixing the Jefferson music in a *peculiar* way: turning down the track on the slavery side and bringing up the sound on the libertine one' (2016; emphasis mine). Although Gopnik fails to mention the other 'peculiar' racial (re)mixing in the form of a black Thomas Jefferson (symbolizing an outdated politics tethered to slavery) and a Latino Alexander Hamilton (the forward-looking, 'ambitious immigrant hustler'), his observation about 'turning down' the sounds of slavery can be extended to the entire musical. For the immigrant-American success story to find its narrative (not to mention its 'ethical') footing, it must forget both the wakes of slave ships (and the bound black bodies) and the tear-filled trails (and the murder of indigenous peoples). The ease in which these violent tracks can be turned down says as much about Miranda's extraordinary skills as a dramatist as it does about America's historical amnesia. Miranda's dramaturgical forgetting allows him to re-member America as an immigrant nation, one where there are no structural impediments; rather, as the musical suggests where 'burdens' and 'disadvantages' can be 'manage[d]' (Miranda and McCarter, 2016, p. 26).

We have explored the treatment of slavery through its omission; let us turn to the third line of the musical where Miranda states he confronts the subject head-on. The line that Miranda references is delivered by the character of Thomas Jefferson (Daveed Diggs). The line does, indeed, reference the daily trafficking and trading of black captives who are 'carted across the waves' (Miranda and McCarter, 2016, p. 16). However, the reference functions, purely, as exposition. It is information that operates, solely, to set the stage and develop the character of Hamilton as a rags-to-riches hero, who is longing to be part of something. In a footnote to the script, Miranda speaks to the function of this line when he says, 'At the top of every musical, it's essential to establish the world. Hamilton's early life was marked by trauma and a firsthand view of the brutal practices of the slave trade' (p. 16). Here the brutality of slavery (which must remain in the Caribbean) is transposed into the 'trauma' of Hamilton's humble beginnings. Hamilton, despite witnessing slavery (as if that is the same thing as being positioned under slavery), is transformed into a 'brother' who is 'ready to beg, steal, borrow or barter' (p. 16). Miranda's use of brother functions to draw a parallel to Hamilton's early life and the violence of slavery. This analogy works to magically redirect any caring energy away from the enslaved and onto the protagonist: Hamilton.

Hamilton's revolutionary setback, as illustrated in its opening lines, is that it answers the question about how he succeeds too quickly, too assuredly. Miranda refuses to meditate on the fact that the ways in which he *remembers* Alexander Hamilton's life and successes *forgets* how they are dependent on those captive bodies that are enslaved and being dragged across oceans. From a different vantage point, the answer to the question that opens *Hamilton* would acknowledge the most critical component of his success; namely, his ability to wield the magic password: 'I am not a nigger.'

OUTRO: The Sound(ing) Below; What Lies Beyond?

In her seminal publication, *Do Not Call Us Negros: How 'Multicultural' Textbooks Perpetuate Racism* (1992), Jamaican poet and critical theorist Sylvia Wynter criticizes the California school system's decision to adopt the Houghton Mifflin textbook *America Will Be* (1991). Wynter analyses the textbook's multiculturalist tendency to restructure historical events into quaint happily-ever-after stories where people of all colours and classes work together to fulfil the dream of America. A central problematic of the textbook, Wynter explains, is that it positions black Americans as one more 'ethnic group' in America and not its 'alter ego', or the 'boundary category' of Western Man (Wynter, 1992, p. 18). Reimagining America and its founding as a nation of immigrants, Wynter argues, 'must ontologically erase the existence of the indigenous inhabitants of the continent, as well as the other founding population group who had come, not as immigrants in search of freedom, but as slaves in chains' (p. 8). In other words, the erasure of the black captive and indigenous population is the condition of possibility for the American immigrant narrative to emerge.

We can contextualize the politics of the textbook *America Will Be* within the debates that animated the 1990s: the criticism of Black Studies programmes, debates on affirmative action, the rise of hegemonic multiculturalism, discussions surrounding the myth of the 'model minority', as well as the smouldering Los Angeles skyline in the aftermath of the 1992 LA Rebellion.[15] We can read the authors' desire to un-race American history alongside the burgeoning liberal colourblind ideology. We can even position the contributors' longing to forget slavery as a constituent element of this nation's founding within the context of a growing fear of the emergence of 'Gangster rap', and a reemerging disdain for the flesh of urban black youth. *America Will Be* could be read, then, as an attempt to return the nation to psychic stability, as well as a phobic response to the sounds of urban Black noise, the presence of young black bodies, and the politics of radical Black thought. Is there a connection between the socio-political context out of which *America Will Be* emerges and the current moment that *Hamilton: An American Musical* appears?

Rather than offer a direct answer, I return to the young black boys that opened this chapter. In a never-ending moment where the list of 'legal' and 'extralegal' murders of black people continues to grow, where the images of brutalized black bodies circulate through the trade routes of social media, what does it mean for them to embody the white founding fathers, to sing that they are called Alexander Hamilton? What does it mean to perform this narrative? What is the nation seeing or needing to see? What (and more importantly who) is rendered absent from such a (re) telling? How does one look for and after, what Jaye Austin Williams terms the 'absences' within plots, story lines, and constructs (Williams, 2016)?

While self-proclaiming a 'revolution' (let us remember that the collected lyrics were published under this title), *Hamilton: An American Musical* is conservative, and its revolutionary imagination is sorely limited. Rather than truly forming a plot 'blacker than the kettle callin'/the pot' calls the pot (Miranda and McCarter, 2016, p. 27) – a plot with the radical potential to imagine a more ethical 'Human' embodiment (to call back to Wynter) – the musical glorifies the Western bourgeois conception of Man (Wynter, 2007), reanimates notions of American exceptionalism, and romanticizes the myth of meritocracy by way of the bootstrap narrative. In doing so, the musical remixes out the suffering of those who continue to experience the nightmare of the American Dream. Finally, it is the musical's refusal to think and be with the captives which results in the project throwing away its revolutionary shot in a time when it matters most.[16]

Notes

1. Two notes here: (1) I sample 'Bonding Over Phobia' from a title chapter of David Marriott's book *Haunted Life: Visual Culture and Black Modernity* (2007). (2) I use the word 'black' with the 'B' capitalized to suggest cultural and racial identification, as in Black people, Black arts, Black aesthetics; the lower case 'b' indicates the descriptive noun, as in black bodies; the terms blackness and anti-blackness are lower case to infer, in line with Jaye Austin Williams, 'a condition that is interpreted, projected (upon) or resisted in a myriad of ways' (Williams, 2016, fn. 1, p. 32).
2. The symptoms of 'Hamiltonitis' are defined by one Reddit commentator as 'an inescapable need to burst into song whenever a phrase or even a word

from a *Hamilton* song appears in normal daily conversation' (www.reddit. com/r/hamiltonmusical/comments/40rvjk/hamiltonitis).

3. Since completing this chapter, a constellation of writings on *Hamilton* has begun to emerge, for example, *Studies in Musical Theatre Journal* (2018) offers an entire issue focused on the musical with a promising range of diverse topics and approaches. On the other hand, there is the collection of essays compiled in *Hamilton and Philosophy* (Rabinowitz and Arp, 2017). Though the contributions are diverse in their analyses on revolutions, specifically the American Revolution, they are extremely limited in their attention to what a radical slave revolt could look like. The tenor of the book, which is described as a self-professed 'love letter to Hamilton, and the hit Broadway show', is emblematic of the book's lack of critical engagement with *Hamilton*, both the musical and the man. The collection of essays that make up *Hamilton and Philosophy* would greatly benefit from engaging more rigorously with Annette Gordon-Reed's work, and by consulting the philosophical writings of Lewis Gordon, as well as Julius Bailey's *Philosophy and Hip-Hop: Ruminations on Postmodern Cultural Form* (2014).

4. For a rigorous and an insightful critique of *Hamilton*'s political and revolutionary limitations, see Donatella Galella's 'Being in "The Room Where it Happens": *Hamilton*, Obama, and Nationalist Neoliberal Multicultural Inclusion' (2018).

5. A fourth element might be the debate around removing Hamilton's face from the 10-dollar bill and possibly replacing it with an image of a Black woman, perhaps even the radical abolitionist Harriet Tubman. After protests and debates, Alexander Hamilton's face will remain on the 10-dollar bill. Some have even attributed the decision's results to the musical's success. I argue that all of these events illustrate a conservative pushback whose main focus is to squelch and quarantine Black movements and radical thought.

6. Here, I am riffing on a statement made by Jeremy McCarter when he describes Miranda's 2009 White House performance. McCarter states, 'The ovation owed a lot to the showbiz virtues on display: the vibrant writing, Lin's dynamic rapping, the skillful piano accompaniment from his friend Alex Lacamoire. But *something else was in the air*, something that would become clearer in the years to come. Sometimes the right person tells the right story at the right moment, and through a combination of luck and design, a creative expression gains new force. Spark, tinder, breeze.' (emphasis added Miranda and McCarter, 2016, p. 15)

7. For examples of analysis that works to trouble the claims to 'colourblind' casting see: Marshall (2007), Gordon-Reed (2016) and Gelt (2017).

8. Davis and Newman's definition poses the difficult questions of: when are such physical features 'necessary' or not? Who determines if race/gender/physical capability influences the play's or character's development or not?
9. The work that the black body is doing on the creative and imaginative level for Miranda should not escape us here.
10. Ron Chernow is the historian who wrote the biography *Alexander Hamilton*, which the musical is based on. Chernow also served as a historical consultant for the musical's development.
11. This statement has been reproduced in a variety of different sources; for some of them see Major, 2016, www.pbs.org/wnet/gperf/hamilton-american-musical-changed-musical-theater/5224, Delman, 2015, and Weinert-Kendt, 2015.
12. Moving in a slightly different direction, Annette Gordon-Reed acknowledges another set of contradictions and problematics in thinking of *Hamilton* as a colourblind production. Gordon-Reed argues that even if elements of the casting are, indeed, colourblind, the 'suspension cannot be total'. The audience is asked to notice that characters are played by black actors, or the central premise of the show fails to work, while at the same time the audience must not become aware of the contradiction of black bodies in the historical context of the musical. Gordon-Reed asserts, convincingly, that if the audience is too 'open' to the actors' blackness, the fact that these black actors dance 'during the sublime "The Schuyler Sisters" proclaiming how "lucky" they were "to be alive" during a time of African chattel slavery' would make them too uncomfortable (Gordon-Reed, 2016).
13. Miranda has stated this on several occasions. I reference an interview from Frank DiGiacomo's (2015) '"Hamilton's" Lin-Manuel Miranda on Finding Originality, Racial Politics (and Why Trump Should See His Show).'
14. A sample, of course, from Toni Morrison.
15. Some might refer to this event as the Los Angeles Riots or Rodney King Riots. I use the term 'rebellion' to mark it as a site/sight of Black ethical demands on the move.
16. See 'My Shot' from *Hamilton* (Miranda and McCarter, 2016, p. 26).

Bibliography

Armento, B.J. & Nash, G.B. et al. (1991) *America Will Be*. Atlanta, GA: Houghton Mifflin Company.
Delman, E. (2015) How Lin-Manuel Miranda Shapes History. *Theatlantic.com*, 29 September 2015. Accessed 10 August 2017. Available at: www.theatlantic.com/entertainment/archive/2015/09/lin-manuel-miranda-hamilton/408019.

DiGiacomo, F. (2015) 'Hamilton's' Lin-Manuel Miranda on Finding Originality, Racial Politics (and Why Trump Should See His Show). *Hollywoodreporter. com*, 12 August 2015. Available at: www.hollywoodreporter.com/features/hamiltons-lin-manuel-miranda-finding-814657. Accessed 15 June 2016.

Galella, D. (2015) Racializing the American Revolution Review of the Broadway Musical Hamilton. *Gcadvocate.com*. Available at: http://gcadvocate.com/2015/11/16/racializing-the-american-revolution-review-of-the-broadway-musical-hamilton. Accessed 20 June 2017.

Galella, D. (2018) Being in 'The Room Where It Happens': *Hamilton*, Obama, and Nationalist Neoliberal Multicultural Inclusion. *Theatre Survey*, 59(3), 363–385. Available at: https://doi.org/10.1017/S0040557418000303. Accessed 15 August 2018.

Gelt, J. (2017) Authenticity in Casting: From 'Colorblind' to 'Color Conscious,' New Rules Are Anything but Black and White. *Latimes.com*. Available at: www.latimes.com/entertainment/arts/la-ca-cm-authenticity-in-casting-20170713-htmlstory.html. Accessed 10 July 2017.

Godinez, O. (2016) Hamilton Uses Color-blind Casting to Shed New Light on History. Available at: www.pacocollective.com/?p=1030. Accessed 1 September 2017.

Gopnik, A. (2016) Hamilton and the Hip-Hop Case for Progressive Heroism. *Newyorker.com*. Available at: www.newyorker.com/news/daily-comment/hamilton-and-the-hip-hop-case-for-progressive-heroism. Accessed 10 August 2016.

Gordon-Reed, A. (2016) *Hamilton: The Musical*: Blacks and the Founding Fathers. *Ncph.org*. Available at: http://ncph.org/history-at-work/hamilton-the-musical-blacks-and-the-founding-fathers. Accessed 20 September 2017.

'Hamilton': The History-Making Musical. (2016) New York: The New York Times.

Hartman, S. (2007) *Lose Your Mother: A Journey along the Atlantic Slave Route*. New York: Farrar, Straus and Giroux.

Hartman, S. & Wilderson, F.B. III. (2003) The Position of the Unthought: An Interview with Saidiya V. Hartman Conducted by Frank B. Wilderson, III. *Qui Parle*, 13(2), 183–201. Jstor http://www.jstor.org/stable/pdf/20686156.pdf.

Hill, L. (1998) *The Miseducation of Lauryn Hill*. [CD] Philadelphia, PA: Ruffhouse Records.

Luthor, L. (2016) Hamilton's Narrative: Colorblind Casting Possibilities and Limitations. *medium.com*. Available at: https://medium.com/@lezluthor/hamiltons-narrative-colorblind-casting-possibilities-and-limitations-2ee37afe2fad.

Marcus, D. (2016) Hamilton Haters Are Why We Can't Have Nice Things. *Thefederalist.com*. Available at: http://thefederalist.com/2016/04/07/hamilton-haters-are-why-we-cant-have-nice-things/. Accessed 2 November 2016.

Marriott, D. (2007) *Haunted Life: Visual Culture and Black Modernity*. New Brunswick: Rutgers University Press.

Marshall, J. (2007) Non-traditional Casting. *Americancentury.org*. Available at: www.americancentury.org/essay_nontraditionalcasting.php. Accessed 12 September 2017.

McMaster, J. (2016) Why *Hamilton* Is Not the Revolution You Think It Is. *HowlRound.com* Available at: http://howlround.com/why-hamilton-is-not-the-revolution-you-think-it-is. Accessed 5 December 2018.

Miranda, L.M. (2015) Alexander Hamilton. *Hamilton (Original Broadway Cast Recording)*, Atlantic.

Miranda, L.M. & McCarter, J. (2016) *Hamilton: The Revolution*. New York: Grand Central Publishing.

Monteiro, L.D. (2016) Race-Conscious Casting and the Erasure of the Black past in Lin-Manuel Miranda's *Hamilton*. *The Public Historian*, 38(1), 89–98. 10.1525/tph.2016.38.1.89.

Morrison, T. (1992) *Playing in the Dark: Whiteness and the Literary Imagination*. Cambridge: Harvard University Press.

Neary, L. (2008) Casting Beyond the Color Lines, interview with Ayanna Thompson. Npr.org. Available at: www.npr.org/templates/story/story.php?storyId=18706620. Accessed 10 May 2015.

Onion, R. (2016) A *Hamilton* Skeptic on Why the Show Isn't As Revolutionary As it Seems. *Slate.org*. Available at: www.slate.com/articles/arts/culturebox/2016/04/a_hamilton_critic_on_why_the_musical_isn_t_so_revolutionary.html. Accessed 15 July 2017.

Piepenburg, E. (2016) Why 'Hamilton' Has Heat. *New York Times*. Available at: www.nytimes.com/interactive/2015/08/06/theater/20150806-hamilton-broadway.html. Accessed 10 July 2017.

Rabinowitz, R. & Arp, R. (eds.) (2017) *Hamilton and Philosophy: Revolutionary Thinking*. Chicago, IL: Open Court Publishing.

Reed, I. (2015) 'Hamilton: The Musical:' Black Actors Dress Up like Slave Traders … and It's Not Halloween. *Counterpunch.org*. Available at: www.counterpunch.org/2015/08/21/hamilton-the-musical-black-actors-dress-up-like-slave-tradersand-its-not-halloween. Accessed 20 August 2017.

Reed, I. (2016) *Hamilton* and the Negro Whisperers: Miranda's consumer Fraud. *Counterpunch.org*. Available at: www.counterpunch.org/2016/04/15/hamilton-and-the-negro-whisperers-mirandas-consumer-fraud. Accessed 10 July 2017.

Rosen, J. (2015) The American Revolutionary. *New York* Times, 8 July. Available at: https://www.nytimes.com/interactive/2015/07/08/t-magazine/hamilton-lin-manuel-miranda-roots-sondheim.html. Accessed 10 July 2017.

Schuessler, J. (2016) 'Hamilton' and History: Are they in Sync? *New York Times*, 10 April. Available at: https://www.nytimes.com/2016/04/11/theater/hamilton-and-history-are-they-in-sync.html. Accessed 5 December 2018.

Sexton, J. (2008) *Amalgamation Schemes: Antiblackness and the Critique of Multiracialism.* Minneapolis, MN: University of Minnesota Press.

Sexton, J. (2010) People-Of-Color-Blindness: Notes on the Afterlife of Slavery. *Social Text*, 103(2), 31–56. doi:10.1215/01642472-2009-066.

Spillers, H. (2003) *Black, White, and in Color: Essays on American Literature and Culture.* Chicago, IL: University of Chicago Press.

Thompson, A. (ed.) (2006) *Colorblind Shakespeare: New Perspectives on Race and Performance.* New York: Routledge.

Viagas, R. (2015) Playwright Katori Hall Expresses Rage Over 'Revisionist Casting' of *Mountaintop* with White Dr. Martin Luther King. *playbill.com.* Available at: www.playbill.com/article/playwright-katori-hall-expresses-rage-over-revisionist-casting-of-mountaintop-with-white-dr-martin-luther-king-com-370896. Accessed 10 June 2016.

Wagner, B. (2009) *Disturbing the Peace: Black Culture and the Police Power after Slavery.* Cambridge: Harvard University Press.

Weinert-Kendt, R. (2015) Rapping a Revolution: Lin-Manuel Miranda and Others from 'Hamilton' Talk History. In *'Hamilton': The History-Making Musical.* New York: The New York Times.

Wilderson, F. & Williams, J. (2016) 'Staging (Within) Violence: A Conversation with Frank Wilderson and Jaye Austin Williams' Hyperriz: New Media cultures. 1-1 10.20415/rhiz/029.e07 www.rhizomes.net/issue29/wilderson/index.html

Wilderson, F.B.I.I.I. (2003) The Prison Slave as Hegemony's (Silent) Scandal. *Social Justice*, 18–27.

Wilderson, F.B.I.I.I. (2010) *Red, White & Black: Cinema and the Structure of U.S. Antagonisms.* Durham: Duke University Press.

Wilkins Catanese, B.W. (2014) *The Problem of the Color[Blind]: Racial Transgression and the Politics of Black Performance.* Ann Arbor, MI: University of Michigan Press.

Williams, J.A. (2016) On the Table: Crumbs of Freedom and Fugitivity – A Twenty-First Century (Re)Reading of *Crumbs from the Table of Joy*. In

Buckner, J. (ed.), *A Critical Companion to Lynn Nottage* (pp. 17–36). New York: Routledge.

Wynter, S. (1992) *Do Not Call Us Negros: How 'Multicultural' Textbooks Perpetuate Racism*. San Francisco, CA: Aspire.

Wynter, S. (2007) On How We Mistook the Map for the Territory, and Reimprisoned Ourselves in Our Unbearable Wrongness of Being, of Desêtre: Black Studies toward the Human Project. In Gordon, L.R. & Gordon, J.A. (eds.), *Not Only the Master's Tools: African-American Studies in Theory and Practice* (pp. 107–169). Boulder, CO: Paradigm.

Index